D1491274

Teaching Your Kids

THE

Truth About Consequences

TEACHING
YOUR KIDS
THE
TRUTH ABOUT
CONSEQUENCES

DR. DANIEL HAHN

MACKEY LIBRARY
Trevecca Nazarene University

BETHANY HOUSE PUBLISHERS
MINNEAPOLIS, MINNESOTA 55438

Scripture quotations taken from the following versions. The HOLY BIBLE, NEW INTERNATIONAL VERSION®. Copyright © 1973, 1978, 1984 by International Bible Society. Used by permission of Zondervan Publishing House. All rights reserved. The "NIV" and "New International Version" trademarks are registered in the United States Patent and Trademark Office by International Bible Society. Use of either trademark requires the permission of International Bible Society.

The Living Bible © 1971 owned by assignment by Illinois Regional Bank N.A. (as trustee). Used by permission of Tyndale House Publishers, Inc. Wheaton, IL 60189. All rights reserved.

The King James Version of the Bible.

Copyright © 1995
Daniel Hahn

All rights reserved. No part of this publication may be reproduced, stored in a retrieval system, or transmitted in any form or by any means electronic, mechanical, photocopying, recording, or otherwise without the prior written permission of the publisher and copyright owners.

Published by Bethany House Publishers
A Ministry of Bethany Fellowship, Inc.
11300 Hampshire Avenue South
Minneapolis, Minnesota 55438

Printed in the United States of America.

Library of Congress Cataloging-in-Publication Data

Hahn, Daniel M.
    Teaching your kids the truth about consequences : helping them make the connection between choices and results / Daniel Hahn.
    p. cm.
    ISBN 1–55661–680–5
    1. Christian education—Home training. 2. Christian ethics—Study and teaching. 3. Children—Conduct of life. 4. Children—Religious life. I. Title.
BV1590.H34   1995
248.8'45—dc20   95–25840
                                                    CIP

To Katie and Kyle

Keep your eyes focused on "the prize"
and one day it will be yours!

DR. DANIEL HAHN is Pastor for Students and Families at Missions Hills Church in Mission Viejo, California. His doctorate in marriage and family ministeries is from Biola University, where he is an adjunct professor. A sought-after camp and conference speaker, Daniel and his wife, Lori, live in California with their two children.

CONTENTS

PREFACE

My buddy Craig and I rode our bikes through town just as the sun was setting. Down Eldridge Drive, past the Catholic church, along the waterfront, up over Sehome Hill, behind St. Luke's Hospital and across the ball field toward the stadium parking lot. Cresting the hill we slowed and looked below. There stretched out in front of us was the Blossomtime Carnival. It came every spring. But this year we were on our own. Thirteen and parent-free! We were going to champion our freedom like never before and hit even the most daring rides.

After polishing off the first installment of cotton candy, washed down with a snow cone, we purchased a long string of tickets and headed straight through the crowds to the Rock-O-Plane. We got settled in our "cage." Seat belts on. Door closed. Motor churned. We were off, spiraling through space, laughing and screaming our goofy heads off as our compartment spun wildly high above a blur of lights below. It was freeing and exhilarating—and then over, way too soon.

Walking up to the ticket booth for another string of tickets I reached into my right coat pocket for my wad of dollar bills. Nothing. I quickly shot my other hand into my left side pocket. Empty. I felt all my pockets as a wave of shock ran through me like an electric current. Zip. "My money's gone!" I shouted at Craig. "We've gotta go back and look for it!" Retracing our steps brought us back to the Rock-O-Plane but there was no sign of the money. I approached the ride operator, who couldn't have cared less about my loss. Craig and I walked away, heads hung low, still searching the ground.

9

The calliope is playing and the lights are on, but the laughter seems hollow. There's an uneasy restlessness. A lot of kids feel ripped off. Why? The answers aren't found in economic recovery or social programs. Kids today feel an emptiness that goes way beyond pocketbooks and programs. It's a narrow dark place down deep inside. Our carnival culture doesn't cut it. The amusements still churn but the amazement is fading. Junior high and high school students increasingly ask the bigger questions—What's it all for? Why am I here? Does anyone love me? Does anything matter? What happens in the end? Those are questions Nintendo doesn't answer.

In a world of competing voices and graying standards, children are searching for some kind of foundation. While they usually can't categorize their needs or their questions, they're searching for values that ring true from one generation to the next. Values described in terms of results. Payoffs. Consequences.

That is what God has given us in his Word, and that is what this book is about: Providing our children with a legacy that lasts a lifetime, and in the process, providing a "lifeline" to eternity.

Having worked with teenagers and their families for many years as a pastor, speaker and college instructor, I was tempted to focus this book specifically toward guiding adolescents. After writing *The Pro-Teen Parent*, I kept hearing over and over that "people need to understand these principles sooner." I agree. What unfolds during adolescence has so much to do with what is melded into their lives much earlier on. So these pages contain the truth about what we as parents plant in kids across the board—elementary-aged children and pre-teens as well as teenagers. It is never too soon, or too late, to consider the legacy we're leaving with our kids.

So where do we start? The studies on parenting are conclusive: kids are shaped primarily by what they observe. While we long for formulas that can be snap-fitted onto our children, God's method is different. First, He says, *These commandments that I give you today are to be upon your hearts* (Deuteronomy 6:6). He invites us as parents to *become* what we so desperately want our kids to be. Then He follows with the logical second step, *Impress them on your children* (6:7). The first necessarily precedes the second.

When God's value system has saturated our own hearts, then we can impact our children. What I hope is that the fifteen "core values" I am about to share with you in this book will sink deep into the soil of your own heart—first.

Since all of us learn through what we see, I have decided to take you with me on my own journey as a person, a trek through images and characters, places and moments, all of them true, in an effort to show you some of what I've seen. Just as Jesus unfolded truth through parables, or pictures, we must be able to help our kids see how the truth matters in the real world. As you read, please do so with an open mind and a ready pen. Jot down your thoughts as they're triggered by what you read. (The ideas that come to you will be far more valuable to you than anything I can suggest from a distance.) And then consider how to best pass these truths on to your children in ways appropriate to their ages and issues. No one on earth knows as well as you do just what will hit home with them.

One last thing. My desire is to travel with you, in all of this, as a friend. Not as an expert who is breezing through the task of parenting and thinking it's a cinch, but rather as a companion who is stepping daily through the goo of family life—and learning much through the mystery in it all. Thanks for joining me.

1

THE HARVEST PRINCIPLE BROUGHT HOME

A farmer went out to sow his seed.

—Matthew 13:3

My father was a farmer of sorts. Not a real farmer, maybe. But he was a farmer in his heart. Early each spring, Dad and I took a walk out on the property behind our house. "Ground's cold and hard right now, son, but you wait. Pretty soon we'll till it up and plant some seeds." We'd walk across the bumpy, hard earth and continue our surveying. "We'll plant some beans here," he'd say, pointing. "I think the squash will work well there." And then my favorite part came. "Where do you want to put the pumpkin seeds?" I loved those pumpkins. That's all that mattered to me.

Spring would come and a silent internal alarm would ring in Dad's head. We tilled and weeded, worked the earth until it was soft and smooth. Then we'd plant. He worked the bean department and I took control of the pumpkin patch. And then came the long wait. More than once I'd ask Dad if we could dig up those seeds to see what they were doing down there. His reply was always the same. "You just wait . . . just wait." It was always hard to believe him. From what I could see nothing was happening.

As sure as the sun came up in the summertime, small green

shoots pushed their noses up through the soil and grew. Small plants in May became strong stocks and long vines in July. "Where's the pumpkins?" I'd inquire.

"Be patient," Dad would say. "They'll come." And they did. Through summer he'd pick his beans and I'd watch my little green pumpkins.

"How come they're green?"

"Just wait. All in good time. Be patient."

And every year, pumpkin season would come just as predicted. Nothing quite paralleled the excitement of the harvest. The biggest pumpkin graced our front porch. My trophy for waiting. And not long after, Dad and I would walk again on the cold hard ground, making plans.

God is a farmer, too. He invented seeds. He invented photosynthesis, germination and a host of other complex components way beyond my scope of understanding. But the Bible isn't complicated like that. God has a way of taking complexities and communicating them simply: Life is a field. We reap what is sown— by ourselves and by others.

Everything about life and eternity is affected by this principle. From beginning to end, Scripture reminds us of this truth. Not as a threat, but as a statement of fact. Reaping is inseparable from sowing, and vice versa. What happens today will affect tomorrow and the harvest of tomorrow, in each of our lives, depending on what has been done in the past.

Whether the issue is the way we drive or the garden we plant or a diet we endure, we make choices based on what we know will follow. When we look ahead, consider outcomes, reckon with results—we're in a better position to choose. Ultimately, we're happier with our lives and our decisions when we choose how we'll live with results clearly in mind.

Unfortunately, kids today aren't being shown the whole picture. From every corner whispers encourage kids to abandon restraint, to follow whatever whim captures them, to do their own thing. God and God's standards are no longer relevant. Absolute truth—isn't anymore. And as for consequences? "Well . . . uh, we're working on ways to get around them. You'll be fine. Don't think about it."

Social mores have changed and are changing rapidly. There was a time when God's truth was upheld by our country as being "self evident," absolutes that were honored. And there was a greater awareness of the consequences that were inevitable if we were to neglect or reject those truths. But over the last few decades there's been an obvious slide, a setting aside of standards, a muzzling of conscience. And the results? We pick up the morning paper, rub our eyes and shake our heads. "People these days. . . ."

Much of what we're seeing in the AIDS epidemic, increased suburban and rural crime, staggering abuse statistics, widespread inner city poverty, drug abuse and the frightening escalation of gang violence, is the dividend paid on decisions we've been making for years. Like rib bones protruding from a Cambodian child, our social ills simply reveal our spiritual malnourishment. When all that is good and right and absolutely true is discarded in reaction to the imagined "restrictiveness" of the past, the baby gets tossed with the bath water. To look at it another way, when our moorings break loose from God's truth, we drift for a time, until we come to a falls. Anyone observing our national "drift" would agree—we're going over. Children go first.

Families are where the sowing begins, where the seed germinates, where all that is eventually produced is cultivated. No one has stated it more pointedly than Chuck Colson in a recent address when he said,

> In response to the increasing, senseless, random violence, everybody wants to get tough; stiffer laws, more prisons, more police on the beat . . . people say, 'We've got to do something to crack down.' But we did crack down twenty years ago. We quintupled the prison population in America, yet in that same period of time, violent crime went up 560 percent. You cannot change the hearts of people with prison bars and more police. So where does conscience come from? . . . How is it cultivated? For centuries, we have understood the answer: in families. Fathers and mothers teach young people the basic rules of civil behavior.[1]

---

[1]Chuck Colson, *Focus on the Family* magazine, January 1994, Vol. 18, No. 1, p. 12.

Our homes are pre-season training camps for life. Home is where morals are modeled. Home is where what is right and what is wrong is reinforced repeatedly—on a daily basis. Home is where consequences can be discussed and truth cemented. No wonder that families seem to be the primary target of our adversary's ballistics.

Reaping and Sowing

The smell of burnt bacon settled on the already simmering heat of an August morning in L.A. I approached Steve's apartment just after 9:00 and pushed the doorbell button encased in the stucco wall. The door swung wide. "Daniel! Great to see you, man." Small talk ensued as Steve slid a couple of fried eggs onto a plate and handed it to me across the bar. After a quick prayer, Steve began to unfold his story. "I didn't exactly *leave* Debbie." He paused. "She sort of kicked me out."

I'd known Steve since our days together in college. We had a couple of classes together and from time to time had collaborated on class notes. As our friendship deepened, studying had given way to batches of Jiffy Pop popcorn and late night discussions of life and, of course, women. He'd dated a number of them even in the first year I knew him. There was Sheri in the fall. Around Christmas time I could recall a Jennifer. Sometime close to summer break there was someone new, I forget her name. Steve would chronicle each phase of each relationship for me as if to say, "Hey, I know you haven't been dating much lately, I'll let you live through my latest escapade." His assessment was pretty accurate.

But after a while the stories became increasingly predictable. Steve and Miss whoever would go out for a while. They'd get serious. They'd end up sleeping together and then, for some reason, they'd break up. He had a pattern.

Off and on I kept up with Steve after those college days. He usually wrote to tell me he was moving, or of a new job he was taking. And then one day I received a wedding invitation. Debbie was her name. I was happy for him, glad he was settling in, putting down roots. There was a note stuck to the invitation. "Daniel, we're moving to Glendale. I'll call you once I get situated." I wasn't able to attend Steve's wedding, but he called about six months later. We decided a Saturday morning breakfast would make for a great reunion.

"She asked you to leave?!" I showed surprise but deep inside didn't feel shocked. There was something so expected, so normal about the news.

"Yah, I can't even believe it happened." There was a long silence. I filled it.

"Well, what *did* happen? I mean, you've been married, what—six months?"

Steve put his fork down and the clang on the plate may as well have been the toll of a death bell. "There's this other woman I've been seeing." Steve looked out the window. The conversation that morning went on for at least two hours after the egg yolk and bacon drippings had dried on our plates.

"I don't know, Daniel, it's like I'm doing exactly what my dad did. I don't understand it. He had an affair when I was seven and ended up leaving my mom and us kids to fend for ourselves. I hated him for that. I watched my mom turn into a different person because of the pain he inflicted on her. I told myself over and over, growing up, that I'd never do that to my wife or my kids." I could have sworn tears were welling in Steve's eyes. I listened almost without breathing. "I may as well tell you too—Debbie is pregnant."

It was a long, silent drive from Glendale back to my home on the other end of the L.A. sprawl. I thought about Lori, my wife, and how much I loved her, and about the choices Steve and I had both made over the years. I thought about the passionate scenes he had described, and I had believed, a decade ago. It all sounded stale now. Traffic snaked slowly through suburbs, and I wondered about all the homes and dads and sons and the decisions they would make that August day in L.A. And the breakfasts to be held and the stories told—in a decade.

Like a billboard over our busy freeway lives, God's Word stands. It speaks even through the noise and clutter of modern life. Social and moral and political opinions start and stop, but its ancient message is so straightforward and strangely fresh. "We reap what is sown." Everything about tomorrow hinges on the investments of today. And, as Charles Kettering put it, "We should all be concerned about the future because we will have to spend the rest of our lives there." Not only concerned for ourselves, but for our children. Long ago God warned Israelite parents that their neglect of the truth would affect *the children and their children for the sin of the fathers to the third and fourth generation* (Exodus 34:7). The same could be stated for our positive influence. Both truth and abandonment of truth have ripple effects that last as a legacy.

The truth stands, but this generation is wobbling badly. Someone has gagged the voice of "natural consequences" for so long that many children and teens don't have any idea that consequences exist. A decade ago some might have labeled that kind of talk an "over-reaction," the stuff religious fanatics are always hot and bothered about. But nowadays heads are popping out of the sand all over the place. Too many people are getting burned to act like there's no fire.

"Sexual Roulette" the headline beamed. The Orange County edition of the *L.A. Times* ran an article recently, stating, "Today's teens face sex-related issues and concerns barely talked about—and even unknown—a generation ago. So how are they coping with their sexuality?" Not well. More than two million teens will contract a sexually transmitted disease this year.

Listen to the words of Susan, a high school senior quoted in the article: "Sometimes my boyfriend and I would use a condom; sometimes we didn't, and I know it was one of the times we didn't that I got pregnant." (And where were her parents through all this?) "My mom always told me that if I ever got intimate with my boyfriend to come to her and she would give me condoms." (Sounds like a solid plan to some parents.) "But when you're having sex, it's not like you're thinking about it. Until you skip a period, you don't think about what could happen to you."

Unfortunately a lot of young people aren't thinking. In too many cases, no one is *teaching* them to think.

Not long ago I was driving a rental car in another major city and made a real bad move. I turned right. Right, that is, onto a one way street going the opposite way. In an instant I saw three lanes of traffic all headed toward me. I whipped the steering wheel to the left and pulled a U-turn in order to go with the flow. The oncoming cars were approaching me as I turned in front of them, forcing them to slow to avoid hitting me. It was then that I caught sight of a police car parked on the side of the street. The officer looked straight at me as I was completing my U-turn. I smiled. He didn't. I drove on and he pulled out. I knew I was had. His lights went on and I pulled over. The policeman turned out to be very understanding but gave me the ticket I deserved. A natural consequence. I drove the wrong way, I impeded traffic, I got fined. Why is that so? Simply because I drive in a country that has laws. Laws designed to protect.

Scripture informs us of laws about our spiritual decisions as well. When we pay attention to them, the rewards are eternal. When we don't, the consequences can be disastrous.

Lessons That Make an Impact

So how do we get our kids to consider the results of their decisions? More lectures perhaps? Make 'em sit still and listen up in church? Ah, you're thinking, "it's not that easy." You're right. Why? Because we don't form convictions on command. Rather, we become convinced of what's true and what isn't by what we see and experience. That is especially so for kids. Ever have someone tell you they love you only to have them treat you as if they don't? Which do you believe—the talk or the treatment? Most kids place their bets on the treatment. "Actions speak louder than words," they'd say. Experience is the ultimate teacher. From mid-elementary age on up, children believe what they *see* over what you *say*.

Throughout my teen years my mother refused to let me buy a motorcycle. I begged. I pleaded. I read her articles about people in motorcycle accidents who *hadn't* been killed. I showed her the cost difference between operating a motorcycle and a car. She wasn't impressed. She described the dangers. She showed me articles about people who *had* been killed. She explained that cost meant nothing compared to my life. She refused to budge.

Then one day I turned eighteen and was more or less on my own. I bought a motorcycle. I was ecstatic. More than that, on a daily basis I could prove that my mom was wrong and I was right.

Then I had an accident. I was driving toward downtown Portland and crossed the Broadway Bridge spanning the Willamette River. It was raining. (What else, in Oregon?) The grooves in the corrugated steel bridge caught the front wheel and my bike zigzagged out of control. Down I went and skidded across the bridge into the oncoming lane of traffic. A lot of thoughts went through my mind fast. But one thing stuck: as far as I was concerned, Mom was right—motorcycles are dangerous.

I lived. (Were you wondering?) Both my bike and my body took a licking, but I survived to tell about it. Now please understand that my point here isn't the dangers of motorcycle riding. What's noteworthy is that Mom's words weren't half as impactful as a mouthful of wet steel. Her words laid a foundation, but *my convictions changed because of what I experienced personally*. When consequences were felt, I changed both my belief and my behavior. I sold the bike.

So do we clam up and wait for life to wallop sense into our kids? Let them touch the stove? Obviously, our job description includes protection. The big problem is that we can't always protect our kids! As they grow older, we can't control who they hang out with at the mall, how well they do in school or what they do on a date. We can beg, plead, scream—we'd never do that!—scold and sermonize, only to discover that the total protection we've given them in the past is impossible to maintain.

For the most part in life, our kids will be forced to draw from within to make some very important choices. There won't always be someone close by to protect or advise. What our kids need, then, is a new system—one that prepares them to choose rightly for themselves. A voice on the inside that triggers responsible, safe decisions.

So how do we as parents go about training them to internalize the law of the harvest? From day one our goal must be to develop that inner voice through the use of real, logical consequences. To raise them on a solid diet of verbal commands or to protect them at every turn is to miss an essential part of preparing them for what lies ahead.

The beautiful thing about allowing real-life experiences to train our kids is that not only do our children learn valuable short-term realities, but a much bigger process begins. Our little adults-in-the-rough begin to understand an eternal principle—choices reap results. Bigger issues, character qualities, values—they all reap an eternal harvest.

Two Kinds of Consequences

For practical purposes, let's think of consequences as falling into two categories—natural and logical. Natural consequences are those outcomes that flow "naturally" from our decisions. Don't study and you'll do poorly on the exam. Spend your money on this and you won't have money for that. Jump from the tenth story, it's curtains. Eat a high-fat diet or abuse alcohol and you'll likely have health problems. And if you drive the wrong way on a one-way street, the natural consequence is a ticket.

While all those examples are very real and tangible, many natural consequences take years to realize. Like planting an oak tree—growth is almost imperceptible for a time. That's certainly the case with most spiritual and character issues. In the short run, a lot of bad people reap some pretty slick benefits. Drug abuse can be a real thrill ride—for a while. Petty theft doesn't seem all that harmful—in the short run. But God says something is taking place. A pattern is being laid. A life is being shaped. A future is being constructed, bit by bit, and those decisions are creating a destiny.

In addition to natural consequences—which often take years to realize—there are logical consequences. These are situations we *design* in order to teach an immediate lesson, to prove the logic of a certain course of action or direct behavior. Logical consequences, when used appropriately, speak volumes and have a far greater impact than any parental lecture ever could. Capitalizing on the influential power of felt results in daily situations helps children see just how real consequences actually are. And here's the real punch: *kids learn to respect the reality of long-term, natural consequences when parents use short-run, logical consequences as a routine part of shaping behavior.*

Certainly there are occasions when a swift rescue is warranted. When your two-year-old is headed into a busy street isn't the time to sit back and let consequences teach a valuable lesson. Yet a few smartly crafted experiences can be worth thousands of words. What we're looking for are those golden moments when we can wisely allow life itself to become an ally in training our children and teens. Parents who rush to rescue even when rescuing is unnecessary or unhelpful short-circuit an opportunity for their child to learn a lesson that sticks.

Here's an example of what I mean by a logical consequence: One mom had become worn out nagging her teenage daughter to get going in the morning for school. The mom normally gave the girl a ride to school on her way to work, using the time to badger her daughter about her tardiness. When the girl was late getting up, or late getting ready, it made the mother late for her job. Yet day after day the mother had continued to inadvertently "own" the problem by playing the role of nag. Over time she realized she was actually enabling her daughter's bad behavior by waiting around for her and giving her a ride no matter how late she was.

Acting on some wise advise from a friend, the mother bought her daughter an alarm clock, gift-wrapped it and gave it to her with the following explanation. "From tomorrow on, you are responsible to get yourself to school on time. I will be leaving for work at 7:30. If you are in the car by 7:29 you'll get a ride from me. If not, you'll have to walk. And if you're tardy for your first period, you'll be making it up at Saturday school. I hope you're in the car by 7:29 because I enjoy my morning commute with you."

The next morning came and the daughter wasn't ready. She walked. "Nearly killed me to drive off without her," said the mother. But you'll never guess who was in the car on day two. Now the daughter rarely misses her ride, and the morning brawl has ceased. Ownership for the problem was transferred from mom to daughter through the use of a logical consequence.

As our kids move through the elementary years and on into adolescence, our parental role shifts. It was so easy when they were little. We hovered nearby—keeping them from falling on their first pair of roller skates, reminding them to practice their multiplication tables or asking them to tell the truth. Much of the time, protection was simply a firm command that brought immediate response. Nice and concrete—black and white.

But kids change. That black-and-white world gives way to the capacity of reasoning. Gradually, most kids question everything. While the process is natural and ultimately necessary, it's bumpy at best. Most of life is still untried so perspectives and decisions are—well, so *adolescent!* Parents face two options. We can keep using the same patterns we used when they were young (and frustrate ourselves to death), or we can realize that our methods must change as our kids develop.

Some have said that when a child reaches adolescence the two best arenas in which to teach personal responsibility are "clothes and cars." One set of parents I know said, "Once our kids became teenagers they got a certain amount from us for clothes every three months. If they squandered it on a 'label' that was their choice. But they had to live with that choice. If they wanted more money for clothes it was up to them to earn it. They were also responsible for washing and ironing their own clothes. It wasn't long before they got tired of running short on funds and wearing dirty clothes. They started considering where their money was going, and when they got new clothes they began taking care of them."

The same kind of strategy could be applied to the use of a car. Maybe "driving issues" are a long way off for you and your child, but the groundwork you lay now will prepare both of you for that day.

As hard as it is, our role must move from controller to consultant. What do consultants do? They ask questions, offer opinions, share experiences, present options and forecast outcomes. Ultimately, however, they step back and allow the client to make decisions. Consultants understand what they can and cannot do for their client, and as a result the client owns the process as well as the results.

The fact is, as kids grow up we can't control much of what they do anyhow. Unless we put them on a short leash and keep them right next to us every minute of every day (and I doubt anyone could handle that!) we can't control them—who they hang around with at school, what they do at the mall or how hard they study. Our best shot is influence. When we decrease our frenzied attempts to control and instead act as a benevolent consultant, we actually find our positive influence increasing. We meet less resistance. Our kids own their behaviors. Internal reasoning gradually takes up where external control decreases. Healthy self-protection slowly develops where parental protection decreases, and kids internalize the harvest principle. They reap what they sow. And instead of controlling, we find ourselves asking, "How can I influence their reasoning without taking over for them? How can I help them develop their decision-making muscles? What situations really necessitate my stepping in? On which issues can I reasonably give them the reins?"

Like the "clutch and accelerator" routine of a manual transmission, we let off the controls gradually, allowing them freedom to move forward. Sometimes we need to clutch a little, or even brake when there's real danger—but more and more our children are accelerating right into their own adulthood. Riding the clutch is as hard on kids as it is on cars. Parents who "hover and rescue" usually create kids who are either overdependent or distant and resentful. Parents who attempt to get obedience-on-command generally find their growing children developing a dual personality, compliant when parents are nearby and hell-bent when they're on their own. Either way, the inner voice is muzzled because parents are unwilling to risk giving up control.

So when do we put on the brakes, so to speak? That's a tough call to make. We need a great deal of instantaneous wisdom on an issue-to-issue basis. There's a tricky balance between freedom and boundary-setting. There's an assortment of preventative and corrective actions we can take, as well as messages we can communicate. As you navigate through daily issues, let me offer a few ideas that help the process work better. Keep these ideas in mind as you read the rest of this book and we look together at teaching the truth about consequences in a variety of life's arenas:

- Discuss boundaries with your child—ones appropriate to their age level. Let them know that you will not allow disrespect for others or behaviors that would clearly endanger their life or basic health. Expectations will vary from family to family, but if they are communicated simply and clearly, you have provided a framework for negotiation—for your child to ask for more freedoms and for you as parent to make clear where you will apply the "emergency brake" if necessary.

- When issues have spiritual or moral implications, point out what the Bible actually says and let your child know how you've applied biblical principles in your own day-to-day choices.

- Consider carefully which boundary battles you want to fight. If you see, for example, five character qualities you wish your child would develop or five behaviors you want changed, decide which one or two are the most important. Are any items on your "parental wish list" life-and-death, non-negotiable matters? Then ask which areas have the most bearing on your child's long-term well-being. Focus your efforts in those areas, and leave less critical concerns for later.

- Don't make your decisions in isolation. Talk with other parents. Find out when they "apply the brakes." It might mean swallowing some pride to ask other parents how they handle touchy situations—and to let others know when you're struggling—but you'll probably both discover that you're not alone in the difficulties you face.

- As you talk with your child use positive language that offers choices rather than wording that sounds negative or demands a certain course of action. This can actually become a habit! Phrases like "You're welcome to come to the mall with me if your room is clean before I leave" work better than "Clean your room or you're not going with me to the mall." Another example would be "I'd like you to be able to go out tonight. If we can agree on what time you'll be home, then you're free to go." That accomplishes more than "Either agree to be in by midnight or forget about going out at all." The goal is to affirm their ability to choose and reduce "the fight mechanism" by using positive rather than negative words.

- When you are the one dishing out a consequence of some type, keep it reasonable (one you will actually follow through with) and closely associated with the problem. An example:

"I want you to be able to drive but you'll need to obey the speed limit. If you don't, I'll have to drive." That consequence is easier for your seventeen-year-old to absorb than "If you don't stop speeding then you can forget about me buying you any clothes when we get to the store." Watch out for extremes like: "If I hear any more swear words out of your mouth you can find another place to live." Your child might just take you up on it!

- Remind your children that your goal is to empower them. Explain that you aren't interested in making decisions for them or nagging and rescuing but in strengthening their decision-making abilities and showing them that decisions have outcomes. On many issues, the choice will be theirs.

- When you are allowing a consequence to run its course, do so with understanding and empathy rather than hostility. Quietly let reality sink in. Retain the relational bond by honestly sharing their sorrow while affirming that grown-up choice-making is a tough job with real-life results. Be sure to communicate forgiveness and love. Never harbor resentment or rub in that "you got what you deserved." Rather, let your child know that even though his poor choice may mean taking some time to regain the same level of freedom he had, you still love him and believe he will do much better next time around.

It takes wisdom and patience to use consequences to shape a life, but the effort is well worth it. A few real-life experiences will do more for your child than a thousand lectures, or, the other alternative, grounding him or her until age thirty.

What issues are on the docket right now? Is it a clean bedroom, or a curfew or a car? Maybe it has to do with washing the dishes in the sink, being honest, getting better grades or feeding the cat. The chapters to follow describe arenas where we as parents can communicate truth. We'll look at choices we all make in small ways every day, not just choices about actions or behaviors, but about how we think—choices we make about what we value, the hopes and dreams and desires behind our actions. How we think about those choices and the decisions we ultimately make will beyond a doubt impact the quality of our life journey, our relationship to the rest of the world and, in the end, our eternal destiny. And I invite you to think about your own life as you read further, because *we* must internalize these truths to pass them on as a legacy to our children. Then we will all realize the harvest of joy attached to each one.

If you're a parent, you're a farmer. Every day, seeds sink deep in the soft soil of your child's heart. Other seeds get in there, too. There's no way to prevent any and all weed seeds from taking root, but there is much you *can* do. No question—much of what grows in a child's life comes from what parents decide to plant.

God speaks to each of us so gently. "Will you walk with me across the field of your life? Feel the earth? Every season is the opportunity for a new beginning. What has been planted in your past? What has it produced? What will you plant today? Tomorrow depends on it. Show me what you're planting and I'll show you the future."

At the end of each chapter we'll have practical tips on how you can pass along a particular truth to your child. Some ideas are things to do, others are things to talk about. Some are best for younger children, others for teens, and some are questions for you to think about on your own. No idea will fit every child, but I hope you'll find some seeds to grow your own ideas of how to communicate the truth about consequences.

Truth or Consequences

- Have your child help you plant some seeds or small plants. As you water, weed, fertilize or prune your plants you can explain the laws of the harvest. Show them how their life is like a garden. What is planted there will someday bring results. Our spiritual lives, our souls, require care just as a garden does. Nothing planted, nothing reaped, and conversely a garden that is planted and cared for produces results.

- Show them a large oak tree or some other slow-growing tree and explain how internal qualities of character take years to realize, but that growth is actually happening each day. Just as a tree doesn't grow overnight, neither does our character.

- From the pages of your newspaper you can find stories that illustrate the principle of consequences. Talk to your child about the headlines—a thief going to jail, a drug trafficker being apprehended, a politician who compromised and was caught. Ask what your child thinks about that person. You could ask, "Do you think this individual thought about the consequences of his or her decisions ahead of time? As a child or teenager, what choices might have been made that led to their present situation? How might their life have been different if they had adopted God's values as a young person? How have other people been affected by the lifestyle they chose?"

- Take three sheets of paper. On one you and your child could write out what you as a parent feel are some reasonable boundaries—limits of freedom. Explain why those boundaries are so important to you and what could result if those boundaries were not honored. On a second sheet, write all the

28

freedoms that the child has within those boundaries—arenas of choice they're responsible for. On the third sheet, write down a number of God's directives, principles or commands for our lives. (You can start with the Ten Commandments and write them down in the child's own words.) If your kid is creative, maybe they'd be open to making the three sheets into posters for their room, complete with magazine clippings or drawings.

2

THE TRUTH ABOUT CHOICES

THE CONSEQUENCES OF INDIFFERENCE

Do not be deceived: God cannot be mocked. A man reaps what he sows. The one who sows to please his sinful nature, from that nature will reap destruction; the one who sows to please the Spirit, from the Spirit will reap eternal life.

—Galatians 6:7–8

As I sit here writing, the city of Laguna Beach, just a few miles from my home, is ablaze. "Worst fire in Orange County's history," I can hear the newscaster relay, ". . . hundreds of homes are burning . . . thousands of acres consumed." Million-dollar mansions that yesterday overlooked the blue Pacific are tonight charred rubble. Hundreds of families have lost every earthly possession. Already they're asking why. The answer? Someone, around 11:30 this morning, made a decision.

From my dining room table I can look out toward the east as dusk creeps across the Cleveland National Forest. A ring of fire tops the ridge of hills across the canyon from where I sit. Another blaze, out of control, visiting the hillsides with destruction. This one, a little closer to home. This one makes me sweat.

My mother-in-law called just an hour or so ago from the edge of Laguna Beach. "We can see the fire getting closer to our home.

Daddy and I are packing a few things—just in case we have to evacuate. We're boxing up pictures . . ." her voice faltered. "You know . . . things we can't replace."

Fires throughout the Southland. Fires begun by choice. While these fires burn on hillsides nearby, I can't help but think that an even more life-altering process is taking place in another realm. The eternal landscape of our own lives and the lives of the people around us will be deeply impacted by the decisions we make today.

Every day we're confronted on numerous fronts. Each of us carries a book of matches around. We can't help but make decisions that at the time seem so small. Yet in the scope of life and eternity they matter much.

Interestingly, much of the Bible is dedicated to those very decisions. It is the world's most complete user's manual on life. It is both clear and profound.

Do not be deceived: God cannot be mocked. A man reaps what he sows. The one who sows to please his sinful nature, from that nature will reap destruction. (Galatians 6:8)

A warning to all of us has been issued. Wait a minute. Wake up. Take stock. Get real. Think about what you're doing. God is no fool. Be assured—rebellion triggers results.

By the same token, the good that we're doing is also taking root. It too is growing into something—something that lasts forever! *The one who sows to please the Spirit, from the Spirit will reap eternal life.* (Galatians 6:8) The Holy Spirit is ready and able to make our daily decisions into eternal investments.

The mandate is clear. What we do makes a difference. Our righteousness is reaping a reward. Don't stop! *Let us not become weary in doing good, for at the proper time we will reap a harvest if we do not give up* (Galatians 6:9).

Throughout Scripture God keeps hammering home a similar principle as if our very lives depended on it. He illustrates and illuminates it in numerous ways, but the point is always the same: We all make choices that will determine much about the course of our lives. The truth about choices is—they all have consequences.

Every year I take a group of students—after rock-climbing in the uniquely hot and dry Joshua Tree National Monument—to a water park in Palm Springs. I really hate water parks. Why? I get the feeling I'm swimming in an enormous tub filled with thousands of children. They sweat and spit and who knows what in the water. As far as I'm concerned, it's a cesspool more than a swimming pool, and these kids love every slimy minute of it.

I usually end up sunning myself on a nice safe bench at the end of one of the slides. From the top of the slide my students scream and wave to get my attention. Then they leap into one of several cylinders that snakes its way down to the bottom where they come splashing out the other end.

Since there are three or four tubes all spitting out kids, I have to really pay attention to which tube *my* kids are getting into at the top. Then I follow that tube as it twists and turns over and under the other tubes. I track it with my eyes all the way to the bottom and—sure enough, each kid comes out of the same tube he entered at the top. If you get in tube #1 at the top, you're sure to come out of tube #1 at the bottom. Happens every time. I've studied it—I know.

Sowing and reaping is like that. Where you head determines where you'll land. The direction you take in life dictates the destination. Choices matter. Here are some good verses to commit to memory. Better yet, race your kids to memorize them. Award a prize to the winner.

Choices are like *crossroads* in our lives; they lead one way or another. *Stand at the crossroads and look; ask for the ancient paths, ask where the good way is, and walk in it, and you will find rest for your souls* (Jeremiah 6:16).

Choices are like *gates* in our lives; they give entrance to the future. *Enter through the narrow gate. For wide is the gate and broad is the road that leads to destruction, and many enter through it. But small is the gate and narrow the road that leads to life, and only a few find it* (Matthew 7:13–14).

Choices are like *investments* in our lives; they add up, day by day. *The wages of the righteous bring them life, but the income of the wicked brings them punishment* (Proverbs 10:16).

Choices are like *paths* in our lives; they carry us to a final destination. *Make level paths for your feet and take only ways that are*

firm. Do not swerve to the right or the left; keep your foot from evil
(Proverbs 4:26–27).

Warnings Should Be Welcomed

The main thoroughfare leading from the freeway to our home
is presently all torn up. Each day as I drive down this street, I see
the signs. First there's the large orange one stating "Construction
Ahead." Farther on, "Lane Ends, Merge Left." Then there's a series
of cones forcing the flow of traffic away from the right lane. Then
there's someone with a flag cautioning drivers to slow down as
they pass. Gazing to my right I see a huge hole in the pavement
where roadwork is in process. Everyone drives on by, never giving
it another thought.

But imagine the same scenario without any warnings. No
signs or cones or flags, just the hole. You're driving along and
BAM . . . SMASH—you hit the hole. No doubt about it, warnings
are there to save our lives. No one would disagree with that when
it comes to road construction, yet when it comes to daily life many
people actually feel offended by a warning. "Who are they to tell
me what to do. . . . What gives them the right? . . . It's none of
their business!" We throw rocks at prophets and push past flag-
men.

In the Fall of 1993, America was shocked to learn of the death
of actor River Phoenix on Halloween night. River had been partying with friends at the Viper Room on Sunset Boulevard that
evening. Then everything went wrong. The cool and casual actor
who enthralled the masses for his roles in *Stand By Me* and *My
Own Private Idaho*, lay outside of the club on the sidewalk. His
lifeless body was found to contain toxic levels of cocaine and her-
oin, as well as traces of marijuana and Valium.

In later interviews, River's mother simply wouldn't admit that
a problem even existed. Despite numerous other accounts of the
actor's ongoing battle with drugs, his mother remained in denial.
As far as his family and close friends knew, she said, River simply
wasn't a regular drug user. Then there was Johnny Depp, co-
owner of the Viper Room. He felt that the story of River's death
was being publicized too much—that we should "get on with our

lives." In every interview with Depp one thing stood out clearly. His primary concern was the image of his club.

There was another person associated with River that most people never heard about. Paul Peterson, a one-time child actor who played Jeff on *The Donna Reed Show* in the early 60's, had learned of River's involvement with drugs nearly a year before his death. He had actually gone to visit River at his home and offered him the support of a group that was meeting to help young actors like himself. He even brought with him a few other performers who had been down a similar road. Together they encouraged River to at least consider their help. River closed the door saying, "There's no problem." Echoes of his mother's words.[1]

Someone tried hard to intervene. Prophets aren't appreciated. Those who warn of impending problems are usually scorned as "fanatical" or "over-reactive." Is River just L.A. coroner's case No. 93–10011? Or does he illustrate a warning? *Don't say "there's no problem" when there is one.* Oh—and *when a prophet knocks on your door, answer it.*

Choice-Making Is a Gift We All Possess

With warnings come choices. Freedom to choose is a profoundly human characteristic. It sets us apart from the animal kingdom. Those who study this sort of thing have come across some amazing distinctions.

Low on the life chain are those cold-blooded beings with only a "reptilian brain stem" which controls their basic functions. Snakes, lizards, frogs (all those things you'd want in your kitchen), live, eat, reproduce—all by instinct. There is no consciousness or choice.

The next stage includes animals that have a "mammalian" layer over that brain stem. This makes creatures warm-blooded, allows them to walk upright and live in colonies. Monkeys are a great example. (My mom thought *I* fit this category.)

The final stage is uniquely set apart by another layer on the

---

[1]*People* magazine, January 17, 1994, "High Life," p. 57–66. And, "When Early Acting Careers Careen to an End" by Kent Black, *L.A. Times* article, January 5, 1994, F–1.

base of our brains. It is called the "cortical layer" or the "cortex." This layer is found only in humans. It controls our conscience. It allows us to make informed choices, to be self-controlled, to be selfless. Only humans have this capacity to RESPOND (with thought and choice) rather than to merely REACT by instinct.

From the Garden of Eden to the grave of the last human on earth, we're all given the means to choose our paths, our priorities, our passions. God gives us that. But he gives it to us with some instructions. The Bible points out that humankind is not only *response-able*, but responsible. Our actions matter.

You may have noticed that in this era of "freedom of choice" there's a strange and powerful message being trumpeted at the same time. Many who herald free choice say in the same breath that we really can't be held responsible for our choices—we're really very powerless when it comes to controlling our appetites.

In his book *The Human Animal*, Phil Donahue describes the sexual pressure that teens are under. His conclusion? They are *powerless* to choose chastity, so it's silly to ask them to wait.

> Today girls reach puberty at about twelve years and boys at thirteen. Marriage is at least seven or eight years away and maybe ten or fifteen. Yet mom and dad and the local clergyman and everybody else says, "Wait." Wait for ten years? How can anyone wait for ten years when the radio is blasting out songs like, "I'm So Excited" and "What's Love Got to Do with It?"; when television is filled with steamy soap operas, "T and A," risqué humor and music videos; when movies lump virgins and nerds in the same category of undesirable; and finally, when that once-in-a-lifetime rush of hormones is lighting fires in all the wrong places?[2]

While there's no question that our modern environment makes it *very difficult* to choose wisely, the fact is we still *do* choose. That is a God-given gift. Kids need to know that. They need to know that they're not simple animals reacting to every knee-jerk impulse. Realizing our power to choose makes us stop

---

[2]Quoted in *How to Live With Your Kids When You've Already Lost Your Mind* by Ken Davis (Grand Rapids: Zondervan, 1992), p. 141.

and think about what we're bringing on ourselves. It challenges our indifference.

Actions Stem From What Is Instilled

I appreciate what one film and video critic cited in a recent report:

> In an editorial comic strip that appeared in the *Orlando Sentinel*, two men are standing on the sidewalk grimacing at the newspaper headlines. "Look, more killings in our schools," observes the first one. "It's a shame," agrees the second. "I just don't understand why kids have such a lack of respect for human life these days," he says. Behind these men are a row of storefronts. One is a movie theater where "Blood Bath III" is playing. "Women in Chains" is the coming attraction. Next door, a large sign points the way to a shop that sells guns. Beneath it is a euthanasia "walk-in" clinic and an "Abortions 'R Us" that boasts being open twenty-four hours a day.[3]

Kids today are submerged in a vat of values. Like it or not, values are communicated everywhere from playgrounds to freeway billboards. That's a given. Sometimes what your child sees and hears is pretty much out of your grasp.

But there *are* arenas of life where you can pull your child's head up out of the soup. School, for example, gets the bulk of your child's prime time and attention. Do you know what your child's school really teaches? Whose values are being planted?

Despite all the rhetoric about "value-free education," it simply doesn't exist. To hand out condoms on school campuses assumes a value. To prohibit cheating on exams presumes a value. To simply *hold* the belief that abortion is any woman's right communicates a value. Who we are and what we believe comes across loud and clear—and kids are listening. You can't lead, educate or even speak without revealing values. Anyone in a position of influence, especially a teacher, who is in that position six hours a day, is

---

[3]Film Report Volume 10, No. 1, January 1994, p. 2.

going to shape values. And what impact do values make on behavior? They literally dictate it! Everything we are and do stems from our beliefs. Choices are based on what I call "value paradigms"—the world of "good and bad" as we believe it to be.

I mention education at this point because kids spend a third of their lives in that arena. Parents simply must become aware of the seed values being planted in that environment of influence. Not only aware, but discerning. I've read curriculum samples which on the surface appear to encourage appropriate goals, such as:

- increases self-esteem;

- promotes greater ability to cope with stress;

- promotes better memory; and

- enhances creativity.

All good end results. The problem is the means to those ends, which in some instances encompass

- meditation, where students are encouraged to consult inner "spirit guides";

- using stories that illustrate that all lifestyles are equally valid;

- the teaching that absolutes are relative, and that we can have moral beliefs but that no one can have moral knowledge;

- the endorsement of a non-divisive, all-inclusive, world religious faith; and

- using chants to help kids get in touch with their higher consciousness.

Just an overreaction by the fanatical right-wing? Every one of the ideologies I just listed are from the global "Core Curriculum" espoused by numerous professional educators, or from the writings of Robert Muller's book "New Genesis: Shaping a Global Spirituality," or from Lynda Falkenstein's paper "Global Education" being distributed by the U.S. Department of Education. (For a more complete development of this issue, pick up a copy of *The*

New Age Masquerade, by Eric Beuher.)

My point isn't to bash public education. Quite the opposite. Many teachers in many schools in many locations are *not* holding or instilling any of the agenda I just listed. The issue at hand is awareness and discernment followed by insightful discussions with your child. What your kids hear at school, even those things we disagree with, can provide a perfect opportunity for learning. In most cases we'd do well to feel less threatened and become more willing to get involved with the material our children are absorbing.

Let's take it a step further. Who is teaching your kids *after* school? The latest studies reveal that the average TV-viewing time of the American child ages 6 to 16 is about 22 hours per week. (If Billy lives to be 80 and continues to watch TV at that rate, he will have spent 8 to 10 years of his life watching television!) Those same realities are true of music. Countless studies report that between seventh grade and graduation an average teen will listen to 10,000 hours of music via MTV, car radios and CD headsets.

With so much time spent wired to school, the television set and headphones, the question is this: Do you know *what* is being taught? Are you aware of the values held and espoused by those holding such huge sway over your child's beliefs? Are you making a connection between worldviews—value paradigms—and the behaviors that ensue from those perspectives?

"What can a parent do about it?" we cry. But if we're honest, most of us will confess that while we hide behind a scarcity of "ideas" what we really lack is action. The real problem isn't what we *can* do but what we *will* do.

- Will we sit down and talk with our children after school and find out exactly what they're picking up?

- Will we take the time to write letters and make phone calls when legislation is being considered that affects what happens in our schools and homes?

- Will we move the couch in front of the TV—in order to block the view, not to improve it—and take back that position of influence in our home?

- Will we listen or read the lyrics that our kids are listening to and use them as a springboard for discussion?

- Will we set real and firm boundaries about appropriate media entertainment, and live out that standard in front of our kids?

- Will we supplant some of what is being beamed into our households with relevant conversations based on God's Word and his principles for life?

- Will we make our child's "Christian education" as important as their "intellectual education"?

Paths always have starting points. Decisions don't just happen. How we act grows from what we believe. And what your kids believe is being hammered out on the anvil of everyday life—with astounding power and influence.

Wisdom Is Acquired Through Daily Opportunities

A number of years ago there was a terrible collision one evening in the intersection adjacent to a church here in Orange County. A few kids from the youth group heard the screeching tires and that all-too-familiar noise of two cars colliding. The students raced over and were actually the first ones on the scene. Victims were pried loose from a mangled pile of metal. Later that week we learned that the cause of the accident was an intoxicated driver. One person had been killed. The students saw it all—and shared with others how they would never forget what they'd seen.

Not long afterward, one of those same kids who'd witnessed the accident was at a party. He left with some friends and got into a car with a student driving who had been drinking. On the way home their car veered off the road and crashed. The boy who'd witnessed the previous accident was killed, the victim of the same kind of tragedy. The one who said he would never forget—forgot. Kicks have kickbacks. Choices have courses. Courses have consequences. Today as I write, I'm deeply saddened that for that one kid the consequences were immediate and final. For the rest of us, there's time. Time to realign and to help our children realign.

I've had the opportunity of sharing that story with thousands of parents and teenagers over the years. On one such occasion I was speaking at a conference in Seattle, and afterward a mother approached me with her teenage daughter lagging a few feet behind.

"Daniel, I'm June. I really appreciated your story about the kid who was at a party." In my peripheral vision I could see the woman's daughter, head down, staring at her own feet. Her hair fell around her head like a veil. "I can't even tell you how many arguments I've had with Chrissy about the people she hangs around with. I know some of them drink. She insists that she never drinks and I insist that she still shouldn't be around these kind of people." She went on describing her situation, after which I asked if I might speak to her daughter alone for a moment. She conceded and I pulled her daughter aside.

After a few minutes together, the girl looked up as far as my shoulder. "I just wish she would let me make my own decisions."

"That's good," I said. I hoped she was catching the smile on my face. "Chrissy, I'll bet you're getting pretty good at making decisions. I'll also bet your mom is running scared. She knows what's out there. She's seen a lot of pain and she's feeling like it's up to her to protect you right now. She hasn't got much time left with you. She loves you more than you'll ever know—"

"No. I don't know!" Chrissy interjected. "She's just worried I'll get drunk and smash her car or something. She doesn't trust me with anything . . ." Her voice trailed.

I ended up walking June back to the convention center lobby that afternoon. We talked about a lot of things. Finally she explained, "Chrissy just doesn't know how to make good choices. She's seventeen and plans to go away to college next year, and I really don't think she's ready to be on her own."

"What big choices is she making on her own right now?" I asked.

June gave me a puzzled look. "What do you mean?"

"I mean, what areas of her life have you handed over to her? What is she completely responsible for?"

Over the next half hour it became obvious to both of us that choice-making was something that had never been nurtured in Chrissy's life. All these years, even more so since June's divorce,

Mom had reserved the right to pontificate on nearly every move Chrissy made. Church, boyfriends, clothes, grades, social functions, you name it—June had an opinion and expected her opinion to be honored. Our conversation became a pivotal point of releasing some rein.

Good choice-making is a learned art, nurtured from birth. The most important role parents play in the process is to allow life itself to teach through consequences, all the way along. Obviously we walk a tightrope. In many instances we need to protect our children for their own health and livelihood. But what about those countless times when we don't *need* to protect—when we simply *want* to protect? Are we giving space for them to fail—space that communicates trust and belief in process? When children are small, protection is everything. But as the years progress, our protective arms and antennae must pull back so that internal strength of character can take over. Face it—many poor choices will be made. Legs fresh out of a cast always wobble. But it's got to happen. It's got to happen gradually. And the baton of life needs to be handed over daily so that when our kids jump out of the blocks, they can run without falling.

Whether it's the media or partying with friends or a debate at school over euthanasia, our job is to help our kids learn to discern—to think through issues and influences and to track them to their natural consequences. Indifference—ours or theirs—to the importance of making choices can cost them everything.

It is now Monday. Laguna Beach burned on Wednesday, last week. The fires were finally extinguished last night at about 6:00 P.M. This morning I took my daughter to Laguna Beach to see what had happened. Places we had hiked were now naked hillsides of black soot. Homes we had admired were reduced to piles of charred wood beams and lonely chimneys. Lush trees that caught Pacific breezes last week were today nothing more than stumps standing like tombstones.

Before leaving to return home we stopped on the side of the road so that I could take a few pictures. Katie stood beside me silently. Finally she said softly, "Why was there a fire, Daddy?"

We made our way back toward the car. "Because, honey," I explained, "someone lit a match."

Lord, *Teach us to number our days aright, that we may gain a heart of wisdom* (Psalm 90:12).

Truth or Consequences

- What major crossroads have you faced in life? Looking back, did you move ahead wisely? Have you shared that junction with your children? Give them an opportunity to see how crossroads, gates, investments and paths all impact the future.

- As you pass by a construction site on the road, initiate a conversation like the scenario described in this chapter. Point out the value of warnings. Imagine what our lives would be like if we didn't pay any attention to warnings. Ask "What warnings have you received from me (your parent) that could make a big difference later on in your life? What warnings has God given to both of us? What could be some of the consequences of ignoring them?"

- Based on what you see on a billboard as you drive down the street, ask, "What values are reflected there?" or "What does that billboard say is important?" Follow up with "What are some of the consequences that could result from adopting that value, either good or bad? How would you describe what you value and why?"

- With your teen, discuss in advance how they'd respond in a typical situation where peer pressure to compromise is intense. For instance, "Say you're at a party where someone begins passing around a bottle of Tequila. What would you do? What kind of internal principles would you think of in making your decision? If you declined the alcohol, how would you be treated? What might your friends be thinking deep down inside? What are some other decisions you might need to make at that point (i.e., not riding in a car with someone who's been drinking)? What are some of the consequences your friends may face and what are some of the benefits of choosing not to participate with them?"

- Take some time to explain to your kids the connection between the good things they're enjoying in life and the decisions you made years back. Show them the correlation, for example, between the education you pursued and the job you were able to get, or the influences you resisted and how that has paid off.

- And most importantly, examine what choices your children are able to make for themselves right now. Take the time to help them see ahead to the natural consequences that result from their decisions. Give them some safe and age-appropriate opportunities to choose for themselves, and experience the results.

3

The Truth About Salvation

The Consequences of Refusal

But Christ has indeed been raised from the dead, the firstfruits of those who have fallen asleep. For since death came through a man, the resurrection of the dead comes also through a man . . . in Christ all will be made alive.

—1 Corinthians 15:20–22

I hate finances. I know some people love this stuff. I don't. Checkbooks never balance for me. Percentages, returns, mutual funds, dividends . . . it all makes me itch. I find financial software programs utterly confusing. "This computer's driving me crazy," I yelled from my desk upstairs down to my wife a few months ago. "Buy an abacus," she shouted back. No mercy. And none of it compares to trying to decipher the hieroglyphics of a medical bill from an insurance company. What are you supposed to pay? To whom? How much goes toward your deductible? Why? And on and on.

A few years ago we decided to invest a small sum of money in the stock market. We picked about five different companies that had a history of growth. "Gotta pay attention to them," said a friend who likes this sort of thing. "You can't just invest and then walk off and ignore them." So I watched. And watched. And waited for my nest egg to hatch into something that would cat-apult me into early retirement. It didn't, by the way. As it turned out, I had invested in the wrong things.

So many people I know approach God the way I took on the stock market. Figure out what God really wants. Pick your strat-egy. Then start making investments in goodness. Do lots of this. Don't do much of that. Pay attention to your life. Do enough of the right and not too much of the wrong and over time you'll amass enough righteousness to get a golden retirement, an en-trance pass into heaven. Do a good job of managing the portfolio of your life and—bingo, you're declared a winner. Slide right past the pit and go directly to the pearly gates.

But God never said that. A buzzer goes off. "Survey says . . . you LOSE! We're so sorry, thanks for playing." According to Scrip-ture, salvation isn't a game, or even a gamble—it's a gift. A gift many people ignore. A gift many people refuse.

Until the Seed Is Planted, There's No Life

A very "good" man named Nicodemus found Jesus one night and inquired about his own celestial bank account. Nicodemus was a member of an elitist group, a sort of first-century "Good Sam Club." These men, called "Pharisees," went above and be-yond the law in their personal righteousness. They were true to form. Perfect in function. If anyone would make it to heaven based on performance they were sure to be the ones. And what did Jesus say to him? "Congratulations, Mr. Nicodemus, you're a winner!" Nope. Jesus said, in effect, "Nick, you're not going to heaven unless you're changed from the inside out." Jesus told him, *No one can see the kingdom of God unless he is born again* (John 3:3).

At first Nicodemus didn't get it. *"How can a man be born when he is old?"* Nicodemus asked. *"Surely he cannot enter a second time into his mother's womb to be born!"* (John 3:4).

And that was precisely Christ's point. It's not a physical thing at all! What Jesus means by being born again is simply this: Apart from the Spirit of God, we're spiritually dead. But when we accept the life that God offers, we're made spiritually and eternally alive by his power. Scripture refers to this as the "second birth" and that is precisely what Jesus had in mind when he taught that we must be born again. *Flesh gives birth to flesh, but the Spirit gives birth to spirit* (John 3:6).

Jesus said, *I am the way and the truth and the life. No one comes to the Father except through me* (John 14:6). Eternal life is a gift from God. It is by the Spirit of God. It comes not from a system, but a Savior. It's not *what* you know but *who* you know that counts.

Jesus went on to explain to Nicodemus, *For God so loved the world that he gave his one and only Son, that whoever believes in him shall not perish but have eternal life* (John 3:16).

Later in the same chapter, a man named John came along and echoed the same truth, *A man can receive only what is given him from heaven* (John 3:27).

So where does the truth about consequences fit into all this? The last verse of the chapter puts it all into one simple, straightforward, all encompassing statement: *Whoever believes in the Son has eternal life, but whoever rejects the Son will not see life, for God's wrath remains on him* (John 3:36).

No truth in Scripture could be more clear. No consequence could be more sobering. Those who admit their inability to "work their way to heaven," who instead put their faith and hope in Jesus Christ, will be given eternal life. Those who don't—won't. That is the truth and that is the consequence.

Amazingly, there's no *strategy* involved.

For it is by grace you have been saved, through faith—and this not from yourselves, it is the gift of God—not by works, so that no one can boast (Ephesians 2:8–9).

There's no *goodness* involved.

Christ Jesus came into the world to save sinners—of whom I am the worst. But for that very reason I was shown mercy so that in me, the worst of sinners, Christ Jesus might display his unlimited patience as an example for those who would believe on him and receive eternal life (1 Timothy 1:15–16).

There's no *human wisdom* involved.

For the message of the cross is foolishness to those who are perishing, but to us who are being saved it is the power of God. . . . God was pleased through the foolishness of what was preached to save those who believe. . . . It is because of Him that you are in Christ Jesus, who has become for us wisdom from God—that is, our righteousness, holiness and redemption (1 Corinthians 1:18, 21, 30).

There's no *chance* involved.

If you confess with your mouth, "Jesus is Lord," and believe in your heart that God raised him from the dead, you will be saved (Romans 10:9).

There's no *worry* involved.

Yet to all who received him, to those who believed in his name, he gave the right to become children of God (John 1:12).

Until the Seed Takes Root, There's No Fruit

The New Testament says that the Word of God is like a seed. When that seed—the truth about Jesus Christ—is firmly planted in our hearts, then a whole new life begins. Without it, expecting fruitfulness is futile.

Jesus told this parable:

A farmer went out to sow his seed. As he was scattering the seed, some fell along the path; it was trampled on, and the birds of the air ate it up. Some fell on rock, and when it came up, the plants withered because they had no moisture. Other seed fell among thorns, which grew up with it and choked the plants. Still other seed fell on good soil. It came up and yielded a crop, a hundred times more than what was sown (Luke 8:5–8).

The four soils, Jesus explained, are like four types of people in the world. Some people are "path people." They know about Jesus, but only in an abstract sort of way. Satan blinds these people from really seeing the Truth for what it is. Others get excited about the Truth when they hear it, but as soon as one of life's storms comes up, they change their mind and decide that it's no longer true or relevant to their present situation. There's a third type of person, Jesus continued, one who believes the truth but then becomes embroiled in the issues of life— solving problems, making money, having fun—and the truth never produces anything in their lives. Then there's a fourth person: *But the seed on good soil stands for those with a noble and good heart, who hear the word, retain it, and by persevering produce a crop* (Luke 8:15).

I'm continually running into people who are forcing, bribing, tricking, pleading, kicking and screaming—trying to get their kids to "be good." They're searching for fruit, longing for goodness in their kids. One father was sharing with me all the strategies he'd tried to get his son to behave. In the course of conversation I asked, "When did your son accept Jesus as his Savior?" There was a pause.

"When did he what?" the father responded. I repeated the question. This dad had no idea.

Becoming a Christian won't make your child perfect. But almost every right choice you want your child to make ties back in some way to this, the most basic of choices.

The most important crossroads people ever face is this decision to "believe in the Lord Jesus." Not simply to give mental assent to the historical Jesus, or to label him a great teacher, but to acknowledge that he was who he said he was—the Son of God, the one who "takes away the sins of the world." It is then and only then that the seed of eternal life is planted, or as Scripture puts it, then "you will be saved."

The verse I'm referring to, Acts 16:31, may be familiar. Interestingly, the verse also makes a profound statement about our faith as it relates to our families. *Believe in the Lord Jesus, and you will be saved—you and your household* (Acts 16:31). In the verses following that text, we read that Paul explained the gospel to the families of those jailers as well. Indeed, they followed the example of their dads in responding to the Truth.

Now, we know from the rest of Scripture that parents can't believe in Christ "for" their kids. Trusting in God's grace for salvation is an individual choice. However, home is where the heart is formed. There was a natural passing on of faith from parents to kids that occurred in the first century, and that dynamic is as powerful today as ever. The biggest influence over a kid's faith is what he observes in his parents.

Maybe you've come to understand the Gospel at some time in the past. Then I invite you to deepen your resolve to make these truths clear to others. But maybe, just maybe, there's still a shade of doubt in your heart. Maybe the seed hasn't really sunk in, or it's there but your faith has grown dry and parched. In either case, the truth about salvation deserves primary attention, because the consequence of refusal is eternally devastating.

Until the Seed Is Internalized, There's No Hope

One of Alfred Hitchcock's haunting TV episodes tells an incredible story that perfectly highlights the truth about salvation. It bears summary.

There was this wicked woman who had lived a terrible life but always seemed to get away with it. Finally she ended up murdering someone and she was sentenced to life in prison. Just as the bus she was being transported on was entering the prison wall, the woman noticed one small detail that would become part of her escape plan. She saw an old man covering up a fresh grave just outside the wall.

The woman discovered later that the old man was the facility's undertaker. He worked in the basement of one of the wards, building caskets and taking care of carting out and burying those who died. She also found out that the old man was going blind and needed cataract surgery but didn't have the means to pay for it.

After offering the undertaker a big sum of money to cover the cost of his operation, the woman coaxed the old man into going along with her plan.

The next time she heard the toll of the prison bell signaling the death of an inmate, she would slip into the basement, get into the casket alongside the body of the deceased and pull the top down over her. Then he, the undertaker, would come along later and wheel the casket out through the prison wall on his cart. He would bury the casket as usual and then, after dark, return and dig the casket up, setting the woman free. She would then reward him handsomely.

Finally the day came. She heard the toll of the bell. Someone had died. This was her ticket to freedom—so she thought. She secretly made her way down the dark steps that led to the undertaker's workroom. Through the dim light she spotted the freshly made casket. She squeezed inside next to the corpse and pulled the top down. It wasn't long before she heard footsteps outside and could feel the casket being loaded onto the cart. After a brief ride, she smiled to herself as the casket was lowered down into the hole and dirt was shoveled on top.

It was silent. She could hardly contain herself with excitement. She waited. No one came. Hours dragged. She began to panic. In a moment of desperation she lights a match and glances at the corpse next to her. You guessed it—it is the old man himself who had died!

As the camera lifts from the cemetery, all you can hear is the eerie, hollow wail of a woman who will never be free.[1]

Our worst nightmare. But a very real one. The woman in this story thought that somehow through her own ingenuity she could outwit death; she could do it on her own. Little did she realize that the one she hoped would save her was himself a victim of the thing she dreaded most. She trusted in the wrong man.

Eternal life isn't found within any of us. It isn't found in the rigors of a religious system. It isn't found by working harder or working smarter or "hoping for the best." It is found when we put our trust in God himself by accepting the Savior he has sent.

Let me speak to you very personally for a moment because this is a decision each of us make—personally. No matter what your background, or what your parents believed, or what church you were raised in, or what good things you've done or what bad things you've done or how hopeless life may seem right now, nothing—I repeat—nothing is as important as this decision to entrust your own eternal destiny to God's ability to save you through the death and resurrection of Jesus Christ.

If you are ready to do that, humble yourself before God right now! Come to him in prayer and admit your sinfulness and need for a brand-new spiritual birth. Acknowledge that Christ's death on the cross was the perfect sacrifice for sin and that you now accept that as payment for your sin as well.

For the wages of sin is death . . . That's the consequence.

. . . *but the gift of God is eternal life in Christ Jesus our Lord* (Romans 6:23). That's the Truth!

---

[1]Charles R. Swindoll, *Growing Deep in the Christian Life* (Portland, Ore.: Multnomah Press, 1986), p. 277–278.

Until We Trust in God's Forgiveness There's No Peace

When I was young my family made a trip from our home in Washington state down the coast to southern California. As a part of our tourist routine we visited Knott's Berry Farm. Soon after entering the amusement park I noticed an attraction that advertised "Panning for Gold." My eight-year-old mind raced with visions of wealth. Mom and Dad agreed and I lined up with the others in front of a trough of rushing water. As instructed, I lowered my tin pan under the water, scooped up some sand and swirled it around. The whole event was over in a moment or two. "Good job," the attendant praised, handing me a tiny plastic vile of water containing a few flecks of real gold. I was impressed.

I carried that thing around with me the rest of the week. I'd pull it out of my pocket now and then to check on it. "Yep. There it was. I owned GOLD!" Then tragedy struck.

We were on our way back to Washington, our station wagon stuffed to the roof with our belongings. In all of the bouncing around (and wrestling around that brothers and sisters do on a long trip) my little clear tube of gold got lost. I hunted for it frantically. Under the blankets. Under the seat. Finally I found it. There it was, on the floor—broken into bits. Someone had stepped on it. The vile had been smashed. The water had leaked out. The gold. . . ? It was gone for good. Even after picking at the carpet for a while I wasn't able to retrieve any of it. I looked for a culprit. "You stepped on it," I accused my brother. And I pouted through the entire state of Oregon!

That childish incident comes to mind when I think about this issue of salvation. So many people view God's love and acceptance like the gold I won for good panning! Do a good job and you'll store up a treasure sure to impress God at the end of the line. But life is an unsure struggle. We try to hang on, toe the line, give up this or that vice, but we fail. Our goodness leaks out through the brokenness of our own errors. We feel devastated by our deviance and deep down inside feel as though our worth has diminished. "God could never love me," we conclude, and we move through life in quiet desperation—never being sure.

Scripture tells us that Jesus Christ is the ultimate "priest." He represents us before God the Father. Even when we fail to act on our new spiritual nature, we can feel confident in coming to God for forgiveness, knowing that we are forgiven because of what Christ has already done for us!

For we do not have a high priest who is unable to sympathize with our weaknesses, but we have one who has been tempted in every way, just as we are—yet was without sin. Let us then approach the throne of grace with confidence, so that we may receive mercy and find grace to help us in our time of need (Hebrews 4:15–16).

If only we understood the magnitude of God's love! With Christ as our Savior, Scripture tells us we are forgiven with certainty. Our eternal life isn't in jeopardy. Sin has real and often disastrous consequences, but losing our eternal life isn't one of them. *If we confess our sins, he is faithful and just and will forgive us our sins and purify us from all unrighteousness* (1 John 1:9). Why? Because our security before God isn't based on what we do in life but rather in what Christ did on the cross.

Let the words of Scripture reassure you of the reality of your eternal life: *Therefore, there is now no condemnation for those who are in Christ Jesus, because through Christ Jesus the law of the Spirit of life set me free from the law of sin and death* (Romans 8:1–2).

As a believer in Jesus Christ, we are given a whole new nature. A new orientation. A new "attraction" to what is spiritual rather than "natural" in this world. Romans, chapter 8 continues: *Those who live according to the sinful nature have their minds set on what that nature desires; but those who live in accordance with the Spirit have their minds set on what the Spirit desires* (Romans 8:5).

How does this happen? It happens because the Spirit of God resides within those of us who have accepted Jesus Christ as our Lord. *You, however, are controlled not by the sinful nature but by the Spirit, if the Spirit of God lives in you. . . . And if the Spirit of him who raised Jesus from the dead is living in you, he who raised Christ from the dead will also give life to your mortal bodies through his Spirit, who lives in you* (Romans 8:9–11).

It is the fact that we now are indwelt by the Spirit of God that makes us "spiritual" people. It is impossible for any of us to live spiritually good lives without the Spirit of God in us. It is the Holy

Spirit that *helps us in our weakness* (Romans 8:26).

Our hope of eternal life is now secure because of that new life we have in Jesus Christ. We've been "born again." We have eternal life! That's the timeless truth with an eternal destiny.

Truth or Consequences

- Which of the four soils of Luke 8 characterizes your own heart toward God? How about the lives of your children?

- Have you planted the seed of the Gospel—the good news of salvation through Jesus Christ, in the lives of your children? Do they clearly understand that eternal life is found in acceptance of a Savior, not in a system of religious activity or in any kind of good behavior?

- It is worthwhile to give each of your family members the chance to verbally express to each other God's great plan of salvation. Help them by encouraging them to memorize verses like John 3:16, Romans 6:23, Ephesians 2:8–9 and 1 John 1:9 and to share with you what those verses mean in their own lives.

- Try illustrating salvation with the use of a gift. Hand your child a small package and then explain that the gift isn't theirs until they accept it. As they open the package, explain that God has given us the greatest gift we could ever receive. It is up to us to accept his salvation through faith in Jesus Christ.

- Our culture hides death, treating it as unreal. Consider taking your child on a walk through a cemetery to see the gravesites of relatives or to hunt for old gravestones. Or revive a lost tradition and celebrate Memorial Day. You can ask, "What's most important in life? All of us are eternal beings—we have souls that live on beyond our earthly existence. Do you know what it means to 'be saved'? Why do we need a 'Savior'? How can we be sure that we have eternal life with our Creator after our bodies die?"

- When a family pet dies, you can use the incident to explain the difference between animals and humans. While we love our pets and they respond in ways that make us feel loved too, God created humans with a "living soul." That part of us that we can't see will be with God forever if we have a genuine relationship with him through Jesus Christ.

- It is amazing how many children have no idea how their own parents came to understand and accept God's plan of salvation for their lives. Share your own spiritual journey with them. If you had a parent or grandparent who was a believer and passed on his or her faith, take the time to pull out the family album and talk about the qualities of that relative. Show your kids how a legacy is passed from generation to generation. Give them a sense that they are connected to a line of believers and will have the privilege of passing that eternal hope on to their children as well.

- You and your child or teenager could come up with a list of three or four friends who don't understand or believe in God's love for people. You could write down those names in a prayer journal and begin thinking of ways to introduce those friends to Christ. Some of the ways could include being Christlike in our example, inviting them to a Christian event where the Gospel is being shared or having them over for dinner and using your prayer before the meal as a simple way of stating who Jesus is and what he's done for us.

4

THE TRUTH ABOUT HUMILITY

THE CONSEQUENCES OF ARROGANCE

Neither can you bear fruit unless you remain in me. I am the vine; you are the branches. If a man remains in me and I in him, he will bear much fruit; apart from me you can do nothing.

—John 15:4–5

"Most scientists now agree that the world as we know it resulted from an explosion of matter in space," the museum guide intoned. "This resulted in the formation of hydrogen, which is one of the main building blocks of our present solar system, planets as well as the sun." Walking past red velvet ropes, our group looked at a large illuminated photo of planets.

"Our planet held the components necessary for life to form, a sort of 'soup' you might say," the museum guide continued. "These components—these gases—mixed with the energy of lightning, resulted in compounds which were basic to the establishment of life." Everyone nodded knowingly. "Of course these molecular structures became more and more complex over the time span of billions of years. This process has continued, has evolved, to result in what we are today. . . ."

"Any questions?" The class of sixth graders looked astounded.

Who could question that? It sounded so well-packaged. But a hand went up in the back anyway. "Where does God fit into all this?" came the inquiry. "Well," the teacher smiled, "I guess you'll have to ask your mom or dad that question."

Chances are the kid's parents probably don't have an answer. For most of our society, God is gone. And with God gone, what "center" is there but ourselves? A natural progression of thought comes from "God gone/self at center" thinking. If God is gone then what follows actually makes a lot of sense:

1. God is either nonexistent or irrelevant. Either way the issue isn't important.

2. Human beings, on the other hand, are vitally important. Humankind's environment, rights and happiness are all that matter now that God is gone.

3. To bring God or God's absolutes into any public arena (government, schools, and so on), is narrow, legalistic, rigid and unwise.

4. Every issue of life consequently needs to be considered in light of my personal desires. With self at the center of my world, marriage, sex, violence, abortion—literally everything—is a matter of what *I* need or want for me and my world.

5. Something only becomes "wrong" when it affects me or someone I care about negatively.

What doesn't make sense is why people across our nation stand around looking bewildered about the state of our society. They blink in astonishment at headlines, gasp at teenagers hanging out in Nazi skinhead militia garb at the mall, stare blankly at urban death tolls and wonder—how come? They can't imagine what could have caused all this chaos.

The Bible begs for a moment of our attention.

When "Self" Replaces "God," We Become Senseless

The one thing most of us agree on is the fact that something somewhere along the line went seriously wrong. That much is obvious. As much as we'd like to say "Oh well, there have always been problems . . . life goes on" the facts reveal otherwise. As noted in a 1993 report by Dr. William Bennett, former U.S. secretary of education, we in America are experiencing a "substantial social regression . . . at enormous human cost." He writes:

> Since 1960, population has increased 41 percent; the Gross Domestic Product has nearly tripled; and total social spending by all levels of government (measured in constant 1990 dollars) has risen from $143.73 billion to $787 billion—more than a fivefold increase. Inflation-adjusted spending on welfare has increased 630 percent, and inflation-adjusted spending on education has increased 225 percent . . .
>
> But during the same thirty-year-period there has been a 560 percent increase in violent crime, more than a 400-percent increase in illegitimate births, a tripling of divorces, a tripling of the percentage of children living in single-parent homes, more than a 200-percent increase in the teenage suicide rate, and a drop of almost 80 points in the S.A.T. scores. Modern-day pathologies, at least great parts of them, have gotten worse. . . .[1]

Romans chapter 1 paints a gray, frightening picture of a society detached from its Source of life. It celebrates its freedom even as decay sets in.

For although they knew God, they neither glorified him as God nor gave thanks to him, but their thinking became futile and their foolish hearts were darkened (Romans 1:21).

In general, Western society has decided that God isn't important or impending, so we exchange attachment to our Creator for another option. Rather than treat God as the Source of existence, most have decided to treat themselves as God and treat God as if he were irrelevant.

Detachment is a foolish move.

Although they claimed to be wise, they became fools and exchanged the glory of the immortal God for images made to look like mortal man. . . . They exchanged the truth of God for a lie, and worshiped and served created things rather than the Creator—who is forever praised (Romans 1:22–25).

---

[1]"The Index of Leading Cultural Indicators," by Dr. William J. Bennett as quoted in *Fifty Practical Ways to Take Back Our Kids From the World*, by Michael J. McManus (Wheaton, Ill.: Tyndale Publishers, 1993), p. 8.

The consequences of human pride are obvious and wide-spread. As if we needed a reminder, the passage lists some of them. It reads like the front page of the daily news.

They have become filled with every kind of wickedness, evil, greed and depravity. They are full of envy, murder, strife, deceit and malice. The are gossips, slanderers, God-haters, insolent, arrogant and boast-ful; they invent ways of doing evil; they disobey their parents; they are senseless, faithless, heartless, ruthless (Romans 1:29–31).

In the second letter to Timothy, Paul offers us the same kind of list with one additional note. This decayed state, he adds, is just how the world will look before Christ returns. Close obser-vation reveals that we're right on schedule:

Remove ourselves from God's love, and we're left with hatred and anger. In the NEXT HOUR about 450 kids in America will be beaten, molested or otherwise abused by their parents. Over 100 will run away from home. And three out of four of the girl run-aways end up selling sex to survive.[2]

Remove ourselves from God's priority on the family, and we're left with brokenness. In 1870, only one marriage in thirty-four ended in divorce. Two generations ago divorce had risen to one in twelve. In the last generation it was up to one in three and at present, researchers place the divorce rate at about half of all mar-riages!

Remove ourselves from God's moral stance, and we're left with immorality. Adult bookstores now outnumber McDonald's restau-rants in the U.S. by a margin of at least three to one. Seventy per-cent of pornography ends up in the hands of kids.[3]

Remove ourselves from God's peace, and we're left with anxiety and pain. Twenty-one million Americans have used cocaine. Two and a half million have continued using it and a million of us are considered heavy users.[4]

Remove ourselves from God's authority, and we're left with an-archy. The riots that shook Los Angeles in 1992 resulted in 53 deaths, 2,400 injuries, 1,400 stores looted and burned, more than

---

[2]Josh McDowell Research Almanac and Statistical Digest.
[3]Ibid.
[4]Vic Sussman, "News You Can Use," *U.S. News and World Report*, September 11, 1989, pp. 70–72.

$1 billion in property damage, and incalculable emotional distress to children and adults.

Remove ourselves from God's values, and we're left with greed. In August of 1989 the Gallup organization released the results of a recent poll which revealed that more than four million 13- to 14-year-olds will have been offered illicit drugs in the past thirty days. It is not surprising then that the average age when kids experiment with drugs is 12.[5]

Remove ourselves from God's plan, and we're left with aimlessness. Suicides among 15- to 19-year-olds have risen over 400% in the last decade with over 600,000 teens attempting suicide in one year. Every minute in America another teenager attempts to take his own life and every hour someone under the age of 25 will succeed. And the biggest reason given by teens for the high rate of suicide? "Feelings of worthlessness (86%) and feeling isolated and lonely (81%)."[6]

Man, left alone, hangs himself. Apart from life infusion by the Spirit of God, we're doomed. Much like Romans chapter 1, Galatians chapter 5 carries the same thought. The fruit of our sinful nature is: *sexual immorality, impurity and debauchery; idolatry and witchcraft; hatred, discord, jealousy, fits of rage, selfish ambition, dissensions, factions and envy; drunkenness, orgies and the like* (Galatians 5:19–21a). I'm glad he stops there.

Or does he? No. Paul takes a breath only to level the final outcome. *I warn you, as I did before, that those who live like this will not inherit the kingdom of God* (Galatians 5:21b).

Pride was the insidious lie in the Garden of Eden, "You can be like God . . ." and it is the lie that pervades our culture today—we are our own god. Self-inflation carries a price tag. There are consequences.

Want a picture? King Nebuchadnezzar. Gazing out from one of the palace corridors. Robed in satin like drapes, stroking his beard as he ponders his loftiness. Babylon stretches out before him. "Mine," he thinks. "It's all mine." To quote him, *Is not this the great Babylon I have built as the royal residence, by my mighty power*

---

[5]Ibid.

[6]*Youth Ministry Resource Book*, Group Publishing, p. 167.

and for the glory of my majesty? (Daniel 4:30). Hmmm. Sounds a tad heady doesn't it? But at the same time it sounds familiar—as if the same self-preoccupation were common not just among Kings, but among us all. "God is gone. So, if it feels good—do it. God is within you. All that matters is what you want. You can have it all. Stand up for your rights. You . . . ME!"

I've always loved this story of King Nebuchadnezzar. It's just so amazing. Suddenly, while *the words were still on his lips,* says Daniel, *a voice came from heaven.* . . . I am sure this was sorely unexpected—this voice. An "uh-oh" moment. Heaven meets earth. And the outcome wasn't pretty. God (whom I'm convinced has a sense of irony that is beyond any of us) turned the king—into the likes of a COW! *You will be driven away from people and will live with the wild animals; you will eat grass like cattle. Seven times will pass by for you until you acknowledge that the Most High is sovereign over the kingdoms of men and gives them to anyone he wishes. Immediately what had been said about Nebuchadnezzar was fulfilled* (Daniel 4:32–33). Have you seen *Beauty and the Beast?* This is the *real* royalty-turned-wretch story. Just as predicted, the king spent seven years in exile, living like a madman, mindlessly crawling about on all fours.

But people have forgotten King Nebuchadnezzar's story and the moral it represents. Daily we sit and stare at our idol, "Mirror, mirror on the wall. Who's the greatest of them all?" The mirror responds on cue. "Oh my, by all means, no question! You are, you are!" We're self-preoccupied but not self-satisfied. Secretly we wonder if there's something the mirror isn't telling us.

I can't resist just one more amazing story from Scripture that underscores this point. We don't know a ton about "the Sons of Korah" spoken of in Numbers 16. But we do know this: they didn't respect God or what He said. And the result of their arrogance? At God's command the ground under them split apart and swallowed them up. (Those of us who live in earthquake-prone areas can relate!) In one big bite they were entombed with everything they owned.

When the Spirit Rules Our Lives, There Is Fruit

There is hope. But contrary to popular polls, it isn't "within ourselves." Hope originates in God himself. When will we come to our senses, like Nebuchadnezzar, and look up from our tufts of grass in the field? When will we realize that all the good we long for is only a by-product of attachment to God—humility before God, surrender to God? The "good life" is found in a whole different orchard. A whole different Vine. Naturally, the result is different fruit—the fruit of the Spirit: *love, joy, peace, patience, kindness, goodness, faithfulness, gentleness and self-control* (Galatians 5:22–23).

Another tour. Not a museum but a mesa. As instructed by our Israeli guide, we all disembarked the tour bus and walked across the dusty road. We found ourselves at the edge of a vineyard. Our American tour host opened his Bible to John 15 and began to read, *Remain in me, and I will remain in you. No branch can bear fruit by itself; it must remain in the vine* (John 15:4).

I looked down at the grapevine in front of me. Jesus would have had a similar scene in mind. I wondered if he and the disciples were standing in a vineyard when he spoke. My mind drifted. I wondered if he was standing in THIS vineyard. (Being in Israel does strange things to a person!) Christ was making a major point: The fruit is only as good as the vine it's attached to. Apart from the vine, carrying life and nourishment up through the plant, the fruit could never grow. Detached from the vine, branches simply wither and die. They're useless and fruitless. The fruit is completely dependent on the vine.

Neither can you bear fruit unless you remain in me. I am the vine; you are the branches. If a man remains in me and I in him, he will bear much fruit; apart from me you can do nothing (John 15:4–5).

Apart from God, we're powerless, purposeless, and hopeless. In Christ, there's fruitfulness. Without Christ, there's futility.

When God Is No Longer "Gone," Perspective Returns

I can hardly wait to tell the rest of the "king turned cow" story. We left King Nebuchadnezzar on his knees (where he should have been in the first place). There, in that miserable condition he'd brought on himself, he finally had a change of heart. From the lowest of lows—living like an animal—God drew his attention to reality. In Nebuchadnezzar's own words, *I raised my eyes toward heaven, and my sanity was restored. Then I praised the Most High; I honored and glorified him who lives forever* (Daniel 4:34). He came to his senses! And God, in his mercy, restored his kingdom for a time. The curtain closes as a truth hits home, *And those who walk in pride he is able to humble* (Daniel 4:37b). No doubt about it.

I wish that this scenario of pride and repentance were confined to self-inflated rulers of kingdoms on earth. Hardly. It's not even unique to the "godless." No, this "God gone, self enthroned" lie lurks in each of our hearts. We too want to be great in our own kind of kingdoms.

It was a nice day in Capernaum and the Lord's disciples were feeling a little smug due to their good behavior, so they approached Jesus and inquired, *Who is the greatest in the kingdom of heaven?* (Matthew 18:1). I can't help but wonder if Jesus ever rolled his eyes up into his head in disbelief. He probably didn't. What he did do was to call over to a nearby child. "Come here for a minute. Let's play Show and Tell. I want these guys to understand something." Jesus said: *I tell you the truth, unless you change and become like little children, you will never enter the kingdom of heaven. Therefore, whoever humbles himself like this child is the greatest in the kingdom of heaven* (Matthew 18:3–4). What a rebuke. What a warning. "Forget about being the greatest, you're not even getting in . . . unless you humble yourselves before God!"

Why have we labored over this point? Because it is flatly overlooked in our country today and our families suffer horribly because of it. This "pride of life" is at the core of our problems. As long as we're living in the delusion that "our happiness is the chief aim in life" we can only expect to foster that same self-engrandizing pompousness in our kids. Until the self is toppled, none of God's commands really matter.

The prognosis on pride isn't good:

Do you see a man wise in his own eyes? There is more hope for a fool than for him (Proverbs 26:12).

By contrast, however:

The fear of the Lord is the beginning of wisdom, and knowledge of the Holy One is understanding (Proverbs 9:10).

And what does that look like on a daily basis?

Trust in the Lord with all your heart and lean not on your own understanding; in all your ways acknowledge him, and he will make your paths straight (Proverbs 3:5–6).

And the results of honoring God?

For the Lord takes delight in his people; he crowns the humble with salvation. Let the saints rejoice in this honor and sing for joy on their beds (Psalm 149:4–5).

Tragically, we don't learn from the past. Modern America is experiencing the heat from choices of the past. At first the pride seemed harmless. History recounts for us numerous small steps taken in our political system, our educational system, in the media, and in our homes. Truth is questioned. Then it becomes relative. Then it becomes unpopular.

This cycle of attitude has been repeated in various forms and in various civilizations throughout history. History does repeat itself. It can be visualized like this:

From bondage to spiritual faith
From spiritual faith to great courage
From great courage to strength
From strength to liberty
From liberty to abundance
From abundance to leisure
From leisure to selfishness
From selfishness to complacency
From complacency to apathy
From apathy to dependency
From dependency to weakness
From weakness back to bondage[7]

Prosperity reigns for a season. People become self-reliant in their thinking. "One nation, under God" slowly ebbs and gives way. Values shift. The slide is gradual but pervasive. And for a time, all seems fine. There's often a quiet before a storm. Even while the storm is brewing.

There's an alternative to the destruction that arrogance inevitably brings. It's humility.

---

[7]Charles R. Swindoll, *Come Before Winter* (Portland, Ore.: Multnomah Press, 1985), p. 321.

Born in Tientsin, China, to Scottish missionary parents in 1902, Eric Liddell grew up loving the Lord. At the age of five, Eric moved with his family to Scotland, where he began running in competitions—and winning! He continued training in track and finally in 1924 qualified to compete in the 100-meter Olympic event. The world was watching "The Flying Scot." But because the race was being held on a Sunday, Eric withdrew. Eric's conviction was that nothing should detract from God getting primary attention on Sunday—so he refused to compete.

The day of the race Eric was in Paris speaking at a church. The race came and went. Later in the Olympics Eric was encouraged to run in the 400-meter, a race for which he had never trained. Amazingly, Eric competed in this race and won in a spectacular time of 47.6 seconds. Instantly, the missionary-turned-runner became Scotland's national hero.

Still, Eric's eyes were focused on a different prize. The following year Eric Liddell returned to China to join his father's missionary efforts. During World War II he was imprisoned by the Japanese. He died in a prison camp on February 21, 1945.

In Eric's life, hero status belonged to God and God alone. Only God was seated in Chariots of Fire. That humility directed Eric's life, his career, and his love of running. Eric put heroism in the backseat out of devotion to his Deity. Another love ruled his life. He knew *God* was God. Eric wasn't. Even to his death in a prison camp, Eric's sights were fixed on his Master. Everything else paled by comparison.

The fruitfulness of our lives depends on our attachment to the Vine.

There's a price on the head of pride. *Pride goes before destruction, a haughty spirit before a fall* (Proverbs 16:18).

But, *The fear of the Lord leads to life* (Proverbs 19:23).

Next time you see a cow, think to yourself, "Wow, that could've been me!"

So, *Humble yourselves before the Lord, and He will lift you up* (James 4:10).

Truth or Consequences

- Who are your heroes? What heroes do your children emulate? Are they being nurtured on an understanding of God's rightful position of authority over everything and everyone?

- When you share stories of Bible characters with your children, don't look only at their successes. Examine their failures and talk about how pride often precedes those failures.

- Look at a rack of magazines with your child to see how our culture exhibits pride—in what we wear, how we look, how smart or strong or rich we are. How does pride seep into our homes? Where does pride control our thinking in certain situations?

- As a parent, how can you exhibit an honest degree of vulnerability and humility to your family members? Are you willing to be real rather than "perfect"?

- We can do all the right things for all the wrong reasons—and often the reason is unbridled pride. Consider having each family member do a status check on his or her attitudes. Look at who is being glorified by accomplishments and who is honored by decisions. Any changes need to be made?

- Take your child into the yard and break a branch from a plant or tree. Talk about what will happen to the branch apart from the tree. Why? You can explain that the tree is the source of life for the branch. Without being connected, the branch will never grow or blossom or produce anything. Point out the parallel truth found in John 15. You could also point out that a branch can be disconnected but still look pretty good for a time, like cut flowers in a vase. Ultimately, though, it will die because it is separated from the source of life.

- In a conversation with your child you can ask, "What results do you see in the world because of people's unwillingness to humble themselves before God and listen to what he says is good? How might the world be different if we lived in submission to God?"

- When you and your child see a preschooler, talk about how small children are dependent on their parents. Imagine if that small child ran away from home. What would life be like for him? (no food, no shelter, lonely, no place to turn when he's scared). In what ways are we dependent on God? How is he like a good Father to us? Why are people unwilling to admit their dependence on him? How will that independence hurt us in the long run?"

- Read Jeremiah 2:19 together with your teenager and discuss what that same truth means in today's world. How is our society suffering due to its lack of respect for God and his laws? Note the connection between the sadness many people feel and the fact that godly values have been ignored.

5

The Truth About Forgiveness

The Consequences of Guilt

"Come now, let us reason together," says the Lord. "Though your sins are like scarlet, they shall be as white as snow; though they are red as crimson, they shall be like wool. If you are willing and obedient, you will eat the best from the land . . ."

—Isaiah 1:18–19

Back in the 1960's a zealous college student named Katherine Powers linked up with a radical activist named Stanley Bond. Those were the days of Vietnam and, despite what may have been good intentions, Katherine became involved in a series of anti-war demonstrations that became more and more aggressive. Then came the turning point of her life. She and her friends were involved in a bank robbery in which a decorated police officer, Walter Schroeder, was shot and killed. Miss Powers was driving the getaway car that day. In one sense, she escaped. In another, the walls of her own conscience simply began moving in on her.

For years, Katherine remained on the FBI's most wanted list as she attempted to run farther and farther away. She changed her name and everything about her life. She ended up as far west as she could get, in Portland, Oregon. She established what appeared to be a whole new life as a wife, mom and even the owner of her own successful restaurant. But the truth followed her, hunted her, haunted her for twenty-two grueling years. Day after relentless day, the internal cords of despair were tightening. She was dying from the inside out.

When she couldn't take it anymore, Katherine Powers, alias Alice Metzinger, did an amazing thing. She turned herself in. As the papers descended on Katherine's unbelievable story, over and over one question was raised: "Why?" "Why did you surrender? Why allow yourself to be sent to prison?" Her reason? To be free. She couldn't live with herself anymore. With tears in her eyes, Katherine told the press, "Finally, I'm free!"

Prisons of the heart are the worst kind. We've all been in them. We have different names for them—disappointment, regret, anger, bitterness—but they all have the same effect. They leave us in bondage.

While it is true that *if the Son sets you free, you will be free indeed* (John 8:36), many of us feel about as free as a caged bird. We feel shackled. We remember our past. We recount the whole thing, as if in slow motion. We can't believe how we failed. We're embarrassed and angry and worried that maybe, someday, we'll do it again. Or something worse.

King David understood that. Guilt from his past weighed him down. It was draining. Sin has a way of doing that. *When I kept silent, my bones wasted away through my groaning all day long. For day and night your hand was heavy upon me; my strength was sapped as in the heat of summer* (Psalm 32:3–4).

When evangelist Billy Graham was in London a number of years ago, a well-known British psychologist told him that three-quarters of the people in the mental hospitals of England could be released if they could find assurance of forgiveness.

Here in Los Angeles we have our own ways of dealing with guilt for what we've done. For two dollars for the first minute and a mere forty-five cents for each minute thereafter, you can call the Apology Sound Off Line and confess your sins. It's a confessional hot line.

"I just can't tell anyone else this . . . I get so enraged with my children. I can't control it. I feel so guilty." *Beep.*

"My wife just wouldn't believe it. She'd never understand. There's this woman I've been seeing . . ." *Beep.*

"I lied to my brother when my dad passed away. Dad actually left a huge sum of money that no one but me knows about . . . in fact I've been living off of it for the past four years." *Beep.*

"There's another woman where I work. She makes me so mad. Well, the other day I met with my boss and ended up telling him a whole series of things about this woman that just weren't true." *Beep.*

"I'm a homosexual." *Beep.*

"I hit a car last week in the mall parking lot. No one was around so I just drove away—fast." *Beep.*

The line receives about 200 calls a day from guilt-ridden people.

During high school I was an exchange student in Germany, where I lived in a small alpine village high in the mountains of Bavaria. The home where I stayed was surrounded by fields dotted with grazing cows. Every one of them had a collar around its neck to which was attached a large brass bell. With every movement the cow made, there was that bell clanging. Head up, *clang.* Head down for another bite of grass, *clang, clang.* Take a step forward, *clang, clang, clang.* All night long, even when I couldn't see them, I could hear them. I used to lay in my bed and listen through the open window of my top-floor attic room and wonder about those cows. I wondered if they ever got tired of it. I wondered if some had gone crazy.

Guilt. It hangs on us. It follows us. The resounding, relentless clanging of past failures. It drives people to alcoholism, it drives people insane and it has driven hundreds of thousands of teens and adults to suicide. The casualty rate is high.

What images must have lingered in the mind of the apostle Paul after he became a follower of Christ.

When Stephen was being stoned to death for his faith, Scripture records,

And Saul [Paul's name prior to his conversion] *was there, giving approval to his death. On that day a great persecution broke out against the church at Jerusalem, and all except the apostles were scattered throughout Judea and Samaria. Godly men buried Stephen and*

mourned deeply for him. But Saul began to destroy the church. Going from house to house, he dragged off men and women and put them in prison (Acts 8:1–3).

In the next chapter, the rampage continued. *Saul was still breathing out murderous threats against the Lord's disciples* (Acts 9:1).

Strangely, though, this was the man who came to understand one of the most profound and liberating truths the world will ever know: God forgives. But he went beyond a mere acknowledgment of it as fact. He took it personally. He let it wash over him and free him. He internalized it and lived it.

I'm sure those images of the past were still fresh in Paul's mind when he penned this now well known verse: *Forgetting what is behind and straining toward what is ahead, I press on toward the goal to win the prize for which God has called me heavenward in Christ Jesus* (Philippians 3:13–14).

Recently I was at a particularly difficult point in my own journey as a Christian. I felt like a failure. In a state of mind where I felt too ashamed to pray and too frustrated not to, I happened to flip the radio dial to a news station. The talk show host began to read a poem someone had sent her. To this day I have no idea who wrote the poem, but I cried when I heard it. I'm not even sure why I cried. I don't cry all that easily. But for some reason as she read I began to envision my heavenly Father encouraging me on despite my failures. In light of its impact on me personally, I called the radio station and requested a copy. I'm anxious to share it with you.

THE RACE

Quit! Give up! You're beaten! They shout out and plead.
There's just too much against you now—you cannot succeed.
And as I start to hang my head in front of failure's face,
My downward fall is broken by the memory of a race.

My hope refills my weakened will as I recall that scene,
For just the thought of that short race rejuvenates my being.
A children's race, young boys, young men, now I remember
  well.
Excitement, sure, but also fear; it wasn't hard to tell.

They all lined up so full of hope, each thought to win that
    race
or tie for first or if not that at least take second place.
And fathers watched from off the side, each cheering for his
    son,
And each boy hoped to show his dad that he would be the
    one.

The whistle blew and off they went, young hearts and hopes
    of fire.
To win, to be the hero there was each young boy's desire.
And one boy in particular, his dad was in the crowd,
was running near the head and thought, My Dad will be so
    proud.

But as he speeded down the field across a shallow dip,
The little boy who thought to win, lost his step and slipped.
Trying hard to catch himself, his hands flew out to brace
And mid the laughter of the crowd, he fell flat on his face.

So down he fell and, with him, hope. He couldn't win it now.
Embarrassed, sad, he only wished to disappear somehow.
But as he fell his dad stood up and showed his anxious face,
Which to the boy then clearly said, "Get up and win the race!

He quickly rose, no damage done—a bit behind, that's all.
And ran with all his mind and might to make up for his fall.
So anxious to restore himself, to catch the pack and win,
His mind went faster than his legs. He slipped. And fell again.

He wished that he had quit before with only one disgrace.
I'm hopeless as a runner now, I shouldn't try to race.
But, in the laughing crowd he searched and found his father's
    face—
That steady look that said again, "Get up and win the race."

So up he jumped to try again. Ten yards behind the last.
If I'm to gain those yards, I've got to run real fast.
Surpassing all he thought he had, the boy gained eight or ten.
But trying hard to catch the lead, he slipped and fell again.

Defeat! He lay there silently, a tear dropped from his eye.
There's no sense in running now—three strikes, I'm out. Why try?
The will to rise had disappeared, all hope had fled away.
So far behind, so error prone, yet closer all the way.

I've lost, so what's the use? he thought. I'll live with my disgrace.
But then he thought about his dad, whom he'd soon have to face,
"Get Up!" an echo sounded low. "Get up and take your place!
You were not meant for failure here, get up and win the race."

With borrowed will, "Get up" it said. "You haven't lost at all.
For winning is not more than this, to rise each time you fall."
So up he rose to win once more. And with a new commit,
He resolved that win or lose, at least he wouldn't quit.

So far behind the others now, the most he'd ever been.
And yet he gave it all he had and ran as though to win.
Three times he'd fallen stumbling, three times he'd rose again.
Too far behind to hope to win, he fought on to the end.

They cheered the winning runner as he finished in first place.
Head high and proud and happy; no falling, no disgrace.
But when the fallen youngster crossed the line, last place.
The crowd gave him the greater cheer for finishing the race.

And even though he came in last, with head bowed low, unproud;
You would have thought he'd won the race to listen to the crowd.
And to his dad he sadly said, "I didn't do so well.
"To me you won," his father said. "You rose each time you fell."

And when things seem dark and hard and difficult to face,
The memory of that little boy somehow helps me win my race.
For all of life is like that race, with ups and downs and all,
And all you have to do to win—is rise each time you fall.

"QUIT, GIVE UP. YOU'RE BEATEN!" they shouted in my
face,
But another voice within me says, "GET UP AND WIN THE
RACE!"[1]

The image of heaven applauding us on is an accurate one! You
can almost hear the roar of the crowd in these words: *Since we are
surrounded by such a great cloud of witnesses, let us throw off everything that hinders and the sin that so easily entangles, and let us run
with perseverance the race marked out for us. Let us fix our eyes on
Jesus . . .* (Hebrews 12:1–2a).

I can't even recount to you how many believers I've met who
feel completely disqualified. I'll share with you just one. Jenny, a
beautiful twenty-two-year-old who had served on our youth leadership team for a number of years, sat next to me at a campfire.
It was the second day of a week-long trip with 40 junior-highers.
For the third or fourth time, she attempted to share what was
really bugging her deep down inside. "I want to tell you . . ." she
stammered. "You just won't believe it."

I smiled, "You wouldn't believe what I'd believe," I said. Tears
started down her cheeks as the dam on her heart gave way. Over
the next hour Jenny shared about a past relationship. One that
had taken her over the edge and had left her there. She had given
herself to this guy completely—soul and body. She had trusted
him completely. That was three years ago. He had long since left—
and left her with the scars.

"But I was a Christian," she reminded me. "It would be different if I could say that I didn't know better. But I did. I've asked
God to forgive me. But I never feel good about myself anymore.
I wanted more than anything to save myself for the person I
would marry someday."

We talked long that night. We talked about the real prisons
that sin builds around our hearts and we talked about a God who
knows all about us and offers real freedom in full view of our
failures. Before the week was over, Jenny had come to stake everything about her past on some overwhelming truths:

---

[1]The poem "The Race" was broadcast by Dr. Laura Schlessinger during her daily talk
show. The author of the poem is unknown.

- God buries our sin in the depths of the sea (Micah 7:19).

- God puts our sins behind him (Isaiah 38:17).

- God sends our sins hurling into outer space—as far as the east is from the west (Psalm 103:12).

- God forgives us for the asking (1 John 1:9).

Blessed is he whose transgressions are forgiven, whose sins are covered. Blessed is the man whose sin the Lord does not count against him and in whose spirit is no deceit (Psalm 32:1–2).

God Has Unlocked the Door—Go Through!

Despite the consequences that ensue from bad choices we've made, God doesn't write us off. In fact, he longs to free us internally. There is a difference between sorrow and guilt. While sorrow is a natural consequence of sin and may linger for a long time, guilt can be washed away the moment confession is made. The choice is ours. And the consequences are profound.

He who conceals his sins does not prosper, but whoever confesses and renounces them finds mercy (Proverbs 28:13).

Satan doesn't want you to read this. As long as he's got you convinced that you're beyond forgiveness, or not worth loving, or a hopeless case, he's got you imprisoned. Guilt is like a bad leg. You drag it around. It slows you down. It keeps you from "running the race set before you." Its cancerous ache makes you bitter and drives you further and further from the Father who loves you—who longs to heal you.

When we refuse to accept God's forgiveness we turn to blaming: "If my parents hadn't divorced I'd be more faithful in my own marriage." Or we turn to sulking: "I can't believe I failed again, I'm not worth God's time. There's no way I'm going to ask his forgiveness again. I'll never change." And all the while his arms are outstretched. He's waiting. Full and freeing forgiveness has already been purchased. All sin; every sin was accounted for and abolished on the cross.

Because of the Lord's great love we are not consumed, for his com-

passions never fail. They are new every morning; great is your faithfulness (Lamentations 3:22–23).

These are the truths conveyed in one of the most compelling stories in all of Scripture. It is the story of a parent and a child—a child who rebels. In fact, the boy runs away from home and the father is left holding only memories. The son ends up spending everything he has and, in a rush of insight, finally realizes that he's made some pretty stupid moves. He also realizes that even the people who work for his father are better off than he is at this point. So he heads for home.

But while he was still a long way off, his father saw him and was filled with compassion for him; he ran to his son, threw his arms around him and kissed him (Luke 15:20).

This is the image God wants us to have in mind, the picture he paints for us of his love despite our failure. When we fail (and we do), God wants us to picture a father who is searching the horizon for his lost child. Day and night he searches, looking for the tiniest movement on the hilltops. Then one day he sees just a faint dot miles away and his heart leaps with hope. The dot takes the shape of a person and then—then, the image of his son begins to emerge. The father catapults off the porch and runs like a madman toward his son. He grabs the boy in his arms and flings him into the air. They circle round and round as the father kisses his son who he has longed for, looked for, prayed for, cried for. The son repents and the father rejoices.

And that is the story God tells, so we'll understand how he feels.

But how different the story would have been if the son had never come home. What if he'd stayed in that foreign land and remained an outcast? What if he'd refused to humble himself and receive the Father's great love? Amazingly, the story has many endings, as many as there are people on the face of the earth. Every one is loved. Some will come home. Some will forever wander. And wonder.

Your home can convey truth about God's offer of forgiveness. You can model God's compassion. Are you teaching your children to come back home—to you and to their Father—when they've been off in a foreign land?

The path home is before us. And our Father is on the front porch.

Truth or Consequences

- How do you deal with the misbehavior of your children? Do you hold grudges or remind them over and over of past failures or use their mistakes as leverage? Realizing that they project their relationship with you onto their view of their heavenly Father, have you considered what they're internalizing about God's love from watching you?

- Share with your family members what the forgiveness of God has meant in your life personally. What have you been forgiven of? What makes it hard to imagine God's great love and forgiveness for us?

- Explain how God's forgiveness is not rooted in our worthiness—that all forgiveness originates in the goodness of the one extending it.

- You may want to ask your kids, "In what area of life is it difficult to believe and accept God's great love and forgiveness?" You can take it a step further and ask, "What are the long-term results of remaining in a state of guiltiness?"

- At any kind of sporting event you can talk about how failures affect the game. Ask, "What would happen if the players just quit whenever they failed? When do you feel like 'giving up'? In what ways does an understanding of God's forgiveness keep us going?"

- If your children are younger, you could act out the story of the Prodigal son described at the end of this chapter. "Why did the son run away in the first place? What were some of the consequences? How did his father respond when he came home? What would have happened if the Son had refused to come home and accept the forgiveness his father had for him? How does God respond to us when we come to him for forgiveness?"

- Along with your child, take note of a baby just learning to walk. How often do they fall? How does a good parent respond? Just like babies learning to walk, God asks us to accept his forgiveness and to keep walking "in step with the Spirit." Just like a good parent, the Spirit of God encourages us and helps us to take the next steps.

- Through the pain of failure can you show your child how you learned, changed or benefitted from some negative experience in your past? How has God's forgiveness changed your own life?

6

THE TRUTH ABOUT GRACIOUSNESS

THE CONSEQUENCES OF BITTERNESS

For if you forgive men when they sin against you, your heavenly Father will also forgive you. But if you do not forgive men their sins, your Father will not forgive your sins.

—Matthew 6:14–15

We entered through a heavy old wooden door. It creaked and caught and cracked as we opened it against dirt that had piled up against the bottom. Peering beyond the door revealed a long dark passageway leading down—down under the castle floor. I took the lead, with fifteen high-schoolers trailing behind, and descended the slope into the blackness, feeling my way along the wall. This Rhineland castle, built hundreds of years before us, had weathered all sorts of invaders. Now we were encroaching on its inner sanctum.

The stonewalled passage continued on, turning corners, dropping lower into the earth. Soon the shaft of sunlight from above was extinguished and darkness enveloped us completely. At first I was sure it was my imagination—the walls seemed to be narrowing, the ceiling becoming lower. But it was true—the farther we walked, the smaller the tunnel. Turning more corners, we were on our hands and knees, crawling on all fours in pursuit of Medieval adventure. We pressed on, but the walls pressed in—the tunnel was turning into a straightjacket.

Finally I could go no farther and the air felt thin. I was breathing hard and attempted to turn around. I couldn't. I needed to back up—but again, I couldn't. Fifteen yelling teenagers were wedged in behind me. Getting a message relayed, around two or three corners, all the way to the back of the line, was a major ordeal. There were moments that panic was grabbing at my heart, electrifying my pulse into a frenzy. Claustrophobia, maybe. The feeling that there's no way out, definitely.

Bitterness is like that. The old heavy door is a thoughtless comment made off the cuff, or a misunderstanding, or a broken relationship, or an outright sin inflicted on us. When we go through that door and hang onto pain, we enter a long corridor. We stumble for a time, not noticing that the path is tightening around us the farther we go. The tunnel turns treacherous. The anger we direct at the failure of another cuts off our own air. We can't move. The resentment holds us hostage like a vice. We want to back out, but the way is cluttered. There are people . . . and people are hard to get over.

We want to be free, to forget that anything ever happened, but forgetting is hard. Our trapped heart jumps and flutters in the dark night, and we lose sleep. We walk corridors in our minds. We even find ourselves reinforcing the walls to protect us from ever being invaded again. And as the dungeon door slams, it is we who are on the inside, longing for release. We're trapped. That's the consequence of bitterness.

The minute we comprehend the incredible reality of God's forgiveness, we must begin to grasp another reality. When we consider that Christ, the perfect one, has forgiven us completely, we're struck with the incongruity of our unwillingness to extend grace to others. If God forgives us, and them, who are we to withhold forgiveness?

That was precisely the point Jesus made in Matthew 18:21–35. A man who owed his master an incredible debt—literally millions of dollars—simply didn't have the money to pay it off. His master had him over a barrel. He legally could have locked him away or even had him sold, along with his family, in order to make good on what he owed.

Then the master did an amazing thing. Realizing the servant could never repay what he owed, the master chose to forgive the man's debt. Not some of it, but the whole thing. Every last penny. Notes were canceled, the ledger burned, the servant forgiven and set free. Then came the twist.

The servant left and found a fellow servant who owed him just a few denarii, equivalent to a couple of dollars. The first servant grabbed this second servant and began choking him. "Pay back what you owe me!" he demanded. Word quickly got back to the first servant's master and he was summoned to appear right away.

"You wicked servant," he said, "I canceled all that debt of yours because you begged me to. Shouldn't you have had mercy on your fellow servant just as I had on you?" In anger his master turned him over to the jailers to be tortured, until he should pay back all that he owed (Matthew 18:32–34).

The parable ends with this haunting warning. *This is how my heavenly Father will treat each of you unless you forgive your brother from your heart* (Matthew 18:35).

Those are sharp words for those holding a double-edged knife. Since we have been forgiven of so much by our heavenly Father, what right do we have not to forgive others? Our obligation is to give people not what they deserve (condemnation), but what we have been given (compassion). In fact, the Greek words translated "forgive" actually mean "to remit, to lay aside," terms applied to the canceling of a financial debt. Another meaning conveyed in the Greek is the idea of "setting a prisoner free." The story makes another point equally clear: without mercy and forgiveness both the one who has failed *and* the one who fails to forgive are in bondage. Both suffer. Both are prisoners. The one who refuses to forgive is as tormented as the one who has offended.

When we stoke the fire of resentment, it is *we* who burn.

A few years ago, I was on a pastors' retreat in the San Bernardino Mountains, not far from my home. I had been recently dealing with someone in the church who, it seemed, did nothing but complain. They didn't like the worship style of certain songs.

They didn't like the youth ministry. They didn't like one of the pastors on staff. And on and on. Their gripes were beginning to feel like Chinese water torture. Day after day the dripping was getting to me. I was beginning to feel resentment setting in. I knew better, but I was struggling.

These issues were fresh on my mind when I sat down on a log at the edge of Lake Arrowhead to read one of Max Lucado's great books. One paragraph stuck in my mind. The imagery not only planted a seed of freedom in my life that day, but I've brought it to mind many times since:

> See the Father's image in the face of the enemy. Try that. The next time you see or think of the one who broke your heart, look twice. As you look at his face, look also for *his* face—the face of the One who forgave you. Look into the eyes of the King who wept when you pleaded for mercy. Look into the face of the Father who gave you grace when no one else gave you a chance. Find the face of the God who forgives in the face of your enemy. And then, because God has forgiven you more than you'll ever be called on to forgive in another, set your enemy—and yourself—free.[1]

In Christ, God gave us the model. In his Word, he gives us the mandate:

Be kind and compassionate to one another, forgiving each other, just as in Christ God forgave you. Be imitators of God, therefore, as dearly loved children and live a life of love, just as Christ loved us and gave himself up for us . . ." (Ephesians 4:32–5:2).

Consider the Rewards for Graciousness, Freeing Others From Their Debts of Failure

Just as we are warned about the results of harboring resentment, the Bible also explains the benefits attached to offering our forgiveness freely. *Forgive and you will be forgiven. Give, and it will be given to you. A good measure, pressed down, shaken together and running over, will be poured into your lap. For with the measure you*

---

[1]Max Lucado, *The Applause of Heaven* (Waco, Tex.: Word, 1990), p. 116.

use, it will be measured to you (Luke 6:37–38).

Give up the resentment and find rest in return. Give up the gossip and find grace. Give up the hostage and find healing. Give it all—then look out! God honors those who obey him!

During a mission trip to Honduras to provide relief to refugees of the war in Nicaragua, I had my first encounter of the personal kind with a real, live, tarantula. We were cruising slowly on a waterway in a motorboat. Heavy foliage lined the stream and arched overhead, almost creating a tunnel for us to pass through. As I sat peering into the jungle, just to the side of our boat a large, jet black tarantula fell from one of the overhanging vines directly onto the pack sitting in front of me. To say I jumped back is an understatement. I nearly leapt into the arms of one of the native boatmen navigating our little vessel.

While I was one beat away from full cardiac arrest, the boatmen were only amused. One of them stepped forward and carefully scooped the tarantula up in his hand and placed him softly on his sleeve. I was mortified. He moved the fury monster right up next to me and asked me if I wanted to hold him. I assured him I'd rather be thrown to the alligators that lurked in the water. He persisted. And after observing that the boatman didn't die, I reluctantly agreed.

He gently set the animal on my arm. I froze. The tarantula slowly moved along my arm toward my shoulder. I begged to have him removed. What had I been thinking? The boatman just smiled and calmly replied, "Don't worry so much. He won't bite you as long as he is free. They only attack if you hold on to them when they are trying to get free. Just let him go and he won't bother you."

Free him and he won't hurt you. It is the lesson I'm learning daily about forgiveness. Bitterness bites the one who hangs onto it. Freeing the guilty is the only answer. Forgiveness is a process of freeing. Freeing the one who has sinned from any penalty you would impose out of personal vindictiveness. Freeing the one who owes from his debt. It is believing that God has his own way of righting wrongs.

Do not say, "I'll pay you back for this wrong!" Wait for the Lord, and he will deliver you (Proverbs 20:22).

In fact, Christ says to endure, to go the distance for your of-fender. Do good to those who persecute you. *If your enemy is hun-gry, give him food to eat; if he is thirsty, give him water to drink . . . and the Lord will reward you* (Proverbs 25:21–22).

And the greatest reward of all? Our relationship with God is right. *For if you forgive men when they sin against you, your heavenly Father will also forgive you. But if you do not forgive men their sins, your Father will not forgive your sins* (Matthew 6:14–15).

When we live in a state of anger and resentment toward oth-ers, we ourselves remain in a state of rebellion against God. When we hold others at arm's length, we distance ourselves from God. But when we are reconciled to others we become reconciled to God.

The principle is so clear. Forgive and you'll end up glad you did. *Blessed are the merciful, for they will be shown mercy* (Matthew 5:7).

Consider the Reality of Your Own Dark Side

Why do you look at the speck of sawdust in your brother's eye and pay no attention to the plank in your own eye? (Matthew 7:3).

Ever had someone try to get something out of your eye? A speck of dust or a contact lens, perhaps? "Okay, roll your eye up. Hmmm. Try looking this way. Hmmm. Wait. Hold it right there. I think I've found it." Then they stick their finger in there and start poking around.

It's one thing if they can see clearly. But what if they were blind? Or cross-eyed! Jesus made a profound point. Some of his followers were professional eye examiners. Only one problem— they couldn't see straight themselves! They had so much junk in their own eyes that they were in no shape to poke in someone else's.

James echoes the same admonition; *But you—who are you to judge your neighbor?* (James 4:12).

When we come face-to-face with our own sinfulness and the enormity of God's mercy for all of us, our perspective changes. The reality we learn about ourselves sheds an enormous amount of light on the situations of others. We're not as shocked when others fail. We're not as offended when others offend. Why? Because we're realists. We know we're capable of rotten behavior. In fact, but for the grace of God we're capable of anything! We're all in the same boat. We all sin. We all need mercy.

I appeal to you, brothers, in the name of our Lord Jesus Christ, that all of you agree with one another so that there may be no divisions among you. . . . Make every effort to live in peace with all men. . . . Honor one another above yourselves. . . . Live in harmony with one another; be sympathetic, love as brothers, be compassionate and humble. Do not repay evil with evil or insult with insult, but with blessing, because to this you were called . . . Don't grumble against each other, brothers, or you will be judged. Forgive as the Lord forgave you (1 Corinthians 1:10; Hebrews 12:14; Romans 12:10; 1 Peter 3:8–9; James 5:9; Colossians 3:13).

Remember, Paul says, we're not the Righteous Judge, we're *accountable* to the Righteous Judge. We are fellow servants. None of us has the righteousness or the responsibility to hold others hostage to our own expectations. *Who are you to judge someone else's servant? To his own master he stands or falls. And he will stand, for the Lord is able to make him stand* (Romans 14:4).

Consider the Results of a Kind Spirit Rather Than a Critical One

The good man brings good things out of the good stored up in his heart, and the evil man brings evil things out of the evil stored up in his heart (Luke 6:45).

Like a rudder steering an immense ship, every great move begins somewhere deep. Deep in the water. Deep down where no one sees. Matters of the heart—matter.

A few years ago my wife, Lori, and I were finishing a day spent walking the silent streets of Pompeii. There weren't any other tourists around, so we felt the eerie stillness of the place and the loss of life that occurred there when Mt. Vesuvius ruptured. On August 24, A.D.79, molten lava was flung a mile high. An angry monster of ash and sulfur, bursting loose from its cage. The city was leveled in minutes. As archeologists have excavated the remains of the lost city, human bones have been found indicating that people were stopped dead in their tracks—literally—as they fled. Whole families were discovered huddled together in their homes. Homes and shops that were filled with chatter fell silent. In an instant all of life became paralyzed. Near the end of the day we stood and reflected as we looked out at the mountain that had destroyed the entire region so long ago. It all started deep beneath the surface. It had boiled for years while Pompeii went about its business. No one thought much of it. But all the while it was brewing, stewing, churning, and then . . . it destroyed everything.

Everything that we are and do on the outside begins on the inside. The inside eventually alters the outside. Attitudes result in actions. Bottled-up bitterness breaks out somewhere.

Consider the Repercussions of the Way You Relate

For out of the overflow of the heart the mouth speaks (Matthew 12:34).

"I find myself swearing under my breath every time he . . ."

"I don't want to gossip, but I can't seem to turn it off."

"I keep coming back with defensiveness. I feel so angry deep down inside."

When we don't forgive, we end up saying things we wish we hadn't. We end up tearing others down. We become insensitive to their needs because of our own self-preoccupation. We hurt the work of the Holy Spirit in our lives and in the lives of those we encounter.

We carry a verbal arsenal everywhere we go, with awful results. Yet that is what we end up with when we refuse to forgive. *Do not let any unwholesome talk come out of your mouths, but only what is helpful for building others up according to their needs, that it may benefit those who listen. And do not grieve the Holy Spirit of God, with whom you were sealed for the day of redemption. Get rid of all bitterness, rage and anger, brawling and slander, along with every form of malice* (Ephesians 4:29–31).

When the grim reaper of resentment takes residence in your life, hope dies. Love dies. Joy dies. Peace dies. Friendships die. Families die. Churches die. Extending grace is costly. Not forgiving is deadly. But when we do forgive, a whole series of things take place. Criticism melts into compassion. Slander is replaced with sensitivity. Spiritual bondage turns into spiritual freedom. Bitterness turns to betterment.

Begin the Process Now!

Given the dire consequences bitterness brings to our relationships with both God and people, it's no wonder that the Bible counsels us to settle matters quickly. In Matthew 5:23–26 Jesus relates a hypothetical situation each of us can identify with. A man in prayer has offended someone else, and they resent him for it. (Have you ever noticed that prayer ignites a status check of your life and relationships? I can ignore a lot of things—until I go to God in prayer. It's as if prayer triggers the conscience to bring reality into focus.) In the midst of prayer this guy noticed a fault in his life, and he wasn't about to act like nothing was wrong.

Jesus commands our friend in the story to stop what he's doing at the temple, to go to the one he has offended, and to be reconciled. In other words, to do whatever was in his power to make things right. Now it is up to us to do the same:

Go directly. Don't just tell someone else how you plan to go. *Don't run it by your friends first.*

Go in humility. Don't go with any expectations. *Don't go for any selfish motives.*

Go in sincerity. Don't attempt to subtly show them how they were wrong. *Don't go with any hidden agendas.*

Go with honesty. Don't go with a partial explanation. *Don't go with a lot of excuses.*

Go immediately. Don't wait until it is comfortable. *Don't wait, hoping they'll forget about it.*

Whether we've offended and need to ask for forgiveness or whether we need to forgive an offense, we are to act immediately to do whatever is going to benefit the relationship.

What model of graciousness are we handing on to our children?

- When we've been wronged, what do they hear us say?
- When our children wrong us, what do they observe from our response?

- When our children have been wronged by another child, what is our attitude toward the culprit?

- When life is hard and unfair, what is our reaction?

Probably the three most healing words your child will ever hear are, "I forgive you." Followed by, "We forgive others too."

As we wrap up this chapter I feel constrained to add a few crucial points I'd like you to consider in your own journey of graciousness toward others.

Forgiveness Doesn't Mean We Release All Boundaries

A woman who has been a friend of our family for years was sexually abused as a child. She's a great mom to her two kids and she has a wonderful marriage, although it hasn't been easy. "I really have forgiven my dad," she relayed to us one evening as we talked. She went on to describe an incident when he had made a obvious sexual comment to her daughter, then a fourteen-year-old, while they were visiting over the holidays. "We cut our visit short," she explained. "I told him that I thought the comment was very inappropriate and that we simply wouldn't be bringing our girls into his home if he was going to talk like that to them. He didn't apologize. He didn't even flinch. He joked about it. It was obvious he had no intention of changing. We decided it wasn't smart to put our daughters through that kind of abuse. We haven't been back. I forgive him, but I don't trust him with my kids."

Drawing lines, setting limits, and knowing when to say no are not only wise but necessary components of forgiveness. The idea of "forgive and forget" is really erroneous. Without boundaries we may actually enable our offenders to continue wrong behavior—hurting both them and us. Jesus forgave everyone but was discerning and selective in his trust. *But Jesus would not entrust himself to them, for he knew all men* (John 2:24).

Forgiveness Doesn't Mean the Relationship Will Be Restored to the Same Place

You can't control other people's reactions, but you can control yours. Romans 12:18 exhorts: *If it is possible, as far as it depend: on you, live at peace with everyone.* Sometimes even when you tr to make things right with others, they may not respond well. Even when we do our best, it may not be good enough for someone else. At that point we are simply to continue to live in a state of grace toward that person, leaving the situation to God to resolve. The relationship may not be salvageable, but we've done our part. We're not responsible for the other person's response.

Even if your enemy makes amends with you and you with them, the relationship may never be the same. That's really okay. So often we can't plumb the depths of why our feelings for someone are altered after we've been hurt. We wonder where the warmth went. We question the genuineness of our forgiveness. It is important to realize that forgiveness is a decision of the will that may or may not restore a relationship to its prior condition. The good news is that in *some* cases, restoration in the wake of failure actually deepens relationships.

Forgiveness Doesn't Mean All the Hurt Will Go Away

Forgiveness doesn't mean that you deny ever being hurt. Neither does it mean that you will necessarily understand why a person acted a certain way. It isn't always an immediate rush of relief! If you've been hurt physically it's normal to admit that "it *really* hurts." Everyone expects that. Why, then, when we've been wounded emotionally do we often try to minimize our pain or pretend that we *don't* hurt? In reality, forgiveness begins when we acknowledge what has happened and how it has felt. Then we can go forward and consciously choose to release others from guilt and failure and allow God to take control of that person's life as well as our own. Forgiveness can be instantaneous but wounds may throb for a long time. Ongoing pain doesn't mean you haven't forgiven.

It was 1947, and Corrie ten Boom had just spoken to a congregation of people in Germany. Her message? Forgiveness. She knew what she was talking about. She and her family had provided a refuge, a "hiding place," in Holland for Jews who were being exterminated by the Nazis. After showing mercy to the helpless, she and her family were captured and imprisoned. She and her sister were tortured, beaten and abused. Years of suffering took the life of her sister, but Corrie was finally freed.

Now here she stood, bringing a message of hope and forgiveness to war-torn Germany. At the close of the service the audience fell silent, moved by her message. People filed out, as usual, attempting to comprehend all the love that Corrie brought on behalf of Jesus. And then she saw him. One solitary figure making his way to the front of the room. Corrie recognized him immediately. How could she ever forget? His long overcoat—while she cringed, naked and freezing on the ground. His cap—with its skull and crossbones that stared back at her as she looked through tears at his face for mercy. The whip—it had cut deep into her flesh. One never forgets. And now he stood in front of her. He identified himself as a former guard from Ravensbrook. She knew. But she hoped he would never remember her among the countless drawn bodies he'd beaten. "Since then I've become a Christian," he informed her. "I know God has forgiven me for the cruel things I did there." Then he stretched forth his hand. "Fraulein, will you forgive me too?"

Corrie stood motionless for what seemed like an eternity. All the images rushed past her heart as if to scream "Never!" and force her to run. "Jesus, help me!" she prayed. And then, mechanically, by the power of God, she lifted her hand to take his. As Corrie recounts, a healing warmth flowed between their clutched hands, bringing tears to her eyes. "I forgive you, brother. I forgive you with my whole heart!"[2]

One far greater than Corrie ten Boom has already been here. He already did all that he could to offer you freedom. As he hung, bleeding and broken from the weight of your sin and mine, his arms were outstretched. They still are. The words spoken that day

---

[2]Neil T. Anderson and Dave Park, *Stomping Out the Darkness* (Ventura, Calif.: Gospel Light, 1993), p. 178.

were, "Father, forgive them. . . ." They are still spoken today. The truth about forgiveness is altogether life altering. God wants to set you free, and your offenders as well. Will you let them go?

The only tarantulas that bite are the ones that we hold.

Truth or Consequences

- What incidents from your past have trapped you in bitterness? Do you harbor resentment—even subconsciously—against a parent or a friend from years ago?

- How have your children observed your spirit of graciousness toward others? What comments do they hear from you when you've been wronged or when you disagree with someone else?

- Are you able to ask forgiveness of your children when you've been impatient or unreasonable? How have you modeled humility in the face of your own mistakes?

- When you've been wronged, let your kids see how you forgive. When someone does something that you consider stupid, let your children hear how you respond with grace.

- Take a common dilemma and use it to help your children learn forgiveness while maintaining appropriate boundaries. Let's say your son is being bullied at school. Walk him through a process of forgiveness while at the same time taking specific steps to prevent further abuse.

- When your child has been wronged by a friend or someone at school help them work through the situation by listing the benefits of acting in "grace" toward that individual. What would it accomplish to harbor resentment instead? How could an unforgiving attitude hurt your child even more than they've already been hurt?

- You could have your child role-play the story of the unforgiving servant in Matthew 18. Then have them act out the same idea in a normal everyday setting or describe how the same type of scenario takes place in their world. Ask "How are people 'tormented' when they refuse to forgive?"

- When you feel it is age appropriate, rent the video *The Hiding Place*, the story of Corrie ten Boom. (Make sure you preview it—while the story is unsettling, it is history we dare not forget.) Or share Corrie's story with your child and ask how they might have responded. Who in their life are they sometimes hurt by and how are they responding? Suggest how they might actually change someone else's life simply by a willingness to forgive.

- Never be afraid to honestly go to your child and ask forgiveness when you've failed them. Children need to see how you handle your failures. When you admit your wrongs, children learn that it is okay to be open and vulnerable with family members. They learn to value humility and honesty. They see they have the opportunity of exercising their own ability to forgive.

7

THE TRUTH ABOUT PRAYER

THE CONSEQUENCES OF INDEPENDENCE

The prayer of a righteous man is powerful and effective.

—James 5:16

We were on the middle fork of the American River, central California, wedged between mountainsides of pines and firs. As forewarned, we arrived at a rapid, appropriately names "Trouble-shoot," where a torrent of whitewater thundered furiously be-tween boulders.

We pulled our inflatable raft into an eddy and walked down-river a hundred feet or so to stand on a precipice overlooking the gorge. Below us the roar was deafening. It was as if the water had been enraged somehow, stirred into an out-of-control frenzy by an unseen demon. "Those boulders—" our guide pointed. "They're treacherous. Once we enter the rapids we have to back-paddle like mad to keep from slamming into them. The last thing we want is to lose anyone at the beginning of the shoot."

Back down by our raft the guide continued to prepare us. "No matter what, once we enter the falls, move to the center of the raft and hang on for dear life. You'll be completely submerged in water for a few seconds before the force of the falls spits you out at the bottom. You won't be able to see anything during that time.

Whatever you do, though, don't allow yourself to be thrown from the boat. This rapid is merciless."

Hearts pounding with anticipation, our raft drifted from shore and gradually picked up speed as it merged in with the current. "Okay, paddle . . . paddle hard!" came the shout from the back of the boat. We neared the top of the rapids. "Backpaddle left, right forward—HARD!" We entered the first section of foaming, cascading water and our boat spun wildly to the left. BOOM! We hit a rock. Whooosh! The boat swept forward with a startling force. We were flying, bodies being lifted into the air and hands clutching for anything attached to the raft. No sound, no voices, no shouts could even be heard over the roar. Nothing was visible. Only water. Like walking through a car wash, water shooting, brushes spinning. In reality the final descent lasted no more than ten seconds, but my mind told me otherwise. It felt like a dizzying Oz dream that made me wonder if we were still earthbound.

I had been in the back of the boat, closest to our guide, and now—something was missing. Our boat was obviously being forced by the current. I could feel the lack of guidance—the missing control. We hit another rock. My mind cleared as the boat emerged from the spray. "The guide!" I yelled to everyone in the boat. "She's GONE!" The current was taking our boat downriver fast. We were spinning again. Everyone wildly searched the water's surface for our guide's orange life preserver. Then we spotted her. Near the bottom of the last set of falls, there she was, moving, swimming toward us. We cheered and paddled hard against the current to hold the boat in place. We grabbed the sides of her preserver and hoisted her into the boat. She was dazed and coughing, but for the most part had come through unharmed.

A good guide is everything when the current is rushing. When we lost ours, we lost our way—we lost our control. It's frightening in the rapids—that helpless, hopeless, sinking sense that the one who can guide and steer is suddenly gone.

In life, it's even worse.

From the beginning of time, God has offered himself as humankind's perfect Guide. He walked with Adam in the Garden and he continued the contact even when the relationship was marred by rebellion. And across the ages, many people have responded to God's grace, his care. God reached out to them, and they reached back through prayer. When the earth was overcome by evil, for example, Noah prayed. *And Noah did all that the Lord commanded him* (Genesis 7:5). Noah knew all about rapids. Water covered the earth, but Noah was saved because of his attachment to the Lifeguard. When Sodom and Gomorrah were about to be demolished, Abraham lifted his eyes to his Sovereign God. *Abraham remained standing before the Lord* (Genesis 18:22), and his life was spared.

Or take Job. In the midst of his miserable, nightmarish life, he looked around at the people who surrounded him. He observed of his culture, *They say to God, "Leave us alone!" We have no desire to know your ways. Who is the Almighty, that we should serve him? What would we gain by praying to him?* (Job 21:14–15). Despite their insolence, Job makes a sobering observation, *But their prosperity is not in their own hands*, and a very wise conclusion, *so I stand aloof from the counsel of the wicked* (Job 21:16). In story after story as the saga of Scripture unfolds through generations of time, certain people prayed while others did not. So what?

What difference, after all, does prayer really make? Does God really hear? Does he respond? Is it essential to our children's well-being—or a waste of breath? Those questions nag us all, even those of us who consider ourselves spiritually mature. Much good material has been written about prayer, but our focus here is singular: why does it matter in regard to our children? What are the results? What value does it have for my family and the future we're all heading in to? What are the consequences of praying or not praying?

Prayer Is Our Direct Link With the Supernatural

Know that the Lord has set apart the godly for himself; the Lord will hear when I call to him (Psalm 4:3).

When we speak to people, there is always potential for problems. We're never sure if they're listening. If they're listening, we're not sure they're understanding. Or if they're understanding, we're still not sure if they actually will respond to what we're saying. And if they do respond, we worry whether it will indeed be a correct response.

Yet speaking to God isn't like speaking to people. Scripture urges us to lay aside the concerns we would have in talking to anyone else and pray without doubt to God, confident of one thing: any humble Christian who longs to speak with God will truly be heard. Period. God is unlimited in his understanding. No problem there. And his response? Perfection guaranteed. He simply cannot err in response to our prayers.

It is this supernatural connection, though, that prompted Jesus to warn people against abusing prayer. Some used prayer to impress others. Their eyes had moved from the throne to the throngs. *"Do not keep babbling like pagans,"* he warned, *"for they think they will be heard because of their many words"* (Matthew 6:7). Maybe the masses were impressed by long-winded prayers, but not the Messiah. Instead, said Jesus, *"When you pray, go into your room, close the door and pray to your Father, who is unseen. Then your Father, who sees what is done in secret, will reward you"* (Matthew 6:6). Prayer is a sacred, intimate communing between ourselves and our heavenly Father. It transports us immediately to his side. And when we comprehend who we're talking to, who is listening, then we begin to feel our prayers become transcendent, meaning they transcend our physical world.

Imagine your son coming home, walking through the kitchen door and immediately getting on his knees in front of you. (I realize some things are harder to imagine than others.) He begins, "Dear Mother, good mom, beloved one, almighty provider and cook and house cleaner and sympathizer. Please hear me. Please be gracious to me and increase my allowance and see that my lunches include more fun food and give me more gas money. Please don't be angry about my grades. Thank you for hearing my requests and I'll talk to you tomorrow. Or I'll call if I get in a lot of trouble." He rises and walks out the door. Silly? Perhaps. But is it any crazier than the way many people talk to God?

God longs for devotion, not dictation. When we realize we're standing before Almighty God there is an inner humbling that happens quite naturally. Scripture says he is "a consuming fire." Certainly there is no other way to approach the God of the Bible than with reverence and awe. But on that holy ground, there should be an equally moving awareness of God's tender, fatherly stance toward his children. We can approach him with delight rather than dread simply because of our sonship brought about through Christ.

Prayer Is Our Deliverance From Stagnation and Sin

When I come to God in honest prayer, it's like a heart-centered oil change. I simply can't pray if I'm harboring rebelliousness against him. That's a feeling birthed by the Holy Spirit in us. Like David wrote, *If I had cherished sin in my heart, the Lord would not have listened* (Psalm 66:18). If we're committed to talking candidly to our Father on a daily basis, the cleansing effect is inescapable. In contrast, when I don't pray I can go for days with the same filthy attitudes, clogging my spirit, squelching his Spirit and generally ruining my effectiveness as his child. Prayer changes all that. It was meant to.

Whenever you hear an "if . . . then . . ." statement in Scripture, you know that what is being said is conditional. God gave the Israelites a condition to prayer being answered. *If my people, who are called by my name, will humble themselves and pray and seek my face and turn from their wicked ways, then will I hear from heaven and will forgive their sin and will heal their land* (2 Chronicles 7:14). If we pray with an attitude of arrogance and disobedience, our prayer amounts to no more than a mockery of God.

On the flip-side, James writes that *the prayer of a righteous man is powerful and effective* (James 5:16). Prayer forces me to face the One who knows me intimately and completely. For some reason, I find myself conned into thinking that my sin is no big deal—until I start praying. That's when confession flows quite naturally. There's something about an encounter with God that makes us want to come clean.

Prayerlessness Leaves Us Alone in Our Helplessness

Give ear to my words, O Lord, consider my sighing. Listen to my cry for help, my King and my God, for to you I pray. In the morning,

O Lord, you hear my voice; in the morning I lay my requests before you and wait in expectation (Psalm 5:1–3). Wait in expectation? Nothing less. When we pray in faith, God *does* respond in perfection. If we're convinced of his love as well as his power—then to trust his response is a natural outcome.

If ever parents needed a verse to hang their hat on, that's it—along with one from James 1:5: *If any of you lacks wisdom, he should ask God, who gives generously to all without finding fault, and it will be given to him.* Then God adds this word of advice: If you're going to ask, you'd better be believing that he'll answer. *But when he asks, he must believe and not doubt, because he who doubts is like a wave of the sea, blown and tossed by the wind. That man should not think he will receive anything from the Lord* (James 1:6–7).

Remember the story of Lazarus? Jesus came late, right? He was callused, right? After all, word came to him that his close friend was deathly sick and yet Jesus stayed where he was two more days (John 11:6). Why would he do that? It was probably a week later that Jesus stood in front of the tomb of Lazarus along with Mary, who was overcome with sorrow. It was there in a dark place of confusion that Jesus brought about the most overwhelming of his miracles. *Lazarus, come out!* There and then Jesus exposed his power over the tomb. The moment shattered any of the small expectations of healing that Mary and the others had held earlier on. Something far more brilliant was waiting to be released by God Almighty. Christ carefully explained, *Did I not tell you that if you believed, you would see the glory of God?* (John 11:40). Indeed!

I've often wondered why God would want his children to seek him. Why not set things up so that a simple prayer delivers an immediate solution? Why the looking and seeking and knocking, that Matthew 7:7, for instance, tells us to do? For me, the answer is less theological than experiential. While the Bible doesn't spell out the answer in a list of reasons, I've found my own list developing as my communion with God has deepened over the years. I've come to believe that my greatest enemy in life is independence. It has been this very process of seeking, believing, trusting, praying continually, waiting, even wondering, that attaches me inseparably to his side.

It is this that he promises: *If you call out for insight and cry aloud for understanding, and if you look for it as for silver and search for it as for hidden treasure, then you will understand the fear of the Lord and find the knowledge of God . . . then you will understand what is right and just and fair—every good path* (Proverbs 2:3–5, 9).

It is in the seeking that I remain where I should—close. When answers are obvious and confusion subsides, I slide away from him. My slide deadens me spiritually, sapping my life. Only the seeking holds me firmly in place. Close attachment is what breeds the spiritual insight and direction I long for. And so I feel challenged rather than annoyed as I wait and trust. *Ask and it will be given to you; seek and you will find; knock and the door will be opened to you. For everyone who asks receives; he who seeks finds; and to him who knocks, the door will be opened* (Matthew 7:7–8).

The Old Testament character Jacob, the "schemer," had many flaws. But one positive trait he displayed was the persistence he showed during an unbelievable struggle to gain God's blessing. During the incredible tug-of-war which followed, Jacob wept and pleaded all night with God (Genesis 32:22–32) as he aggressively sought the Lord's blessing on his life. It was not until after this severe struggle that Jacob received a new name (Israel) and a different character. Physically, Jacob won the match, but his hip was supernaturally dislocated, causing Jacob to remember that he was to be permanently dependent upon God. He was never the same again. Now, having found power with the Lord through dependence upon God in prayer, he became powerful among men. His persistence with God was rewarded.

Prayer Is Our Daily Source of Spirit-Filled Power

Paul said that the first line of spiritual defense is prayer. What, for example, did Peter and John do right after they had been released from prison? They gathered with their friends for a prayer meeting. *After they prayed, the place where they were meeting was shaken. And they were filled with the Holy Spirit and spoke the word of God boldly* (Acts 4:31). Talk about results! They were filled with the Spirit, and that empowered them to share the truth about Jesus with others! How many of us feel puny and peculiar and powerless when given the opportunity to speak up about our love

102

for God? Could there be a direct link between our lack of zeal and our lack of prayer?

Not only is prayer our link *with* the Spirit, but the Spirit is our link *in* prayer. When we pray "in the Spirit" as we're commanded to do (Ephesians 6:18; Jude 20), the Spirit inspires our prayers and actually guides us in our prayers so that we pray in a way that is consistent with the desires of God himself. *In the same way, the Spirit helps us in our weakness. We do not know what we ought to pray for, but the Spirit himself intercedes for us with groans that words cannot express. And he who searches our hearts knows the mind of the Spirit, because the Spirit intercedes for the saints in accordance with God's will* (Romans 8:26–27).

Prayer places me in a spiritually sensitive state. When I go through those stretches of prayerlessness, I'm simply not aware of the Spirit's infilling or his work in and through me. It is as though I'm deep-sea diving and there's a kink in my air hose, spiritually speaking, and prayer is the only way to breath again.

Jude encourages us that prayer will resuscitate and enliven us. *But you, dear friends, build yourselves up in your most holy faith and pray in the Holy Spirit. Keep yourselves in God's love as you wait for the mercy of our Lord Jesus Christ to bring you to eternal life* (Jude 20–21).

The Bible highlights several ways that we cut ourselves off from the power God wants to grant us through prayer:

1. Harboring sin will thwart God's attention.
If I had cherished sin in my heart, the Lord would not have listened (Psalm 66:18).

2. Rejecting Christ will shut out God's provisions.
We have confidence before God and receive from him anything we ask, because we obey his commands and do what pleases him. And this is his command: to believe in the name of his Son, Jesus Christ, and to love one another as he commanded us (1 John 3:21–23).

3. Ignoring Scripture will impede our requests.
If you remain in me and my words remain in you, ask whatever you wish, and it will be given you (John 15:7). *The Lord is near to all who call on him, to all who call on him in truth* (Psalm 145:18).

4. Ignoring God's ability will stop his hand.
Let us acknowledge the Lord; let us press on to acknowledge him. As

surely as the sun rises, he will appear; he will come to us like the winter rains, like the spring rains that water the earth (Hosea 6:3).

5. Asking selfishly will close doors.

When you ask, you do not receive, because you ask with wrong motives, that you may spend what you get on your pleasures (James 4:3).

6. Relating wrongfully will hinder our prayers.

Husbands, in the same way be considerate as you live with your wives, and treat them with respect as the weaker partner and as heirs with you of the gracious gift of life, so that nothing will hinder your prayers (1 Peter 3:7).

7. Lacking persistence will short circuit God's power on our behalf.

And will not God bring about justice for his chosen ones, who cry out to him day and night? Will he keep putting them off? I tell you, he will see that they get justice, and quickly (Luke 18:7–8a).

Prayer Is Our Duty to the People We Love

As for me, far be it from me that I should sin against the Lord by failing to pray for you (1 Samuel 12:23).

When I really have a need, the phones of some good men and women start ringing. Why? Because when godly people pray God responds. Is any one of you in trouble? He should pray. Is anyone happy? Let him sing songs of praise. Is any one of you sick? He should call the elders of the church to pray over him and anoint him with oil in the name of the Lord. And the prayer offered in faith will make the sick person well; the Lord will raise him up. If he has sinned, he will be forgiven. Therefore confess your sins to each other and pray for each other so that you may be healed. The prayer of a righteous man is powerful and effective (James 5:13–16).

There's a valuable lesson here. We need to pray for each other more. God has promised that our neediness stems from our prayerlessness and that the greatest gift we can give another human being is to intervene for him or her through prayer.

God really wants us to talk about our kids behind their backs. He's our father. He's their father. And he wants to be involved in the rigors of each daily trial we as parents endure. The whole idea of putting parents in charge of children, after all, was his idea from the start. He wants us to come to him for wisdom, for encouragement, for help.

The father of James Dobson wrote this to him on one occasion: "I have observed that the greatest delusion is to suppose that our children will be devout Christians simply because their parents have been, or that any of them will enter into the Christian faith in any other way than through their parents' deep travail of prayer and faith."[1]

Prayer Is Our Direction in the Face of Confusion

Call to me and I will answer you and tell you great and unsearchable things you do not know (Jeremiah 33:3).

When we do pray we often want immediate insight. Like a child coming to his father with a list of demands in hand, we think we know what is best and we think that "clear direction and lots of yeses" must certainly be the best he can give us. While we know yes isn't always the best when it comes to the requests of our own children, at times we act as though it's the greatest way God could respond to *our* desires. After all, what we want is good. We want our kids to shape up, our financial needs to disappear, our illnesses to be resolved, or our Sunday school class of sixth-graders to exhibit a greater degree of sainthood. Whatever it is—we're convinced that God's best answer is going to be yes and it is going to be now and it is going to be complete. I've learned from those who have walked with God far longer than I that God's good answers are not nearly that tidy or trite. There is a process happening above our heads that we don't often see. It is to that far larger reality that we must become committed.

Part of me longs for a candy machine sort of God. I insert a request, out pops the treat exactly as I envisioned it. Sure, the satisfaction is short-lived, but it's predictable, safe, and functional in a small sort of way. It shrinks God and elevates my sense of control. It makes me the master and God my slave. Amazing how we get so turned around.

I see more and more that God's designs are focused on the

---

[1]James Dobson, *Straight Talk*, p. 49.

eternal transformation of people. It's obvious that many times God can accomplish his goal of changing us while answering some immediate desire. But more often, I have noticed, God does something far-reaching—even when my prayers are stubbornly small. As one anonymous writer put it:

> I asked God for strength that I might achieve;
> I was made weak that I might learn humbly to obey.
> I asked God for health that I might do greater things;
> I was given infirmity that I might do better things.
> I asked for riches that I might be happy;
> I was given poverty that I might be wise.
> I asked for power that I might have the praise of men;
> I was given weakness that I might feel the need of God.
> I asked for all things that I might enjoy life;
> I was given life that I might enjoy all things.
> I got nothing that I asked for
> But everything I had hoped for.
> Almost despite myself, my unspoken prayers were
> answered.
> I am among all men most richly blessed.

Hebrews, chapter 11, the trophy room of God's Word, paints a vivid picture of how God might choose to answer our prayers. The passage lists the outcome of the lives of these who were faithful. It is pretty glorious, describing those *who through faith conquered kingdoms, administered justice . . . shut the mouths of lions . . . escaped the edge of the sword . . . became powerful in battle* (Hebrews 11:33–34a). Wow! But wait. The list continues. *Others were tortured . . . some faced jeers and flogging, while still others were chained . . . they were sawed in two; they were put to death by the sword . . . destitute, persecuted and mistreated* (11:35–37). Hold on! What was the difference between the first group and the second? Nothing! *These were all commended for their faith* (11:39a).

These were men and women with great faith in God. They probably all prayed to have their suffering alleviated. It's safe to assume that every one of them asked God to spare their life. But every one of them had a much greater goal at the core of their being. They yielded to the will of God. They wanted God's bigger picture more than they wanted him to honor their limited perspectives. The result? Some accomplished great things through their lives—and others accomplished great things through their lack of life. Either way, they entrusted themselves to God and their faith wasn't limited to what they could see!

This is so important. Charlatans claim that those who really have faith will see their prayers answered with a yes no matter what. They claim that if you're sick, or poor, or being oppressed—or your child's life doesn't overflow with all the good things you could hope for—then, brother or sister, it's you and your lack of faith that's to blame!

Did Satan rip Hebrews 11 out of their Bibles? Having faith means desiring that God will bring about good and glory and greatness far beyond the scope of our tiny needs or earthly lives. It doesn't in any way diminish the properness of praying for what would be most desirable for ourselves, as long as the overarching, far greater desire is that whatever God deems good will win out! What a lesson we'd learn to meet one of these martyred believers *now*, and find to our amazement that not a single one would wish God had worked for his glory in any other way.

Faith in the midst of confusion isn't just for people in the Bible. Each of us faces opportunities to learn a "no matter what" kind of trust.

Erika, absolutely beautiful in every way, was the precious first child of my brother Dave and his wife, Lauren. Around the ninth month of Erika's life, Dave and Lauren noticed she was having trouble. At first the change was almost imperceptible. She wasn't moving as quickly. There seemed to be an effort in her movements that wasn't there before. Then the doctor's office visits began. "She's probably got a virus of some sort . . . hard to tell really. She'll be fine. Just watch her." They did. But the downhill slide continued.

Erika's first birthday came and went, but the problem, whatever it was, wasn't going away. Her growth had stopped. She wasn't gaining any weight. She was stumbling and falling—not walking at age one like every parent plans. "There's definitely a serious problem. Seems to be a chemical in her system. The blood test shows that something isn't right . . . we're just not sure." The testing continued. Day after excruciating day. Questions nagged. Dave and Lauren watched. Their daughter was in agony and no one was coming to the rescue. They felt a screaming pain in the silence.

June arrived and kids were out running through sprinklers, and moms toting their little ones down the street. Lauren was pregnant again, so there was the prospect of better days ahead. Together the couple sat on the front porch, hand in hand, watching the world and hoping. Erika came through the doorway. She stepped forward, turned awkwardly on her leg—and fell.

Santa Monica Hospital. "She's broken her femur."

One night in August, Dave and Lauren walked into Erika's room to check on her before turning in for the night. An eerie stillness lay in the room. Erika's breathing was shallow. A cold steel gray had washed over her. Dave grabbed her in his arms and rushed her to UCLA Medical Center. She was admitted and diagnosed with congestive heart failure. EEG's showed seizures in her brain. Doctors inserted a tube in her neck to monitor her heart and placed her on a respirator. Her tiny chest, rose and fell. Despite the doctors' efforts she descended into a coma.

Then came the prognosis. "Lauren, Erika has a genetic enzyme deficiency that also threatens to affect the child you're carrying now. We seriously recommend that you abort the pregnancy at this point."

Lauren froze. There are those moments in time that seem as if there is no time—that everything you ever believed in, hoped for, dreamed of, lived for—vanishes. But there was no internal debate. One reality was clear to Dave and Lauren even through tears—life belongs to God, not us.

The days that followed were quiet. Feelings were too severe to be spoken. In the dark confusion, only one light remained: prayer to a faithful God. "We believe that God allowed for what has happened," they said. "Both Erika's life and the life of our unborn child are in his hands."

One angel went home on October 19, 1981. The machines were shut off, the curtain closed. I flew to Washington to carry Erika's casket. We set her tiny box down on gold and brown leaves in a country cemetery—"Evergreen" was the name. There we stood, with my brother and his wife, believing with them that God is good and hates the bad of this fallen world more than we do. Then we let go. We released what we could hold no longer.

On April 19, 1982, Lindsey Joy was born. *The prospect of the righteous is joy* (Proverbs 10:28). "She's our gift for as long as God wants her to be ours," Dave said.

From day one, she was a surprise. "She's exceptionally strong," the doctors puzzled. "We can't find a single trace of a problem."

Then there was Cathy. Then Johnny. Then Melanie. At Christmas 1993 our whole extended family was together for the holidays. "It is amazing when you see what God does," Dave told me. "We're not sure exactly why, but each of our kids have been given an exceptional amount of capability, all in different areas. All of them seem to just naturally excel above the norm in academics, their athletics, and even in their social relationships. It's as though God is having his day with them—despite what the doctors predicted. He's doing things his own way. And Erika—she changed our lives more than anyone ever could have. It was so hard to hold on during those days when we couldn't see the future. All we knew was that God's plans are good and that his agenda is an eternal one. All we could do was pray and hang on—despite the fact that we couldn't see."

Much of the time as we care for our children we can't see what God plans. We don't know exactly how he will choose to answer our prayers. What we do know for sure is that God sees and he hears and he responds when we pray. As someone has said, "I don't know what the future holds, but I know who holds the future." He waves us close to his side. "Hold my hand" we hear him say. "I know what I'm doing. Trust and obey."

Truth or Consequences

- How is prayer given a priority in your home? Is it relegated to a quick prelude to meals or is it also a meaningful part of your family time?

- Have you shared with your children how the power of God has been evident in response to your prayers?

- When your kids come to you with fears, needs, or concerns, do you take the time to pray with them about those feelings? Help them to understand how much their heavenly Father desires to hear from them and respond to them in perfect love.

- When God seems silent—when you don't see visible evidence of God responding to your prayers—how do you help your children understand God's bigger picture? Are they able to recount how character has been built or how good has come about even through times of suffering?

- What do your children hear you pray for? During your times of prayer with your children, be sure that they experience various facets of prayer—worship, confession, intercession on behalf of others as well as personal requests. It is worthwhile to lead your children explicitly through each of these aspects during your prayer times so that they will come to understand the full scope of communicating with God.

- Keep a simple prayer journal so that you and your children have a tangible way of seeing God's faithfulness in many different situations.

- As you experience conflict or misunderstanding between family members, praying together is a powerful way to resolve those hurts. It's amazing to see how prayer provides perspective and healing in relationships.

- Younger children enjoy going on a "blind walk." After they're blindfolded, lead them through the house or into the yard. Encourage them to ask you for more help as they need it. At some point let them try to walk without your assistance. Then talk about how this experience illustrates our walk through life. God can see "the big picture." He spots what's ahead and sees the dangers. Prayer is how we communicate our needs to God and express our trust in him to guide our lives.

- As challenges confront your family members, start a habit of spontaneously praying together right on the spot. Going to God first with issues communicates to our children the importance of prayer in our lives.

8

THE TRUTH ABOUT CONTENTMENT

THE CONSEQUENCES OF INNER CHAOS

The mind of sinful man is death, but the mind controlled by the Spirit is life and peace.

—Romans 8:6

July 1973. Ghana, West Africa. My father and I, along with a friend of his, were traveling northward toward the border of Upper Volta in a beat-up station wagon bound for the village of Wa. That's not a typo. The village of Wa, in the northern most territory of Ghana, actually exists. We found it.

Even more impressive, however, than Wa's tiny existence is its king. In the local vernacular, he was the "Na." That's right. The "Na of Wa" was he, and he presided on a throne made of nailed boards located under a thatched roof quite some distance from the bustling village of Wa.

We'd heard of the Na, and now we were in Wa, so it was time to visit the king. My father's friend, who was acquainted with the king, instructed us as we hiked the dirt path leading toward the palm-branch palace. "It is very important that you not look directly into his eyes. I'll introduce you and he'll give you some kind of greeting. Out of respect, though, don't look directly into his eyes. Look past him to the right." I couldn't believe what I was hearing. *Out of respect?* I thought to myself. *Who does this Na think he is?*

From the thick of the jungle we neared a clearing, and there in the center were four poles and a thatched roof. And there was the chair—and the very old king. An attendant stood close by and welcomed us. I stood looking off to the right as I had been told and only saw him with my peripheral vision. A few words were exchanged and then our friend indicated that our visit was up and we should leave. I couldn't help it. While turning to go I glanced directly at the king. It was obvious in an instant. He was blind. Apparently the attendant hadn't seen me look or really didn't care because nothing ever came of it, except a split-second snapshot forever burned in my mind.

Here was an old man, blind and incapacitated, sitting in a dusty shed, never doubting for an instant that he was the king. Why? Because he *was* the king and neither his health or his wealth had anything to do with it. He knew it and so did everyone else. As I left that day, I came away with a strange appreciation for the Na. He didn't let his outward circumstances dictate his inner condition.

Nearly every day I speak with someone who is troubled from the outside in. Circumstances are beyond them—their families or jobs or health or finances are falling apart. Disappointment hits them and leaves them in a state of inner disrepair.

Here's a fact: Everyone gets hit. Live long enough and walk far enough and you're going to stumble . . . or be tripped by someone.

Jesus wanted his followers to understand that inner peace and contentment results from the inside out, not the other way around. *Come to me, all you who are weary and burdened, and I will give you rest* (Matthew 11:28). The "rest" he offered was obviously not an easy ride through life. He modeled just the opposite. Christ's own peace and the peace he offers us is spiritual. It has the capacity to transcend even the worst of circumstances. But whether or not we experience that "contentment at the core" depends on our perspective.

As a man thinketh, so is he. It is as though each of us carries on an internal dialogue that guides our words and behaviors the way a script guides a theatrical production. The lighting, the words, every movement—they all depend on the script. Our internal script, that inner dialogue—what we tell ourselves is true—has been shaped by years of input. Our parents, our teachers, our friends, our experiences, the media all have written countless words. This drama is enormous!

Our mind rehearses the script: "You'll never amount to much. . . ."

"God is a cosmic kill-joy."

"Why can't you do anything right?"

"People can't be trusted."

"Religion is a crutch."

The book of Proverbs tells us that how we think

- will affect us physically (Proverbs 14:30);

- will affect our moods (15:13);

- will affect what we say (16:23);

- will affect everything about us (27:19)!

And Jesus taught in Mark 7:21–22 that what is inside us directs our wrong actions; *For from within, out of men's hearts, come evil thoughts, sexual immorality, theft, murder, adultery, greed, malice. . . .* and the list goes on! Conversely, it is through the *transformation* of our thinking that we're able to break free from the drag of sin on our lives: *Do not conform any longer to the pattern of this world, but be transformed by the renewing of your mind* (Romans 12:2).

No wonder God is so concerned about what goes on in our minds! It dictates everything we are and do.

The fourth chapter of Philippians speaks directly to our longing for inner congruity, to the benefits of a mind transformed by God. It points the way to a harvest of peace.

When Our Minds Are Centered on His Presence, the Result Is Peace

The Lord is near. Do not be anxious about anything (Philippians 4:5–6).

It was quiet as we loaded the last of the donated relief supplies and our own provisions onto the three old motorboats. Only the muffled voices of the boatmen and our tiny band of Americans could be heard. With the jungle behind us, we pushed out into the Caribbean Sea just past 5:00 A.M. I sat on the tarp that covered boxes of supplies destined for the remote refugee encampments of war-torn Nicaragua. There were 60,000 of these homeless people, many of whom had fled from their villages after Sandinista guerrillas had burned their homes to the ground. Stories abounded of the tortures these families had endured. All their valuables had been confiscated. Soldiers raped women and children and many men were shot on sight. Some of their number had died while fleeing through the treacherous jungle on their journey north toward the Honduran border.

A blast of water jolted me awake. The ocean was to our left, and in the distance to our right, a wall of vegetation reaching right to the sea. The day had been long and the sun merciless but finally the boatmen began to speak of nearing the mouth of the Coco River, where we would turn inland from the sea. As evening closed in we saw ahead of us the river's wide expanse.

A wind had come up and was whipping the water into whitecaps. Earlier in the day the boatmen had explained that moving from the sea going inland could be tricky. The waves resulting from the river rushing into the ocean often created a lot of turbulence. What they hadn't anticipated was a storm.

Waves battered our boat from all sides as the rain beat down on us. Laying face down on the piles of supplies, I held on tightly to the side of the boat. The front of the boat would fly up high and then hit the water with a loud crash as it descended. In the noise of wind and splashing water I could barely hear what the boatmen were hollering about. And before I could quite comprehend it, the boat took one last dance upward and plunged down hard, filling the boat with water. Amid the force of it all, my eyes closed tight, I could feel the boat sinking away as I was submerged in water.

Show me, O Lord, my life's end and the number of my days; let me know how fleeting is my life. You have made my days a mere hand-

breadth; the span of my years is as nothing before you. Each man's life is but a breath (Psalm 39:4–5).

Before leaving home, I had detailed all of this trip's possible dangers to the friends I had recruited to join me. I really loved these guys and now for the first time I truly feared for our lives. As I floundered in the water all I could wonder was *Where is everyone? Are they above the water?* With each crest lifting me upward I scanned the waves trying to see them.

Save me, O God, for the waters have come up to my neck. I sink in the miry depths, where there is no foothold. I have come into the deep waters; the floods engulf me (Psalm 69:1–2).

Before our boat had sunk one of the boatmen had untied the rubber raft being towed and I caught sight of it about twenty feet away. Treading water wildly I made my way toward the raft and was pulled in by others who had reached it before me. My mind raced as I mentally took roll call. Everyone had made it. But again we were sinking. The boatmen frantically attempted to start the waterlogged motor. As if making a desperate offering to some enraged sea god, the rest of us tossed box after box of valuable provisions into the churning water to lighten the load.

Give ear to my words, O Lord, consider my sighing. Listen to my cry for help, my King and my God, for to you I pray (Psalm 5:1–2).

With the current of the river flowing seaward, we were drifting away from land. We knew if the motor wouldn't start we would continue to be pushed out into the gulf stream, which moved south into Nicaraguan waters. Without power we would be carried away, no telling how far. There was nothing to stop us—other than the Sandinistas positioned in gunboats off the shore of Nicaragua.

Out of the depths I cry to you, O Lord; O Lord, hear my voice. Let your ears be attentive to my cry for mercy (Psalm 130:1–2).

At this point it was completely dark and we couldn't be sure which way shore lay. Then, out of nowhere, we could make out something protruding in front of our raft. We were drifting by and paddled hard with our arms to draw closer. It was a tree snag buried in a sandbar. One of our team members grabbed on to it from the front of the raft and hung on tenaciously against the current. We held on for life.

116

Turn your ear to me, come quickly to my rescue; be my rock of refuge . . . (Psalm 31:2).

It took us nearly an hour to get the motor started. With considerable hesitation, it began to propel us forward and we headed in what we thought was the direction of land. We ended up on a large island of sand. Stepping out of the boat onto any sort of land was exhilarating.

He turned to me and heard my cry. He lifted me out of the slimy pit, out of the mud and mire; he set my feet on a rock and gave me a firm place to stand (Psalm 40:1–2).

We were completely soaked and covered with sand and mud. Using the tarps that had survived with us we covered ourselves and slept under the wind and driving rain until dawn. The other boats in our group had made it to the same island and we were all reunited. One of those boats was still seaworthy and was able to travel inland that morning. By noon they returned, followed by three long native canoes.

We knew at that moment that God had renewed our contract on life. We were going to survive.

My salvation and my honor depend on God; he is my mighty rock, my refuge. Trust in him at all times, O people; pour out your hearts to him, for God is our refuge (Psalm 62:7–8).

Crying out to God. It's what the Hebrews did in Egypt. It's what we did on the Coco. It's what war refugees do every day. It's what battered children do in the stillness of the night. It's what alcoholics do when they watch their lives and families slipping away.

It's what I do. But not as often as I should. Just imagine what it would be like if all of us decided to live daily with an awareness of God's presence. What if we were to always lean hard into him— as though our life depended on it, each and every day. Maybe, just maybe, our life does.

When the demands of your job seems relentless—the Lord is near.

When you receive that property tax bill and the same week your company is talking about layoffs—the Lord is near.

When a very special friend has shared some private infor-

117

mation about you with someone who already thinks the worst of you—the Lord is near.

We live in a pressurized world where anything can change in an instant. The causes for alarm are always alarming. *Where is God's peace in all of this?* we wonder. God reminds us, "I am right here. I'm in the storm too. I can hold you if you'll let me." And if God is your place of strength, then your children will also see that he is their refuge.

You will keep in perfect peace him whose mind is steadfast, because he trusts in you. Trust in the Lord forever, for the Lord, the Lord, is the Rock eternal (Isaiah 26:3–4).

Not only is God our secure place, he's our eternally secure place. I've found in my own life that focusing on the "foreverness" of God's nearness makes a huge difference for the present. I think this is part of what Paul was expressing in 2 Corinthians 4:18. He's been discussing the afflictions and anxieties his readers were experiencing. Then he writes, *So we fix our eyes not on what is seen, but on what is unseen. For what is seen is temporary, but what is unseen is eternal.*

If our thinking is primarily focused on this life, disappointment is inevitable. Why? Because everything breaks down! Our cars, our computers, our kids, our looks, our health, our most treasured relationships—they're flawed. They don't work perfectly. Life, as it stands, is a letdown. But when we look to what and to Who is ahead, everything in the here and now, even the hard stuff, isn't as crushing.

His presence means protection. His power is our means of peace. Our only hope is faith in the fact that God is here and he's aware and he's able to control anything in his own way and his own time. It is a simple faith that requires sustained trust, even against the whirling blast of life's storms.

I constantly need to come back and lodge this truth in my mind: "God is with me. His love is unconditional. Nothing I do can make him love me any more or any less. He doesn't leave me when I act sinfully. He's fully aware when my life caves in. He understands storms and he is the only one who can calm them."

When Our Minds Are Centered in Prayer, the Result Is Peace

But in everything, by prayer and petition, with thanksgiving, present your requests to God. And the peace of God, which transcends all understanding, will guard your hearts and your minds in Christ Jesus (Philippians 4:6–7).

There's a great little bumper sticker that reads, "As long as there are tests, there will be prayer in schools." While on one level that slogan is funny, it surely points out our tendency to pray best when we're in a jam! When life falls apart, I pray. When I think I've got everything under control, I put my prayers on autopilot. Other than "scheduled" prayers (such as meal times, church or tucking the kids into bed) most of us fight a tendency toward independence. Unless we blow a tire on the freeway or one of our kids threatens to run away from home, most of us live busy lives with little space for the supernatural.

Yet it is just this communion with God through prayer that is foundational to inner harmony. It requires coming away from the noise long enough to hear his voice. When I come into that quiet sanctuary of prayer, I find my heart held in his hands. When I bring his Word to bear on my life, I find my mind focused again on what is true. Nothing is more necessary or healing in our world of conflicting messages.

Augustine could have penned these words in the spiritual journal of any busy Christian living today:

> I find no secure place for my soul except in you. And in you, I pray that what is scattered in me may be brought together, so that no part of me may be apart from you. Sometimes when you are working within me, bringing my scattered self to you, you draw me into a state of feeling that is unlike anything I am used to, a kind of sweet delight. I know that if this spiritual state were made permanent in me it would be something not of this world, not of this life.[1]

My inability to rest in the Lord often results from my own

---

[1]Augustine's Confessions, as quoted in *Early Will I Seek You*, by David Hazard (Minneapolis, Minn.: Bethany House Publishers, 1991), p. 15.

chaotic mind. "The Lord wants me to work hard for him," I think. "The more I work, the more good I'll do." The problem is that the needs are never-ending. There are always countless tasks at hand—what someone has coined the "tyranny of the urgent." So I plunge ahead, forgetting to pray, neglecting to rest, all the while ignoring the truth that my greatest accomplishments will happen on my knees.

Christ knew it was imperative to pull away, to retreat—to pray. The one who calmed the sea looked for ways to calm his schedule. *After he had dismissed them, he went up on a mountainside by himself to pray. When evening came, he was there alone* (Matthew 14:23). As he approached the cross, he didn't cram another seminar into his itinerary; he went to the garden to pray. And there Christ found the resolve to move ahead as directed by his Father.

When Our Minds Are Centered on What Is Good, the Result Is Peace

Finally, brothers, whatever is true, whatever is noble, whatever is right, whatever is pure, whatever is lovely, whatever is admirable—if anything is excellent or praiseworthy—think about such things. Whatever you have learned or received or heard from me, or seen in me—put it into practice. And the God of peace will be with you (Philippians 4:8–9).

Where your mind is, there will your life be also.

"Five-year-old sets trailer on fire, killing sister," the *Wall Street Journal* caption read. The five-year-old was imitating behavior she had just viewed on MTV. The article that followed observed this: "Not only is society itself more violent today, but local news, network news, the front page of the newspaper and magazines reflect that violence is back into the nation's living rooms." Violence has always been a part of programming, but as the article pointed out, TV now gives children uncontrolled access to cable, video on demand, rental videos and other media.[2]

What are you exposing yourself to? What are your kids exposed to? Are there consequences?

---

[2]*Wall Street Journal*, "Stamping Out TV Violence: a Losing Fight," October 26, 1993, B1.

Ephesians encourages us to rid ourselves of the rotten and replace it with the righteous. Paul says to put out of our minds the stuff of the old life and to *Be made new in the attitude of your minds* (Ephesians 4:23). The same idea is brought home in Colossians 3:1–2 as well: *Since, then, you have been raised with Christ, set your hearts on things above, where Christ is seated at the right hand of God. Set your minds on things above, not on earthly things.*

I can still hear my art teacher. In our class of hyper-tense, hyper-distracted high school artists he constantly yelled one word: "CONCENTRATE!" If you're going to paint an apple, he would explain, you've got to get your mind clearly focused.

I can hear the apostle Paul shouting the same admonition. Concentrate on what is good! If you want good things to flow from your life, put good things in your mind. Good in—good out. Christians in the city of Galatia had slipped back in their walk with God. What was the problem? They were listening to old lifestyle philosophies and rhetoric. *How is it that you are turning back to those weak and miserable principles? Do you wish to be enslaved by them all over again?* (Galatians 4:9). The very same words apply to much of what fills our minds these days.

And the minds of this generation of kids? What have we given them to concentrate on? A couple of typical findings:

American children spend 5,000 hours in front of the TV set prior to the first grade. By the time they graduate they will have seen more than 200,000 acts of violence, including more than 40,000 murders. In an independent study *TV Guide* found that 1,846 acts of violence occurred on ten channels in a normal eighteen-hour broadcast day.[3]

Researchers from Michigan State found that the average soap opera contains two "intimate sexual acts" per hour. They also found that 94% of all daytime copulations (including rape and prostitution) occur between unmarried couples.[4]

---

[3]M. Zuckerman, "The Victims of TV Violence," *U.S. News & World Report*, August 2, 1993, p. 64.
[4]Randy C. Alcorn, *Christians in the Wake of the Sexual Revolution* (Portland: Multnomah Press, 1985), p. 94.

Does soaking our minds in sex and violence have any effect? Scripture says it does. People who spend time with young people see the effects every day. And television isn't the only source of mind-numbing immorality.

Our first task is honesty about what we are ingesting day after day. Is it truth? Is it pure and honorable and lovely?

Everyone has to decide what kind of stand they're going to take. But take one! In our house our television is more or less a video monitor. Apart from an occasional newscast or "Sesame Street" or a special now and then, we only watch good videos that reflect the values of Philippians 4:8. We fix our minds and spend our time on things more valuable than TV. We feel free! Without the TV-habit we have time and freedom to enjoy God's Word, to invest prayer and time and energy in our kids, and to submerge ourselves in all of the people and activities God has placed in our lives.

So take a tomahawk to your television and go walk with your kids in the woods. Then watch your life take a turn!

When Our Minds Are Centered on Positives Rather Than Negatives, the Result Is Peace

I have learned to be content whatever the circumstances. I know what it is to be in need, and I know what it is to have plenty. I have learned the secret of being content in any and every situation, whether well fed or hungry, whether living in plenty or in want (Philippians 4:11–12).

There's a mind game most of us play without recognizing how debilitating it is. Some can call it "scarcity thinking." I call it "looking at what is lacking." It's a rut of negativity and its consequences are severe.

When self-talk is negative, you are creating a toxic environment for yourself. What's more, you will carry this internal environment with you, regardless of your physical location. How a person reacts to a particular stress is very much related to that person's own self-talk. To the exact same circumstance, one person will react with depression: "It's hopeless, I'll never succeed," another with anger: "It's all their fault," and a third with optimism: "You can't win them all. I'll do better next time."[5]

As a kid one of my favorite stories was *How the Grinch Stole Christmas*. It's about a miser in the mountains who thinks he can steal Christmas joy by taking away all the presents. But on Christmas morning—as the "Who's down in Whoville" start singing anyway—the Grinch discovers something. Joy, in other words, depends not on the externals of life but on the internals.

Discontentment works for the Grinch. He's a miser who kills joy from the inside out and couldn't care less how many good things surround your life. When he takes up residence within you, you lose all. He moves in on your family and the quarreling escalates. He creeps into your career and makes you hate going to work. He takes control of your assets and—no matter how much is there—he twists the numbers until they're red. He wraps his bony fingers around your soul and squeezes out every ounce of joy.

Contentment is that quality that says your external environment is less important than the inward realities of faith. To paraphrase Paul, "In good times, I've been content. In bad times, I've been content. Outside, circumstances change all the time, but my inner calm is consistent. I can handle any and every kind of situation because God strengthens me from within." It's an inside job.

If discontentment has moved into your life, I can almost name the door by which he entered—a belief in "entitlements." We feel we're entitled to good things, that life, after all, should be good to us: "Others should be nice to me." "My kids shouldn't cause me so much stress." Entitlements. Shoulds. They're different than desires or hopes or wishes. They're demands, things we expect from life and others. When we don't get them discontentment moves in with his load of ugly baggage.

There's only one antidote—a thankful heart. Thankfulness at its core is an "abundance mentality." It sees all that is and can live well with what is not. It's a frame of reference that accepts all of

---

[5]Pamela Butler, *Talking to Yourself* (San Francisco: Harper, 1981) pp. 7, 9.

life—the good as well as the bad—with the belief that God is ultimately good. It's not a happy-go-lucky skip in the park in the midst of tragedy. It's an acceptance that in a world depressed by sin, bad things happen even to good people. Evil hits us all. And while the impact of genuine hurt is beyond our control, it is we who ultimately choose to hold on to the hurt or lean into the Healer.

I was digging through a dusty old book when I came across one author's thoughts on the attitude of gratefulness. I love the images it brings to mind:

> Think of the delights that have come to us through the avenues of sight and hearing; recall the joys of lovely scenery, of pictures, of sunshine, of music. Think of the gladness of life, of health and strength and work.
>
> With every year that is added to my life I feel more keenly the inadequacy of my appreciation of God's wondrous world. Every year the spring is more precious, the summer more delightful, the autumn more glorious. And many times I marvel that so many years have passed me by and I have learned so little, wondered so little, enjoyed so little all these everyday marvels of creation.
>
> One day I was visiting an insane asylum and a patient there asked me quite suddenly, "Did you ever thank God that you are not insane?" I never had.[6]

When Our Minds Are Centered on God's Power Rather Than Our Own, the Result Is Peace

I can do everything through him who gives me strength (Philippians 4:13).

This is the *how* behind the *what*. This is the cause behind Paul's contentment. Peace has come by way of a realization, Paul affirms. It's an abandonment to a greater power that far exceeds my limited endurance. Contentment comes when we admit that we can indeed handle life, no matter what—but through God's power, not our own.

---

[6]From a sermon by Bernard J. Snell, as cited in the compilation of sermons entitled *Jesus in the Cornfield* (Manchester, England: James Robinson Press, 1908), p. 163.

A desire for personal control plagues us. We drive ourselves crazy trying ever harder to live up to demands imposed from without and within. That's not God's design. Paul's intention here was to reassure us that life doesn't depend on our resources. The battle is the Lord's.

I have found that the less I feel I can count on God's power, the more I expect from myself and others. For instance, if I doubt that joy comes from my relationship with God, then I replace what I lack by looking to others to make me happy. If I doubt God's love, then I to turn to others in hope that their love will fill the void. If I'm not convinced of God's ability to take care of me, then I turn to any number of material things, "health and wealth" stuff, to make me feel secure.

Many of our inner conflicts arise from our tendency to hold people or things responsible for our inner sense of well-being. "If they would just shape up or ship out, then. . . . If my job were. . . . If my child only. . . . If my spouse was. . . . If my health would. . . . If I just had. . . ." It's always something on the outside that will fill the inside. Untrue! Paul proclaims. It is God within you that gives you strength. Needing others to change is a no-win way to live. We simply can't control most of life's circumstances, nor can we control what others do or don't do. What we can control is how we respond to them.

God is the one, the only one, who fills all of our inner voids. His power is sufficient to strengthen every part of us. Damaged emotions begin to heal as God's love makes up for the failures of others to love us. Damaged feelings of worth begin to change as God's acceptance takes root inside our hearts. Damaged confidence is built up once God's power is realized.

The next time you're feeling angry, depressed or scared, ask yourself who or what you're depending on for your inner peace. If the answer lies in something or someone other than the Lord, you have good reason to be upset!

We impose a lot of "If . . . thens" on ourselves. "If I'm a good mother, then my kids will obey me. If I'm competent on the job, then others will appreciate my efforts. If I'm a good enough writer, then everyone will want this book." It's a bizarre pass/fail system where we're either perfect performers or worthless failures. More than anything else, it's a control issue—if we can control our world then we feel we'll find the contentment we desire.

Another consequence of this "me in control" mentality is a tendency toward rescuing. I've seen it in doctors, teachers, social workers, some moms and dads, and, of course, pastors. Many of us in helping professions chose our jobs because of a subconscious desire to rescue people. We rightly shoulder our responsibility when we do what we can to help others, yet it's unreasonable to attempt to completely control the lives of others, including our children's. When we struggle to take the reins for another's life, both of us lose our grip.

No one struggles with rescuing as much as a parent. We spend every moment of our kids' first years of life yanking them away from this, or guarding them from falling into that. Rescuing is what keeps them alive. But then they grow. And when they're grown—or even when they're gone—parents can still be easily trapped in a pattern of rescuing.

To all of this God replies, "Not you, but me. I can fill you with strength even if—even *when*—life lets you down. I can also work powerfully in the lives of others. You're not the Savior. I am. Point them to me."

I find that as I meditate on these truths I come back to reality, to an accurate appraisal of my life and God's great power. As my inner dialogue becomes untangled I say to myself, "Daniel, you are not God. God is God. You are just Daniel. You have permission to be human. Stop playing God. Stop acting like you can control everything. You can't. Let God be God and you go back to being a faithful servant! God will meet your needs, and the needs of others, with the truth of his sufficiency."

The implications of this for life and joy are many. If I am no longer God then I'm allowed to be mortal. I am allowed to be in process. I'm allowed to have imperfect children who sometimes need to learn things the hard way. I'm allowed to fail and to be forgiven. I'm not required to save anyone. I don't have to be "all things to all people." I even have permission to rest. (Remember, even God did it!) I can do all the things God wants me to do, because his power is completely sufficient.

Last week I got a call from a mom of one of the middle-schoolers in our ministry. "Daniel, I feel like I've lost control and I feel like I'm losing my mind!" After a good hour together on the phone, we both came to a point of peace in a situation that indeed was beyond control. (We were even laughing!) Before hanging up, this woman added, "I guess perspective is everything. I still don't feel like I've got control but I suppose that's not as important as knowing God does. Oh, and my mind. I guess I can live without that too."

There was another boat in another storm on another day. You and the other disciples are doing your best to navigate while the storm intensifies from restless to raging. Strong breezes knock the boat back and forth. Waves spill over the sides. Suddenly gusts turn to gales. The boat isn't just rocking—it's rolling! Everyone panics, and for good reason. Everyone—except one. Jesus is asleep in the bow of the boat. "Jesus, wake up! Don't you even care that we're going to capsize! Jesus, we're going to drown! Do something!" And he does. He turns to the sea, and with complete control speaks to it: *"Quiet! Be still!" Then the wind died down and it was completely calm.* While you're still trying to comprehend what you've seen, Jesus speaks again. This time his words are for you: *"Why are you so afraid? Do you still have no faith?"* (Mark 4:39–40).

The words of the Savior on the sea still come whispering across life's waves: "I'm here. We're in this boat together. Peace— be still."

Truth or Consequences

- How have your children seen God's peace control your life and emotions even in the midst of chaos? When you are at peace, do they know where it originates? Have you told them how dependent you are on God's provision of peace?

- Does your schedule include times of solitude, reflection and meditation? Do you build it into the schedule that your children keep? You may want to explain how even good things in life can prevent them from enjoying God's best things in life. Take them through the story of Mary and Martha in Luke 10:38–42 and show them how special it is to take time simply to meditate on what the Lord has to say in his Word.

- Take daily opportunities to show your kids the connection between what they put in their minds and what results in their lives. If they watch a horror film on TV, there's a good chance they'll feel frightened afterward. If they listen to music laced with angry, rebellious lyrics, it only fuels bad attitudes. Help them make the connection in every area of life. What kind of positive substitutes could you offer?

- Are negatives a large part of your family's conversations? Do a status check. Are there ways you may be communicating to your children that your happiness is contingent on what others do or don't do? How could you model contentment even in the face of adversity?

- To help children visualize the "garbage in—garbage out" principle of our minds, get a hold of a couple of shoe boxes and a pile of magazines. Clip pictures that represent God's values and place those inside one box. On the outside of the box glue or tape pictures that illustrate the outcomes of those positive values. Find just the opposite kinds of pictures to use on the second box—pictures on both the inside (causes) and outside (effects) that illustrate bad decisions or Godless values and their results. Talk about the two boxes representing two kinds of lives. What goes inside eventually will be reflected on the outside.

- Tour your home and look for things that cultivate discontent. Are your magazine racks full of slick mail-order catalogs for things you can't afford—and don't need? You can unprogram the shopping channels from your TV, and toss out ads that pressure you or your children to spend unwisely. (The fliers that come inside children's toys and videos, for example, shout that happiness is only found in acquiring every last piece in a set.) Think through other habits that breed dissatisfaction—living at malls, comparing yourself to neighbors, or even working for a company or attending a church that promotes endless accumulation of "stuff."

- Do a biography dig on some famous people of the past who supposedly "had it all." Take Howard Hughes, for instance, a man who had every imaginable worldly possession and yet never achieved contentment. How could that be? God says there's more to life than what this world has to offer. Consider what your family is doing to invest in real contentment as God defines it.

9

THE TRUTH ABOUT REALITY

THE CONSEQUENCES OF DECEPTION

Blessed is the man who fears the Lord, who finds great delight in his commands. His children will be mighty in the land.

—Psalm 112:1–2a

A good friend of mine works in a bank. One evening he and another teller were working at the drive-up window just as it was getting dark outside. Something about the lighting—apparently some of the outside lights weren't working—caused a glare on their window so they couldn't see customers well. Mrs. So and So pulled up at the farthest island from the window. She was typically short-tempered, and this evening proved no exception. Whatever it was she said came through loud and clear over the speaker inside the bank. Then she put her banking in one of those plastic tubes and shot it to the tellers through the vacuum pipe.

Now remember that my friend and his fellow teller couldn't see Mrs. So and So very well due to the glare, but they could see the silhouette of her large poodle—who often accompanied her to the bank—sitting in the seat next to her, also facing the bank window. The dog had curly hair and long floppy ears. (That really is pertinent to the story!) Here's where the plot thickened.

The bank, wanting to spread goodwill, had a bowl of large,

130

dry doggie-bones they gave to customers with dogs in their cars. So upon shooting the plastic flask back through the vacuum pipe, my friend's associate cheerfully sent the woman on her way by saying, "Thank you, Mrs. So and So. Here is the receipt for you . . . and here is a bone for your dog." There was a pause. Then, over the loudspeaker inside the bank, came the most raucous, disgusted, punctuated reply. "THAT'S . . . NO . . . DOG! THAT'S . . . MY . . . DAUGHTER!!" Both tellers cupped their hands around their faces and pressed their noses to the glass for a better look. Sure enough. It was the woman's young daughter sitting next to her—pigtails and all!

Things aren't always what they seem. There's truth—and then there is our perception of things. We tend to make decisions and operate our lives based on what we perceive as being true even though, often enough, what we perceive is inaccurate.

A few years ago *Rolling Stone* spent a great deal of money trying to change its image in the marketplace of magazines. It ran a series of ads using just two words. On one side of the page was a picture of a guy with long hair wearing a tie-dyed T-shirt. Underneath the picture was one word: "PERCEPTION." On the other side of the page was another picture—this one of a clean-cut businessman in a nice suit, holding a briefcase. Underneath was the ad's second word: "REALITY." The magazine's promoters wanted people to change their perceptions to match what they felt was the truth about *Rolling Stone* readers.

From the beginning of time, God has been bringing people back to truth. The reason? What we ultimately think about God, the Bible, the past, the future, ourselves, our actions, others, and literally everything else in life—how we view it, or perceive it, or think about it—will have dire consequences. As the prophet Hosea wrote, *My people are destroyed from lack of knowledge* (Hosea 4:6).

Interestingly, Jesus described Satan as having one primary character quality: deception. *He is a liar and the father of lies* (John 8:44). The Bible also states his primary objective: distortion. *The god of this age has blinded the minds of unbelievers* (2 Corinthians 4:4). And he doesn't let up—don't be fooled. *For we are not unaware of* [Satan's] *schemes* (2 Corinthians 2:11).

We're So Vain

Go back in your memory for a moment. It was a bright crisp morning in the garden. Remember? God had given you every-thing, along with one simple instruction. He asked you not to eat of that one fruit off that one tree. Why? One tree represented a whole other side of reality. A side God never wanted you to know about or experience. It was the reality of evil, of life without him, of all that is opposed to what is good.

But the choice was yours.

Long before you, God had given his angels the same type of option. He had no desire for obedience by obligation. He longed for more than rote response. He wanted a love relationship. And love always contains a choice.

Some of his created heavenly beings chose to oppose him. They decided to take their chances at separation. They disowned him, with disastrous consequences. They were no longer destined to share in his glory. They were forever lost—an option God him-self allowed for.

Back in the garden there was a rustling in the bushes. A snake appeared. Someone was out to destroy God's greatest creation. The first whisper out of his mouth was a lie. "Did God really say, 'You must not eat from *any* tree in the garden'?" Right off the bat, a major distortion. God had given you everything but the *one* tree that would destroy you! Satan was out to make God look stingy, harsh and unloving, but he had to confuse you in order to do it.

Remember what you said next? You fumbled God's command. You misquoted God. "God said I must not eat fruit from the tree that is in the middle of the garden, and I must not touch it or I will die." Don't touch it? He never said that. Things were getting hazier.

"You will not surely die," the serpent lied again. Then he hissed his promise. If you ate of the fruit of the tree in the middle of the garden, your eyes would be opened. You would be enlight-ened. You would know everything! With God no longer interfer-ing, you could have it ALL! So you ate.

Something felt different. Suddenly you noticed you weren't beautiful anymore. You covered yourself. God came near and you hid. You were the very first case of a "bad self-image." You had been fashioned perfectly in the image of God, but the image was now marred by sin and the results were just beginning to show.

Little did you know, however, that on that day God instituted a plan to make you beautiful again. He was going to send you his Son—the Savior.

In the beginning God created . . . and Satan set out to destroy. Satan did it by deceiving us then and he does it the same way now. *There is a way that seems right to a man, but in the end it leads to death* (Proverbs 14:12).

In our culture "the way of death" appears to be a pleasant day in the park. But the park is real foggy. *It seems warm*, we think. *But the haze. Too bad it's so hazy. Oh well, guess that's just how it is. Always a little hazy:*

- We should accept alternative lifestyles no matter what.

- No one knows for sure what happens after death.

- Don't be too dogmatic. There's more than one way to look at mercy killing.

- The media just mirrors what's real. It doesn't add to the problem.

- Teaching kids to use condoms is the answer to teenage STDs (sexually transmitted diseases) and pregnancy.

This haze . . . I'm having trouble seeing straight. Is it any wonder?

Even the worst of behaviors have become commonplace, normative, through gradual inoculations of perversity. Whatever your kid sees over and over and over again will gradually seem normal to him or her—whether it's true or not. To kids, the truth or goodness of a thing or an action doesn't make half as much difference as the fact that something is considered "normal" and therefore "acceptable."

What I'm saying here is really important. When you analyze what is being purveyed as normative in our culture, it should make us long, yearn, reach for God's Word. In this era like never before untruth is being normalized on a grand scale. The fog is getting thicker.

Since eternal life with God is found in the one and only truth of the gospel, it naturally follows that Satan's "first strike" is to create blindness, because only through blindness can he keep us in the dark. *The god of this age has blinded the minds of unbelievers, so that they cannot see the light of the gospel of the glory of Christ, who is the image of God* (2 Corinthians 4:4).

Now I wish I could say that once our blindness breaks and we embrace our Savior that we don't struggle anymore with distorted perceptions. The reality is that we're influenced by Satan's schemes until the day we receive our eternal bodies and enter God's presence. While he's lost the battle for our eternal state, he still affects our state of mind. By confusing the truth about who we are and what we are in relation to God, he can render us powerless as God's children.

Neil Anderson has carefully defined some of the delusions that hold even Christians captive. In his book *The Bondage Breaker* he presents a straightforward list of "Who We Are in Christ." It's worth getting a hold of a list like this, or better yet, doing a study with your family to uncover these truths straight from the pages of Scripture. Let me give you a sample of truth statements about our identity as believers:

- I am indwelt by the Spirit of God (1 Corinthians 2:12).

- I am a citizen of heaven (Ephesians 2:6).

- I am chosen of God, holy and dearly loved (Colossians 3:12).

- I am no longer ruled by sin (Romans 6:1–6).

- I am a child of light not of darkness (1 Thessalonians 5:5).

- I am only a visitor to this world in which I temporarily live (1 Peter 2:11).

- I am an enemy of the devil (1 Peter 5:8).

That's just a few from a much longer list. No "self-image" confusion when it comes to Scripture. The more we and our kids focus squarely on the truth about who we are, the more our character will be reshaped to fit that mind-set.

Let what is real—instead of just what you feel—shape what

you believe! *Impress them on your children. Talk about them when you sit at home and when you walk along the road, when you lie down and when you get up* (Deuteronomy 6:7).

What philosophy—whose philosophy—are your kids being impressed with on a daily basis? If you're watching for opportunities you can use life's daily routine to trigger some terrific "truth dialogues":

- When you're lounging at home (even if the TV is on—okay, I admit, it can be good for something!)

- When you're talking to your son after his little league game

- When your daughter gets dumped by "some jerk" she liked

- When you're tucking your kids into bed

- When you're sitting at the breakfast table in the morning looking over the headlines.

That's what Deuteronomy chapter 6 is saying. Watch for those moments when truth can be impressed. Then start discussing!

Contending With Counterfeits

The world presents an alluring alternative to what is real and what is lasting. It's pretty well summed up in 1 John 2:16: *For everything in the world*—here it is—*the cravings of sinful man, the lust of the eyes and the boasting of what he has and does—comes not from the Father but from the world.* In other words, the sensualism and the materialism and the egotism of humankind is a facade. It isn't from God and it isn't going to last. As foundations go, they're a surefire crumbler. *They followed worthless idols and became worthless themselves* (Jeremiah 2:5). As gods go, they're nothing but propped up trinkets fashioned by man himself. The answer is to forego the prevailing opinions of humankind, and trade them for the truth that is grounded in our Eternal Lord himself. *Do not deceive yourselves. If any one of you thinks he is wise by the standards of this age, he should become a "fool" so that he may become wise. For the wisdom of this world is foolishness in God's sight* (1 Corinthians 3:18–19).

The wisdom of this world often laughs at that wisdom from above—for a time. And then the laughing ceases. From an earthly vantage point, Esau had everything going for him. He was a first-born, which in the Jewish system entitled him to his father's legacy—his blessing, his family name and his inheritance. In fact, his particular heritage was incredible. Esau's grandfather Abraham had been given the promise that the whole Jewish nation would come through his lineage. Esau was right in that line.

One day Esau was out hunting and he came home famished. Really famished, like *starving* famished. Stew was on the stove and his brother, Jacob, had on the chef's hat. "Gimme some stew!" But Jacob refused. He sensed how hungry Esau was and decided to take advantage of the moment. Jacob cut him a deal. "Swear to me that I can have your birthright and I'll give you all the stew you could ever want!"

"Okay, okay, take the lousy birthright. Just give me some dinner!"

So the birthright was sold for a bowl of bean soup.

Esau missed out because he sold out. He traded what was infinitely valuable for what was insignificant. We look at that story in Genesis 25 and shake our heads in amazement. How could anyone be so shortsighted and stupid? How could he trade something so far-reaching for a momentary sense of satisfaction? What was he thinking? How could he be so blind?

How could he?

How could *we*?

People do it every day.

Later on, in Genesis 27:34, we hear a lonely wail rising out of the desert. Indeed, Jacob was given his father's blessing, and *when Esau heard his father's words, he burst out with a loud and bitter cry and said to his father, "Bless me—me too, my father!"* But the key had already turned in the lock. He had chosen his course and now nothing was able to reverse it. One decision changed the course of history. Granted, Isaac was conned by Jacob. But he had felt around in the dark and grabbed hold of the wrong thing. Deception is like that. It dulls our perception and hooks us with some worthless alternative. It's not until later, until the morning after, until someone knocks on our door, that we regain consciousness.

Don't be deceived, my dear brothers, James warned. *After desire has conceived, it gives birth to sin; and sin, when it is full-grown, gives birth to death* (James 1:15–16).

The world laughs at that and snubs "Not true! We'll find a way out! There's got to be a way to have it all—all the sin with none of the side-effects." But the warning stands.

Choosing the Most Excellent Way

When my mom and dad retired from their careers in education, they could have done what some people do when they retire: buy a motor home, travel the country, watch old movies on video and show off pictures of their grandchildren. Now before you snap this book shut, please understand I'm not implying that any of those things are bad in themselves. It's just not what my parents chose. Instead, they packed up their belongings and moved to Africa, where they served for the next thirteen years as missionary educators, spending in the process a good portion of their retirement "fun money."

Halfway through that time, my mom contracted a severe disease in her stomach and could well have died. Nevertheless, she had a vision, and after recouping remained right in the center of that vision. "They're crazy," some might say. "Should have taken it easy. Should have joined the Moose lodge and learned lawn bowling and enjoyed themselves." But mom and dad were marching to a different drummer, seeking a different kind of wisdom, operating from a totally different set of values.

My dad is now in his 70s and he's doing volunteer tax preparation for "other people who are old," as he puts it. I understand that what my parents chose isn't for everyone. The choice before all of us, however, is to decide how *we* are going to live beyond the confines of this world's value system—how we're going to grasp what will outlast us! That is wisdom from above.

Do not turn away after useless idols, the great priest Samuel warned his people. *They can do you no good, nor can they rescue you, because they are useless* (1 Samuel 12:21).

Let's face it. Idols abound. An idol is anything or anyone that consumes your time and attention in place of God. Think about it. Do you have an idol in your house? In your efforts? In your dreams? Who or what is your heart's desire and where does your time and money go? That is your god. But anything less than the Lord God is a worthless, lifeless, hopeless deception. It consumes your days—and when your days are spent you'll have nothing on the other side. Prosperity as the world reckons it is pretension.

It is in light of this reality that David wrote Psalm 119:37: *Turn my eyes away from worthless things; renew my life according to your word.* Don't be fooled.

The Bible dramatically reorients my thinking. Like a spiritual tune-up, it clears the mixed messages and false messages that lodge like old dirty oil in my soul. And faulty thinking is at the root of most of life's problems. My anxieties, more often than not, are a result of my limited perspectives. According to God even the worst of events can bring about good. Truth has phenomenal consequences. It changes your thinking, and that will change your life.

The Only Protection Is Perception

Someone once said regarding the history of nations that "slavery is always preceded by sleep." That's also true in our own lives. Yet a keen perception of truth as revealed by an all-knowing God defeats the devil's agenda of deception and bondage. Lies hate the light. Look at the focus of Christ's prayer for us as recorded in John chapter 17. *My prayer is not that you take them out of the world but that you protect them from the evil one* (17:15). And how will that be accomplished? *Sanctify them by the truth; your word is truth* (17:17). When we go to God's Word we get realigned with what is true. While the world is filled with a dizzying disarray of half-truths and outright lies, God brings us back to reality through his Word. It's a spiritual de-fogger.

The employees at the Bureau of Engraving use special ink, special paper and special presses, all to create money that can't be perfectly duplicated. They know the tricks used by counterfeiters, but their skill is most perfected by a thorough knowledge of the real stuff. They know cold hard cash when they see it. Those who can spot counterfeits learn how by studying the real stuff. Counterfeits just stick out.

What's the best way to protect your kids from the world's counterfeits? Ship them to a monastery? There's always the way of Simeon the Stylite, who for thirty years lived atop a pillar to avoid being ensnared by the world. Or how about St. Francis of Assisi, who walked naked through town as a protest against the trappings of materialism.

With all due respect, I think there's a better way: Know the truth. Drink deep from the well of God's Word and everything else will begin to look dry and dingy. Will you do it? Will you be so bold as to turn off the TV and the CD and the PC and talk to your kids? Will you open the Word, play memory games with the Word, engage in challenging dialogue by discussing the Word, look for answers to current problems by studying the Word? Is God's truth getting inside or being set aside? Jesus asked the Father not to remove us from the intimidation of the world, but to make us internally strong so that we might impact the world. Inside out. The Word of God offers that inner arsenal.

The Bible says it straight out. There's only one safety net for our kids that is ultimately going to hold them: *How can a young man keep his way pure? By living according to your word* (Psalm 119:9). Better to face it now than later. Realistically, we can't remove our kids from the world. Reasonably, we can't follow our kids everywhere they go. But responsibly, we can outfit them with the internal armor of God *so that when the day of evil comes,* [they] *may be able to stand* [their] *ground* (Ephesians 6:13). Are we preparing them? Internally? Have we buckled a belt of truth around their waists? (Ephesians 6:14).

God wants our children to be *mighty in the land,* not removed from the land. Yet the only way that comes about is when parents decide to *fear the Lord* and *delight in his commands.* Notice, as always, it begins with us parents! When you've got some leisure time, what's your "delight"? (I know I'm shooting at sacred cows here. Hang on.) Sports? Movies? Honestly, I'm not trying to be cruel or legalistic about this. I love all those things too—I ski, I take vacations, I read novels. That's not the point. Here's the issue at stake: Are we also taking a "great delight" in the Word of God?

Can our kids tell? Do we dig around in there long enough to unearth "delightful truth" and show it to our kids like a diamond discovered in the backyard?

Can I take this a step further? What is the atmosphere around your home on Sunday morning? Is going to church a burden? When you're asked to give your time or resources is it an imposition? A prayer meeting . . . or a walk held in protest of killing unborn children . . . or the chance to care for an AIDS patient . . . are these opportunities or inconveniences? What attitudes are seeping across to our kids? *This is how we know that we love the children of God: by loving God and carrying out his commands. This is love for God: to obey his commands. And his commands are not burdensome* (1 John 5:2–3). No, they're not. But sometimes we treat them as if they are. Every day our children learn by watching us what they should delight in and what they can expect to simply endure.

There's a promise here. Don't miss it.

Rote Answers or Real Discernment

How can we help our children internalize the truth in a way that results in good behavior? Honestly good behavior, that is— the kind that happens even when the "authority figure" is nowhere in sight. That's what we want, right? The only way I know to internalize truth is through friction. Challenge. *Use* of truth rather than simple *assent* to truth. In other words, kids parroting back learned responses to our questions is only minimally effective in the process of developing true character and changed behavior. In order for internalization to take place, we must habitually challenge our kids to think for themselves, and then to go out and act on what they've said they believe. Thinking makes it theirs. Acting makes it stick.

When children are young concrete answers are appropriate. But as kids progress beyond their elementary years we need to challenge their beliefs if ownership is to take place. Instead of asking, "Do you know who the Savior of the world is?" try asking, "Why would God say that Jesus is the only way of salvation?" Instead of saying, "Suffering actually is a part of our growth as believers," try asking, "Why in the world would God allow a believer to suffer?" Instead of asking, "Do you believe that the Bible is really God's Word to humankind?" why not go a step further and challenge them with this: "Take a stab at showing me one line of evidence for the validity of the Bible."

This is when family devotions get fun for everybody. If you as a parent are challenged and your kids are challenged then you're off and running. Studying the Word will become a delight rather than a drag because you're looking for real answers to real questions. Inspire your kids to think! Keep asking *why!*

Build on that by getting your kids to act on what they say they believe. It is through the hands that the heart takes shape. I've been to the inner city, so my tears are real when I hear about the mother of a gang member burying her son. I've held the hand of and cried with a fourteen-year-old just informed she's pregnant. Everything about the compassion I have for others has been shaped by what I've experienced—by what I've seen and been involved with. One of the greatest problems facing young people today is their lack of hands-on experience with the real grit of other people's lives.

You pick the experience. Options are limitless. Spend a day at an orphanage. Work with the handicapped. Take sandwiches to the inner city homeless. Go to Mexico and work on a building project. Do free housework for a shut-in. How about a work-day at the church? Or gleaning fields in order to feed the poor? Or having each of your children choose a toy that they no longer use—or one of their nice new toys—and taking them to a home for abused children?

Are you willing to act on your beliefs? Until you do and your kids do the truth will ring hollow. Unless truth is true enough to change what we do it will make little difference to our kids once they're out from under our charge. To nod in appreciation of the truth but to live a lifestyle of doing little is to live in deception. *Do not merely listen to the word, and so deceive yourselves. Do what it says. . . . The man who looks intently into the perfect law that gives freedom, and continues to do this, not forgetting what he has heard, but doing it—he will be blessed in what he does* (James 1:22–25).

In light of all this, what "value system" is being handed down from you to your kids? What is printed on that baton you are passing off to them? Are you giving them a legacy of truth or something else? The warning is worth our attention. A worthless and empty way of life is quite naturally handed down from one generation to the next (1 Peter 1:18). But depending on the choices we make, our kids can learn a new desire, a desire that draws and prods them toward an eternally rich destiny.

Truth or Consequences

- In what ways are you protecting your children from the negative influences of the world? By contrast, how are you allowing friction and challenge to strengthen their ability to live righteously in the real world? Have you explained this balance to your kids?

- Help your kids compile a list of "who we are in Christ." Have them pick one aspect to focus on during the week and ask them how what they believe about themselves could alter their behavior.

- Through what your children observe in the media or their peers or at school, are they learning to be discerning? Take one popular social norm they're encountering and try applying some tough questions to it—actually, help your child frame the critical questions. Then assist your kids in finding scripture references that apply. Lead them through a logical flow of thought on an issue and help them arrive at a God-honoring perspective that reflects his truth.

- Take time to share how Scripture has impacted you this week—how it has shaped your thinking in some area. Ask your kids to choose one passage of Scripture and concentrate on "tuning" their life according to the passage they've chosen.

- If your child watches a particular TV sitcom or plays a video game with characters, get them used to doing a little reality check. Discuss questions like these: "What did the characters value?" "What was positive or negative about their actions and attitudes according to God's standards?" "Did the characters 'laugh at sin' or did they think honestly about the consequences of what they said or did?" "Were the characters self-centered or concerned for the welfare of others?" "Did the show realistically portray life?" "Would you want to be like the characters? Why or why not?" "Did you gain anything positive from watching the show or playing the game?"

10

THE TRUTH ABOUT GENEROSITY

THE CONSEQUENCES OF HOARDING

Remember this: Whoever sows sparingly will also reap sparingly, and whoever sows generously will also reap generously.

—2 Corinthians 9:6

The taxi pulled up in front of a hedge of tropical foliage. Through a small white gate we could see the garden party in process. "Change? You want change, meestarr?" I was feeling a little nervous. "Keep it. Thanks." My wife, Lori, and I got out of the backseat. Piak, our Thai friend, led us through the white gate as inquisitive eyes moved across the lawn to greet us. "Welcome, Americans! Come in, come in. Welcome to our home." Piak's middle-aged father extended his hand and held mine for a long time as he spoke. "You've never been to a Thai birthday party before, no?" One by one we were welcomed again and again by aunts, uncles, cousins and others whose associations escaped me. Gracious handshakes. Warm smiles. Gestures that defied our language barrier.

As much as they worked to include us, clearly, we were the "outsiders." Different country, culture and customs. Different skin color, different dress, different language, different palate—I'll tell you about the seafood stew another time—and different families.

We were foreigners and everything was foreign. One other difference stood out as well. By American standards, these people were considered poor. Their home, food, clothing . . . nothing but the necessities—nothing lavish. While I had never been a part of the "upper crust" back home I knew these kind folks were living off of a whole different crust. Not a single car was parked out front. All the guests had walked.

After dinner, everyone moved from the lawn into the living room. Without paying close attention to what was going on around us, Lori and I moved right on into the house. Shoes and all. That's when we noticed everyone else had taken off their shoes before walking onto the bamboo mat carpeting the floor. Big oops! Right away our gracious hosts understood our faux pas. "No problem. Keep the shoes on in our house," they assured us. We tried to take them off anyway but they insisted. "Leave the shoes on. No problem." Embarrassed, we consented. The party began. I kept looking at everyone's small, brown, bare feet next to my big shoes. "Dumb American," I thought to myself. "What are these nice people thinking?"

The game of "Best Lucky Man" commenced. Father reached into a wicker basket and pulled out a plastic tab and read off the name. Everyone shouted, laughed and clapped. The first person was "out."

Let me take a moment here to explain the game. On the wall hung a large poster with twenty-six numbered boxes—one box for each guest at the party. All the guests' names were written on twenty-six little chips of plastic and placed in a bowl. Each name was to be drawn randomly and stuck onto the poster beginning with box number twenty-six at the bottom and working on up toward the number-one slot. Piak explained, "The last five drawn will each be lucky prize winners. Father has placed money in five envelopes for these winners. Fifth prize, 100 baht. Fourth prize, 200 baht. Third, 300 baht. Second, 500 baht. And first prize— 1000 baht!" Piak's eyes sparkled with anticipation. I calculated in my head. 1000 baht. $40. "Father has saved up to honor his guests."

I knew the average daily wage for these people would be somewhere in the realm of $5 per day. Father was giving away nearly a month's wages. "He does it for the family every year. Everyone is excited." That was obvious. Everyone *was* excited, except Lori and I. I could read the same dread on her face that I was experiencing. *What if we* . . . the thought was horrid. Surely our names would be drawn in the first twenty-one rounds. Surely we'll be eliminated early on. At the moment I could think of nothing more disgusting than having to take money from these poor, beautiful people. More names were called. I looked down at my shoes and prayed, *God, make him call my name . . . pleeeease.*

With each name, hoots and cheers burst forth from all in attendance. The anticipation of winning and the letdown of hearing one's name called was the pinnacle of thrill for these who had so little. More names were called. Finally, Lori's name was announced. With a sigh of relief I erupted in clapping. No one else clapped. I stopped clapping. Everyone looked toward Lori as if to say, "We're so sorry . . . we really had hoped you would win."

One down, one to go, I thought to myself. More names were called. The air was electric with excitement. The numbers were getting smaller. Number seven, number six, number . . . my heart was pounding. I was sure the family members must be able to read my face. I kept trying to smile. Now it was certain. I couldn't escape. I, the guy who never wins anything, was locked into winning. I sat mortified. *Oh, God,* I pressed, *please, oh please make him pick my name next.* At least to be a small prize winner would help greatly at this point.

Number four, a name. Number three, a name. Number . . . *Oh God, act now. Act NOW!* Number two, not my name. As the shouting quieted all eyes turned toward me. Mr. Big Shoes. Mr. Rich unknown foreigner who had more money in pocket than most of these would see in a year. I was stunned. Normally not one to be easily embarrassed, I was overcome by an unbearable redness beyond words. Number one, my name was called out with a distinctive Thai accent. It was too much. I covered my face and bowed low as I was handed the envelope containing 1000 baht. *Three cheers for the pirate,* I thought, as all in attendance clapped in my honor. They worked at making me feel okay about it but none of their efforts had any effect. I tried giving the envelope back. I tried leaving it with his wife. I tried disappearing. Nothing helped. There was no way around the fact that I deserved nothing, had been given everything, had been served by the one who should have been honored and left that evening with the most that this "Father" could have possibly given. If you're a child of God, this probably sounds familiar.

Sometimes we get what we don't deserve. Even that is a part of the sowing/reaping equation. Someone else has done all the work and we reap all the benefits. I once lived near a guy who didn't work because he didn't have to. His father had died some years before leaving him a sizable inheritance. He went to the beach, played his guitar, even volunteered for a few charities— but he never held a job. His father had left him everything.

Let me ask a question here that I've asked myself countless times in the past. Do I have anything, really, that hasn't been given to me by my Father in heaven? Life, breath, food, air, fire for warmth, others for love . . . isn't it all his? What do we have that isn't a loan? Every penny I hold is another deposit he's made in my hand. It seems that God is concerned with his investment, too. The Bible refers to prayer about 500 times, to faith less than 500 times but to material possessions about 1000 times!

My daughter owns a pig. Mrs. Pink Pig sits on her chest of drawers near her bed and at night before she snuggles in she gives the pig a good shake. If you asked Katie she would tell you in no uncertain terms who owns the money. She does. No question. But if you asked me, I would tell you the truth. Everything inside that pig really came from me. I'm her dad.

I wonder what God thinks when we're stingy. Actually, I know what he thinks. He told us. Go back with me for a moment to a frightening and dark period in the history of the Jewish nation. The prophet was Amos and the problem was selfishness. Some of the most biting and angry words ever penned in Scripture were written toward those who were hoarding in the face of those who were hurting. I'm warning you, it's not pretty. He begins by calling these wealthy people a bunch of overstuffed cows!

Hear this word, you cows of Bashan on Mount Samaria, you women who oppress the poor and crush the needy and say to your husbands, "Bring us some drinks!" (Amos 4:1). Cows of Bashan? They were the well-marbled—the best-bred and the best-fed in the pastures of the northern Transjordan region of Palestine.

But these were "good church-going cows." They went to Bethel to worship. They went to Gilgal to worship. Wasn't God impressed with that? *Go to Bethel and sin; go to Gilgal and sin yet more. Bring your sacrifices every morning, your tithes every three years. Burn leavened bread as a thank offering and brag about your freewill offerings—boast about them, you Israelites, for this is what you love to do, declares the Sovereign Lord* (Amos 4:4–5).

To round out the picture, Amos offers a few visuals along with a warning of the coming judgment for such selfishness. *You trample on the poor and force him to give you grain* (5:11) and *you lie on beds inlaid with ivory and lounge on your couches. You dine on choice lambs and fattened calves. You strum away on your harps like David and improvise on musical instruments. You drink wine by the bowlful and use the finest lotions . . . your feasting and lounging will end* (6:4–7).

All of their pious ceremonialism was worthless as far as God was concerned. They were whistling, "Ain't Life Grand" as they marched to their religious gatherings, stepping on the bony out-stretched fingers of the world's poor. *I hate, I despise your religious feasts; I cannot stand your assemblies. . . . Away with the noise of your songs! I will not listen to the music of your harps. But let justice roll on like a river, righteousness like a never ending stream!* (5:21–24).

And through the torrent of God's disgust, he keeps reminding them of the Truth. *Seek me and live* (5:4); *Seek the Lord and live* (5:6); *Seek good, not evil, that you may live. Then the Lord God Almighty will be with you, just as you say he is* (5:14). In the words of the Psalmist, *Blessed is he who has regard for the weak* (Psalm 41:1).

The book of Proverbs warns us against turning our eyes and our hearts away from those who are suffering. To do nothing is as bad as to do the wrong thing. *Rescue those being led away to death; hold back those staggering toward the slaughter. If you say, "But we knew nothing about this," does not he who weighs the heart perceive it? Does not he who guards your life know it? Will he not repay each person according to what he has done?* (Proverbs 24:11–12). And again, *He who gives to the poor will lack nothing, but he who closes his eyes to them receives many curses* (Proverbs 28:27).

The Pretense of Giving While Privately Hoarding Is Costly. Stop Pretending!

One of the most startling stories from the annals of the early church is the account of Ananias and Sapphira—the pretenders. This couple had a piece of property they decided to sell so that the money could be used for the Lord. They claimed they had received a certain amount for the land and were giving that amount to the ministry. That would have been just great, except for the fact that they lied. They claimed to be giving one amount (the price of the land) when in reality they were only giving a part of it. The rest they kept for themselves.

It's a short story. Both of them were struck dead the same day. Right on the spot.

Ouch! Given a scant reading, the sentence seems rather harsh, doesn't it? It does until we really stop and consider that our friends, A and S, had allowed Satan to fill their hearts (Acts 5:3) and were attempting to deceive God. *You have lied to the Holy Spirit* (5:3). *You have not lied to men but to God* (5:4). The problem wasn't the money; it was the mockery of God—the delusion that God doesn't see or care what goes on in our private affairs. Ultimately we all give. We give an account. As Romans 14:12 says: *Each of us will give an account of himself to God.* It is foolish to think that God will never know or ask us why. He will.

Remember too, the land was theirs. No one compelled them to give the money to God's work. The problem wasn't a *lack* of generosity but the *pretense* of generosity. They were posing as generous while they were privately greedy. Paul may have even had this event in the back of his mind when he wrote, *Each man should give what he has decided in his heart to give, not reluctantly or under compulsion, for God loves a cheerful giver* (2 Corinthians 9:7).

I believe a timeless picture was painted that day. A stark picture that would strike at the core of all of us for generations to come. *God will not be mocked.* Giving is never simply a horizontal act. To give to anyone is to give to God himself. Remember the words of Jesus when he said, *Whatever you did for one of the least of these brothers of mine, you did for me* (Matthew 25:40).

This is one area where children especially do as we do, not as

150

we say. If we ask them to be generous with their toys, with their words of appreciation and with their time, do we model generosity for them? What do they see in us? Would our children describe us as "lavishly generous"? David wrote of giving people: *They are always generous and lend freely; their children will be blessed* (Psalm 37:26). Oh, and while we're asking some lean questions: Why does God say, *A greedy man brings trouble to his family*? (Proverbs 15:27). I wonder if Ananias had any kids.

Generosity isn't something stingy people reap in their kids. Our kids take on the attitude they observe day after day, whether we like it or not. Generosity, or a lack of it, seeps into them on a daily basis. If we hoard because we secretly long for the status that money offers, our kids will pick up on that.

> Make no mistake. Children will in some form reproduce our efforts to find significance and security. If we really believe that money and achievement bring significance or that compliments and attractive clothing bring security, we can preach all we want about the joys of knowing Jesus. Our kids will learn to depend on what we really are depending on for our satisfaction in life. No amount of teaching, family devotions, or trips to church will effectively counter the message we convey with our lives.[1]

If the local news had taken a picture of Ananias and Sapphira on the day of their death, they well could have captioned the shot with the following: "God is never fooled by the pretense of generosity when the heart is filled with greed. Don't be deceived into thinking otherwise. *Here lies proof.*"

One Purpose for Giving Is to Change the Giver. Reap Joyfully!

God doesn't need your money. Honestly. He never has. Remember, he owns the cattle on a thousand hills—and he owns Saudi Arabia and Manhattan and Fort Knox too, for that matter. God could build his church and feed the hungry and send mis-

---

[1]Lawrence Crabb, *Effective Biblical Counseling* (Grand Rapids: Zondervan, 1977), p. 118.

sionaries overseas by any means he wanted to. He doesn't have to use his people to do it. While God isn't hurting for cash, you might say he's hunting for givers. He's interested in giving his love to a lost world through Christians who will share his heart and his wealth. He's looking for people who will simply obey him and become like him in this common bond of giving.

It was in connection with this issue of giving that Paul wrote, *Remember this: Whoever sows sparingly will also reap sparingly, and whoever sows generously will also reap generously* (2 Corinthians 9:6). There are those who teach that the more *money* you give, the more *money* God will give you—that God wants you to be dripping rich. I disagree. If giving up earthly possessions for the kingdom of God made a person rich on earth, Jesus would have been the wealthiest man ever to walk the planet! Rather, the seeds of sacrificial love that are planted will grow and produce in the lives of another. It's a whole different mind-set.

At the same time our Father will keep on supplying what we need so that we're able to continue in our mission of mercy toward those in need:

God is able to make it up to you by giving you everything you need and more, so that there will not only be enough for your own needs, but plenty left over to give joyfully to others. It is as the Scriptures say: "The godly man gives generously to the poor. His good deeds will be an honor to him forever." For God, who gives seed to the farmer to plant, and later on, good crops to harvest and eat, will give you more and more seed to plant and will make it grow so that you can give away more and more fruit from your harvest (2 Corinthians 9:8–10, TLB).

God actually takes our small seed of investment and turns it into changed lives for His glory. *Yes, God will give you much so that you can give away much, and when we take your gifts to those who need them they will break out into thanksgiving and praise to God for your help* (2 Corinthians 9:11, TLB).

And when others are touched by our love, God is paying attention. In reference to the gifts that the believers at Philippi had sent for Paul's ministry he wrote, . . . *the gifts you sent. They are a fragrant offering, an acceptable sacrifice, pleasing to God. And my*

God will meet all your needs according to his glorious riches in Christ Jesus (Philippians 4:18–19).

When we sow in generosity, we actually reap an internal change. Our capacity for joy expands. Like the metamorphosis that took place in the life of dear old Scrooge, there's a life-change that takes place in us when our hearts are freed from selfishness and stinginess. I'm not saying God won't bless you materially. I'm saying that it doesn't really matter that much. Solomon, who had a pretty good handle on being rich, wrote, *A generous man will prosper; he who refreshes others will himself be refreshed* (Proverbs 11:25). But the clear indication in Scripture is that when we give, what boomerangs back is way MORE than a "good material perk." Something far more profound is being logged in eternity. Paul wrote to Timothy, *Command them . . . to be generous and willing to share. In this way they will lay up treasure for themselves as a firm foundation for the coming age, so that they may take hold of the life that is truly life* (1 Timothy 6:18–19). You start to get the feeling that everything we give in the Spirit of Christ is actually going into some celestial bank account that will last for eternity.

When you and I were young our minds were consumed with getting from others. The here and now and material was all there was, right? There were, perhaps, dolls and bikes and toy trucks and trinkets . . . and about three hours into Christmas morning there were tears over the stuff that was already broken or didn't come with batteries. And there was the disappointment of not getting what you really wanted or not getting what your brother got. Being a "getter" is fairly limiting. The joy is short-lived at best. But now that you've grown older, haven't you noticed a change? There's a quiet joy that spreads out like a cozy blanket in your heart—not from getting, but from giving to someone who desperately needs you and can never pay you back. It's a feeling that you can't duplicate by any other means. Generosity is its own reward.

Most parents understand that principle quite well. Nothing rivals the thrill of participating in the miracle of bringing a life into the world, of giving food, shelter, clothing, guidance and kisses—lots of kisses. The deep and internal satisfaction of having kids is an example of the strange sort of reciprocity that comes from being a giver. Kids—they cost hundreds of thousands of dollars, often keep mothers from their careers, steal your sleep, spit up on your shirt, spill cokes in your car and then ultimately go off and marry someone else.

Talk about giving! If you boil down the process of being a good mom or dad, it's this: Parenting=Giving. Period. But the returns—now that's something that would take volumes to write about. Maybe not—maybe it's simply indescribable. Either way, the internal joy far exceeds the external expense. Giving is like that. I suppose that's precisely what Jesus meant when he said, *It is more blessed to give than to receive* (Acts 20:35), or Solomon when he penned, *A generous man will himself be blessed, for he shares his food with the poor* (Proverbs 22:9).

The Priority of Giving Is a Generous Spirit. Sow Freely!

The scene is a church foyer, a number of years ago. The players don't even know they're being watched. A number of people from the wealthier set walk by. They toss their offering into the receptacle without a break in their conversations. They've done well again this week. Stock market's been good to them. Business is up. They gave a lot. Plenty to give. "Do lunch?" "Sure!" "My treat. The Temple Promenade Room for a bite?" "That'll be fine. I'll have my chauffeur drop me there at noon." Conversation fades as they pass.

The watcher keeps watching. Another figure approaches the scene, another character altogether. She's quiet. She moves more slowly. Her head is covered, her robe old and faded. She pauses as she places two very small copper coins carefully, deliberately, into the plate.

She too passes and the focus turns to Jesus, the watcher. He calls over his followers and teaches them something he wants recorded for all time, *I tell you the truth, this poor widow has put more into the treasury than all the others . They all gave out of their wealth; but she, out of her poverty, put in everything—all she had to live on* (Mark 12:43–44). Two impressive men who give a great deal and a single widowed woman who had nearly nothing to give. What mattered wasn't the size but the sacrifice.

The same thing is echoed in 2 Corinthians, where Paul is encouraging the believers to give. He points out, *Last year you were the first not only to give but also to have the desire to do so.* He's glad for the gift, but expressly notes their spirit in giving. He continues, *For if the willingness is there, the gift is acceptable according to what one has, not according to what he does not have* (2 Corinthians 8:10–12). It isn't the amount of the gift, but the attitude of the giver.

Have you ever noticed what happened after that famous story of the widow and her two cents' worth took place? Mark 13 begins with these words, *As he was leaving the temple, one of his disciples said to him, "Look, Teacher! What massive stones! What magnificent buildings!"* As if Jesus the Son of God should be impressed with what humans had built. Jesus replied, *Not one stone here will be left on another; every one will be thrown down* (Mark 13:1–2).

Yes, Jesus was referring to the coming destruction of Jerusalem. But it has always been intriguing to me that this conversation took place moments after the Lord had pointed out the widow and her tiny gift. Could Jesus have been trying to show the disciples again that what appears so impressive on the outside may not matter as much as we think?

The Potential of Giving Is Enormous. Start Sowing!

Kids. You can't live with 'em and you can't—feed 5000 men without 'em. Ever feel small and ordinary? That's okay. God uses the small and the ordinary. He certainly did that day on a hot hillside in Galilee. The people had assembled for an all day conference and it was time to eat. Everyone was hungry. The disciples were panicking when they should have been praying. When Jesus asked for what was available for him to use, the disciples produced a kid with a lunch box. That was it. *Here is a boy with five small barley loaves and two small fish, but how far will they go among so many?* (John 6:9). Their perspective was like mine would have been. "The needs seem endless . . . so many problems, so few solutions . . . world hunger on the rise, what difference can I make. . . ." I love what came next. Jesus simply said, *Have the people sit down* (John 6:10). That's right. Sit!

Maybe he wanted them sitting because he knew they would fall down if they saw what he was about to do. He was going to take what the kid had and make it into more. He did it then and he does it now.

Look in your wallet. It's probably got a little fish in there. Or a piece of old bread. What are you doing with what you have? Are you hoping for great returns? Let me offer a poem that has rocked my perspective on what giving could accomplish:

> Five thousand for my convertible,
> Ten thousand for a piece of sod.
> Twenty thousand down for a house,
> A dollar I gave to God.
> A sum to entertain
> My friends in endless chatter;
> And when the world goes crazy mad,
> I ask: "Lord what's the matter?"
> Yet there is one big question—
> And for its answer I now search—
> With things so bad in this old world,
> What's holding back my church?[2]

What have you got? A talent? Some money? A vacation? A life? Where are you going to invest it? What good will it do? According to the Lord it is "seed-sized" faith that moves mountains and small lunches that feed an amphitheater of people. How will your kids describe you?

If you don't plant the seed it won't grow. If you're not willing to part with your lunch box you'll miss the banquet.

---

[2]John Lawrence, *Down to Earth* (Portland, Ore.: Multnomah Press, 1975), p. 81.

Truth or Consequences

- What are some daily ways you could demonstrate that God is the source of all things? Giving thanks before meals is one way. What other ways are you helping your kids make the connection?

- Do your children see evidence of your care for people who are in need? How are you cultivating in them a heart of compassion? If your kids receive an allowance, encourage them to set aside a certain amount of that each week for a ministry that serves people in need.

- Contact Compassion International (1–800–336–7676) and link your children with a child who needs sponsorship to provide for food, water, shelter, education and spiritual instruction. You'll receive a photo of your sponsored child. What a powerful and practical way to teach your child the truth about giving.

- As you discuss money and possessions with your kids, what attitudes are they picking up? Are they being shown that security and significance both come from our relationship with the Lord rather than from what we own?

- Are your children learning that giving is a joy or an obligation? In what ways are they watching you give your time and talents as well as your finances? Have you told them about the eternal investment you're making?

- One family we know uses a series of jars to teach the principle of stewardship to their children. One jar is marked for giving away, one is marked for saving and one is designated as spending money. With each earning or allowance, a third is placed in each jar. From early on, their children are learning to value money according to God's priorities.

• You and your children could plan to skip a meal each month and send that money to an agency that helps those who are hungry. In our youth group at Mission Hills Church we sponsor a planned famine and make sack lunches to take to the homeless in the urban centers of Los Angeles and San Diego.

• If you and your teenager go into a jewelry store, a car dealership, or pass by a row of new luxury homes, you might be able to bring up the fact that you've had to make some tough choices as a parent about what you value and where your money goes. Quite possibly you're a mom who has been able to opt for being at home over a career or you've purposefully decided against certain luxuries in order to have the money available for your child to go to college or for a friend to go to the mission field. Kids need to know how you've used your money in a positive way and to see that many important things we value are only within our means if we're willing to make financial sacrifices. Finances offer a terrific training ground for showing how the cause-and-effect principle works in our choices.

11

THE TRUTH ABOUT DISCIPLINE

THE CONSEQUENCES OF NEGLECT

He who fears the Lord has a secure fortress, and for his children it will be a refuge.

—Proverbs 14:26

"I could never do enough to please my mom," one man shared with me. "No matter how hard I tried to please her, I never felt like I was good enough. I've always felt like I had to perform perfectly to win her approval. If she didn't like something I was doing, she'd give me the 'silent treatment' for hours. If I did enough good things, then she was happy—for a while. She made me feel like I was responsible for her happiness, so consequently I was always rescuing her by trying to please her. Even today, at forty-two years of age, I find myself asking, 'What would mother want me to do?' The worst part of it is, now I find myself repeating those same patterns with other people. I am constantly worried about pleasing them. When anyone is unhappy, I take it very personally. I feel responsible for their feelings and, quite frankly, it wears me out!"

We live in a world of competing expectations. Our parents had expectations of us and gave us their "rules for behavior." While many of those were positive and helpful as children, we must each come to a point of personalizing what we believe to be important for our own lives. Many grown adults still try to please a demanding mother or a distant father. Those messages from decades ago can rule lives. I've seen it *ruin* lives!

Discipline, however is different than having expectations. It's true that good training involves reasonable expectations. But discipline is a process that has the good of the one being disciplined clearly in view. Expectations, on the other hand, tend to be self-serving. Discipline views change as a gradual process rather than a standard to be immediately met. Those distinctions are crucial when it comes to both our understanding of God's discipline of us as well as the discipline we use with our kids.

Young children depend on their parents as their primary source of discipline. When parents neglect that vital role, children aren't able to develop a healthy sense of "response-ability." God calls us to train, shape, correct—in essence, to teach a disciplined, controlled, thoughtful way of responding to choices. As our kids grow, parental discipline must gradually give way to personal discipline. Rather than hearing our voice shaping or commanding responsibility, kids need to rely more and more on an inner voice that has been cultivated through logical consequences. Discipline is not only something we do *to* our kids but it is something we create *within* our kids. On both counts, Scripture says that discipline is an essential part of God's value system.

The writer of Hebrews teaches candidly about the importance of discipline, of its ramifications in a parent-child relationship, and of its consequences. The whole of chapter 12, in fact, is a primer on parenting. Weaving themes back and forth, God makes a clear parallel between his role in our lives as Father and the roles we play as parents.

Discipline Is the Sign of Love, Significance and Acceptance

My son, do not make light of the Lord's discipline, and do not lose heart when he rebukes you, because the Lord disciplines those he loves, and he punishes everyone he accepts as a son (Hebrews 12:5–6).

A few key characteristics of discipline beam right off the page here:

THE TRUTH ABOUT DISCIPLINE

Discipline is obviously not a sideline—it is essential.
   do not make light of it . . .
Discipline isn't meant to discourage—it is to build up.
   do not lose heart . . .
Discipline is a sign of love—it communicates care.
   the Lord disciplines those He loves . . .
Discipline is a mark of sonship—it proves security.
   he accepts as a son.

Have you ever explained these principles to your kids? If we don't share with them the role of discipline in their lives, chances are they won't figure it out on their own.

As one kid put it, "If I didn't have you, Dad, I'd have to lecture myself!" Obviously discipline isn't about lecturing, but the point is well-taken nevertheless. Kid's can't be expected to "pull themselves up by their own bootstraps." They need parents who have experienced more, have learned more, can see more, can discern more. Kids need parents to train them toward what is wise—to steer them toward what is excellent.

Parenthood, as with any kind of discipleship, is a blend of loving comfort accompanied by loving direction. We want to understand and identify with our child (that's the comfort) while we impact (that's the direction). Good discipline involves both. The verse *Faithful are the wounds of a friend* (Proverbs 27:6, KJV) captures both components. The "wound" is that necessary rebuke, that jerk of the leash, the stern explanation of misconduct. But notice who is doing the "wounding"? It's the friend.

Some object to the idea of being a "friend" to your kids. "Kids need parents to be parents. You shouldn't try to be their friend." So they say. I heartily object. The best parent is a first-class friend. A loving, caring, intimate, fun, rowdy, outrageous friend who also has a calling from God to be a consistent guide. Jesus worded it well when he said, *Those whom I love I rebuke* (Revelation 3:19). Discipline is far more effective if the one on the receiving end is deeply convinced of and often reminded of the love that brought it about. Harsh insensitivity or discipline in an environment where the deep well of relationship has run dry only serves to harden hearts, not win them.

Discipline Is the Right and Responsibility of Parenting

Endure hardship as discipline; God is treating you as sons. For what son is not disciplined by his father? If you are not disciplined (and everyone undergoes discipline), then you are illegitimate children and not true sons (Hebrews 12:7–8).

The proof of ownership is discipline. The very mark of great parenting is a willingness to help kids make constant course adjustments. Every one of us, child or adult, benefits from instruction, training, correcting, improving—the elements of discipline. Don't sweep under carpets or shirk under pressure or shy away from opportunities. Even as you lengthen your child's leash, your model of discipline as well as your willingness *to* discipline when necessary will make a profound impact.

There's a passage that was originally directed at fathers but applies to mothers equally well. *Do not exasperate your children; instead, bring them up in the training and instruction of the Lord* (Ephesians 6:4). Somehow I got through seminary without anyone ever explaining to me the connection between the first half of this verse and the second. In fact, it has been experience itself that has rendered an understanding of what Paul may have had in mind here.

Over the years I have had contact with thousands of teenagers who have *not* been brought up in the training and instruction of the Lord. And—in general—they are *very* exasperated. When God's Word is thoughtfully applied in everyday life it shapes and guides and nurtures and comforts and controls. In effect, it shores up life. It disciplines and sharpens our inner selves. I'm sure you've noticed it in your own life already. When guidance increases, frustration decreases. When proper control increases, panic decreases. When spiritual discipline increases, inner chaos decreases, and so on. Parents! If you're willing to make "the training and instruction of the Lord" a priority in your home, there *will be* less exasperation. I've seen how true it is over and over again.

My own mother was a walker. Every day she walked when I was a kid, and often I walked too. We walked and talked and sometimes she brought up something that I needed to think about. The subject varied according to the need of the day—homework or chores or feeding the dog or bedroom management or an attitude I was or wasn't displaying. Walking for us was, perhaps, less confrontational than a frank chat at home. We were looking ahead, moving in the same direction. On a walk, the correction somehow was easier to take. Then once, I came across a verse that reminded me of my mom: *He who walks with the wise grows wise* (Proverbs 13:20). So now I walk—my kids and I.

Discipline Is the Foundation for All Respect

Moreover, we have all had human fathers who disciplined us and we respected them for it. How much more should we submit to the Father of our spirits and live! (Hebrews 12:9).

Ever heard the line "Kids nowadays—no respect!"? The assessment isn't just a critical jab. It's true. Respect for parents, teachers, law enforcement personnel, for God himself has declined dramatically. Wonder why? Scripture tells us that part of the problem is a lack of discipline. Loving correction fosters respect.

Without personal discipline, there's no self-respect. Without parental discipline, there's no parental respect. And when it comes to a relationship with our heavenly Father—he, too, draws us up to a respectful stance toward himself through discipline. It's a respect that will save our lives.

God commands children to *honor your father and your mother* (Deuteronomy 5:16). He even promises that doing so leads to a long and prosperous life. Yet even though kids are called to honor parents, parents are the ones who build honor into their kids.

Our job as parents is to teach respect by example. We should always discipline, in fact, with an attitude of respect for the thoughts and feelings of our children! Some examples of what I mean: Have we given them ample space to share their perspective? Have we affirmed our belief in them as persons despite their behavior? Are we willing to let them vent the frustrations they feel at being corrected—still standing by our correction while holding their feelings with gentle hands?

Discipline develops a healthy submission that primes a child

163

to accept a heritage being passed down. Parent to child, teacher to student, coach to athlete, God to human beings—without respect there's no chance for improvement. When submission is gone and respect is gone the opportunity for imparting good from generation to generation is also gone. Discipline reverses the process.

There's a flip-side to all this as well. Not only does discipline benefit kids, but it will come back to bless you, the parent, as well! Cultivating respect and honor in kids is good for them; it's a present they will hand back to you over and over again throughout life:

The rod of correction imparts wisdom, but a child left to himself disgraces his mother (Proverbs 29:15).

Discipline your son, and he will give you peace; he will bring delight to your soul (Proverbs 29:17).

She watches over the affairs of her household . . . Her children arise and call her blessed (Proverbs 31:27–28).

There's a family we know whose children are all growing right out of the nest. All three kids are at various points in college and graduate school. Knowing these parents for years, I have observed the discipline and respect they modeled and expected from their children. Even when their teenage children disagreed with them, the parents maintained an underlying sense of respect even in the hottest debates. They didn't expect to be agreed with—but they always expected to be respected, even in disagreement. And they respected their kids as well. These parents worked hard at balancing freedom of rein with high standards of responsibility.

Today two of their three children hold their parents in the highest esteem you could imagine. For the most part they have internalized the values handed off to them by their mom and dad. The third? I spoke with Krista recently. She's the youngest and attending community college close by.

"I'm not what my parents wish I was—yet," Krista relayed. "One thing is, I know where they stand and I respect them for that. I feel like I need time to discover things for myself. Like—I don't hold their conservative views on some things." She paused and smiled at me. "But I gotta hand it to them. I always have this sneaking suspicion in the back of my mind that they're right."

Discipline Is Necessary for Spiritual Maturity

Our fathers disciplined us for a little while as they thought best; but God disciplines us for our good, that we may share in his holiness (Hebrews 12:10).

Earthly parents face some major limitations in this role of "child trainer." Limited time, limited understanding, limited supervision. But that's where the translation from human father to heavenly Father is so key. If children learn over time to respond to their parents' correction, then they have the inner tools necessary to respond with submission to their heavenly Father. The good news is that God's training is perfect! Our job as parents is to foster the ability to submit and respond to loving discipline (even though ours isn't always perfect). Perfect or not, all training that is done with wisdom and love takes us from superficiality toward spirituality.

Since parental discipline builds the ground floor for spiritual discipline later on, it's essential that we as parents mimic the role of our heavenly Father toward us.

- The way we accept our kids should mirror God's acceptance of us.

- The way we listen to our kids should reflect the patience and understanding God extends to us.

- The way we forgive our kids should mirror God's forgiving grace toward us.

- The way we speak to our kids should mirror the "truth in love" way that God deals with us.

Discipline Pays Off!

No discipline seems pleasant at the time, but painful. Later on, however, it produces a harvest of righteousness and peace for those who have been trained by it (Hebrews 12:11).

There's fruit. Again! Discipline produces a harvest. Ask any athlete. The rigors of discipline in one season produce a win in the next. That is equally true both in parenting and in our walk with God. At the moment, resistance makes life tough. We balk at the pain. But press on! There's a reason behind rigors—rewards! Look at them! "Righteousness and peace." What more could we want for our kids?

The consequences of a lack of discipline are only too obvious. We're seeing it in the teens we encounter and we're watching the ramifications spread like cancer across our nation. Kids with no inner resolve, no firm core, no self-control, no willingness to submit to any kind of authority—it adds up to confusion, chaos and anarchy. But when kids feed on a diet of discipline, resolve, control and strength, the results are profound. Scripture is thick with encouragement on this issue. Over and over we're told that the fruit of discipline is something all of us want: happiness!

Parents, if you have young children, start disciplining now. It's easier to teach self-control when they're three years old and the issue is stealing candy or angry outbursts. It is much more difficult once they're older and the stakes higher. Take a moment to reflect on the exciting benefits that await your kids if you're willing to hand them a heritage of self-discipline and godly boundaries:

Respect God—it will build security into your home.

He who fears the Lord has a secure fortress, and for his children it will be a refuge (Proverbs 14:26).

Respond to God in obedience—it will end up blessing your kids.

The righteous man leads a blameless life; blessed are his children after him (Proverbs 20:7).

Reprove when necessary—it will instill and nurture an appropriate maturity.

Folly is bound up in the heart of a child, but the rod of discipline will drive it far from him (Proverbs 22:15).

Responsibly correct and guide—it will affect the future of your kids.

Discipline your son, for in that there is hope; do not be a willing party to his death (Proverbs 19:18).

Route your kids toward the Lord—it will be a guidance system for life.

Train a child in the way he should go, and when he is old he will not turn from it (Proverbs 22:6).

Some dramas are comedies, some tragedies. Some are an ironic blend of both. So it was with the Old Testament priest named Eli and his pathetic sons. From all we gather, Eli no doubt was a pretty good priest. Maybe too good. Maybe he spent too many nights at committee meetings and temple potlucks to pay attention to the monsters growing at home. In any case, Eli lacked initiative. And as a consequence, his sons lacked discipline. It was a deadly mix. The boys were skimming the offering and sleeping with the women serving in the temple.

Here's the kicker. Even after being warned, Eli didn't do anything about the problems mushrooming before his eyes. "Your sons are out of control!" came the truth. But Eli responded like an old lion warming his belly in the sunshine, petrified by old patterns, unwilling to take any decisive action with his sons. Oh, he probably yelled at them. Scripture says that he talked to them about what people were saying. But that was it. There were no teeth left in the old lion. Eli let them continue working in the temple; the boys went back to their ruinous ways as soon as the canned lecture was over. No control—of them or in them.

Yet finally God and the people of Israel had endured enough. *See, I am about to do something in Israel that will make the ears of everyone who hears of it tingle. At that time I will cry out against Eli everything I spoke against his family—from beginning to end. For I told him that I would judge his family forever because of the sin he knew about; his sons made themselves contemptible, and he failed to restrain them* (1 Samuel 3:11–13).

While all of this was going on, there was another young man in the temple—Samuel, Hannah's son. From day one Hannah had prayed for Samuel. She had brought him to the temple. She had reminded him continuously that he belonged to the Lord. She had completely given him over to God for his glory. What a contrast! See for yourself: *This sin of the young men* [Eli's sons] *was very great in the Lord's sight, for they were treating the Lord's offering with contempt. But Samuel was ministering before the Lord—a boy wearing a linen ephod* (1 Samuel 2:17–18).

While Eli's sons stole from the temple, Samuel served. They

snuck women behind the altar. He prayed in front of it. The boys were all living out what had been built in from birth—Eli's sons were living a tragedy, Samuel a legacy.

There's an intriguing point about Eli's style that stands out in the drama. Eli, despite the fact that his own house was collapsing in a moral earthquake, was deeply focused on preserving temple relics. Over and over Scripture slides in snippets about Eli's concern for what was happening to the ark of the covenant—a symbol of God's presence among the people. Translated into a modern equivalent, he was all wrapped up in preserving church traditions and maintaining religious relics. All the while the lives of his own children were toppling.

I can't even begin to tell you how many times this scenario plays out in our churches today. I can show you pastors whose kids *hate* God because "God stole daddy away from the family." I could list people who so fervently try to protect church facilities and traditions that they refuse to allow the church to minister to young people in a relevant way—and the young people consequently *hate* the church. I can line up parents who are so legalistic and adamant about their own idea of how their kids ought to worship the Lord that their kids end up not wanting to worship at all. Here we are again—on the same issue: fixated on externals. Missing what matters most.

Parents, wake up! Take hold of your responsibility to discipline and disciple your children. It's not the school's job or the church's job or a family counselor's job. It's *your* job! And when you have a say in what takes place in the church, go to bat for the lives of young people. Don't sacrifice tender hearts for tending traditions. Reach out to those kids who deeply need Christ. Be willing to relegate relics and reform religious technique in whatever way is necessary to do the real work of the ministry—which is simply to help young people be transformed from the inside out.

Eli should have taken a Sunday off. He should have skipped church once in a while and taken those boys of his backpacking. He should have set up an altar just for the three of them. He should have lit some candles and conducted a worship service for no one but them. He should have talked turkey with them, confronted them, hugged them, cried over them. He should have committed himself to a plan of integrity, accountability and restoration for the family first and foremost.

Discipline begins on the inside of us. When our inner core is maintained then we find God giving us wisdom to know how to pass the baton. If ever the kids of a nation needed parental authority, it is here. It is now.

A postscript. In the end, the Ark of the Lord was captured by the Philistines. Eli's two sons were killed in battle (just as God had warned). And Eli (who was old and overweight) fell off his chair, broke his neck and died.

The curtain slips shut to finish the final scene of a tragedy of misdirected attention and unwillingness to discipline.

Yet wait! The curtains are rustling! Samuel, the son of discipline, is taking his place on stage. . . .

Truth or Consequences

- It might be worthwhile to read Hebrews 12 with your children and show them how love involves discipline. The story of Eli and his sons could make for a great devotional some evening as well.

- Do your children know the whys behind your directives? Do you "just say no" or do you "also say why"?

- What kind of loving, involved relationship are you fostering so that proper discipline will be interpreted through the grid of love?

- In your mind, have you differentiated between discipline (focused on future inner character-building) and punishment (focused on past behavior)? Is your parenting primarily done in a positive spirit of discipline rather than a negative spirit of punishment?

- Be careful to discern willful disobedience from mistakes of ineptitude. A full measure of understanding and patient guidance should be applied when honest mistakes are made. On the other hand, willful disobedience should never be ignored. It should be met with natural and logical consequences severe enough to make your child never want to act that way again.

- There are so many ways you can show your children the benefits of personal discipline. If your child comes home with a poor report card, help them own the process for getting better grades. You can begin with the end in mind and work your way back to the present level of responsibility. It's a process that sounds something like, "What kind of a career would you like to have someday? Having a career that you like usually requires special skills or even a college education. In order to pull that off, what you do now in school is going to make a big difference. What sacrifices are you willing to make now in order to accomplish what you want someday? You'll have a new opportunity tomorrow to make better decisions about your use of time, discipline in studying and so forth, but ultimately it will be up to you. No one can do it for you. I believe in you and your ability to do well."

- If you and your child have the opportunity of observing, say, a skilled pianist, it makes for a terrific discussion about discipline. Often we think of discipline as the opposite of freedom to do what we want. In actuality, discipline is what allows us to do what we really want. For instance, the pianist has the *freedom* to play well because of his willingness to discipline himself early on. In fact, he continues to discipline himself to follow the notes, keep the rhythm, apply music theory and practice a lot in order to produce what we love to hear. Total freedom, in this instance, would have never given this pianist what he really wanted. Think about it together and apply the example to various areas of life where discipline is required.

12

THE TRUTH ABOUT PURITY

THE CONSEQUENCES OF COMPROMISE

Blessed are the pure in heart, for they will see God.

—Matthew 5:8

The Lummi Indian tribe of Washington state lives on a scrap of land between Puget Sound and the Nooksack River. The Lummis are a quiet remnant of Native Americans tucked away on a jetty of land surrounded on three sides by water. Their lives and livelihood are found in that water.

Snaking inland from the sea, the banks of the Nooksack are dotted with tiny homes. Most are little more than shacks. Many have a dock out front with a boat attached and nets with buoys stretched out for drying and mending. Life is quiet on these banks. especially in winter when the river freezes over and the fishermen go into hibernation. Then comes the thaw.

As winter gives way to spring, the snow fields of Mount Baker to the East begin to melt into a thousand tiny tributaries feeding the Nooksack. More and more water merges until the Nooksack becomes a swirling torrent as it moves toward the Sound—and the flatlands where the Lummis live. There the water rises and begins to pour over its banks. Like the claw of a monster, the current uproots dwellings perched on the river's edge. Homes built back from the river also drown in the water pouring beyond its usual borders. Pastures turn into lakes with cows crowded onto mounds that have become islands. The shape of the landscape changes. Roads are closed.

On the one hand the river is a conduit of life—the very center of sustenance for an entire civilization of people. But once the banks are broken, it reclaims what has been given and more.

It all has to do with boundaries.

Of all the changes that have taken place across America over the last generation, none have impacted us more than this one: our moral boundaries have given way. The protective borders God established for the well-being of humankind have been bulldozed down by no one other than ourselves. The flood of consequences has just begun.

Not long ago, for example, former U.S. Surgeon General Dr. Joycelyn Elders vehemently kicked at the few moral boundaries still clear. "We've taught teenagers what to do in the front seat of the car," she's famous for saying, "and now it's time to teach them what to do in the backseat." She outspokenly supported abortion on demand and homosexuality as a lifestyle. Until she was terminated, she hammered away at parents, whose values stood in the way of "freedom," and whose beliefs she relabeled "prejudices."

While it's an established fact that condoms have a failure rate as high as twenty-five percent, so-called leaders like Elders advocate distributing condoms on campuses so that sex will be safe. Is a loaded gun safe if it only fires every fourth time? The agenda of moral license is not only obvious but deadly.

God isn't mocked. As a nation we aren't even challenging that immoral agenda as it advances step by step—not even realizing that our borders have been penetrated. *Like a city whose walls are broken down is a man who lacks self-control* (Proverbs 25:28).

For years Doogie Howser was a popular teen hero. In the beginning the show was decent, but then, about the time that ratings were through the roof—and millions of kids were watching—Doogie took his girlfriend to bed. When executive producer Vic Rauseo was asked about it, his answer was simple and sad: "All we tried to do was be honest . . . Doogie's been involved with this girl for two years . . . it would make him kind of weird if nothing happened."[1]

Any illustration I offer here is going to be outdated by the time you're holding this book. So pick up the morning paper and find out which walls are being demolished this week.

While Doogie—and he was simply one example among many—was showcasing the normalcy of premarital sex to our kids nationwide, they were following suit at home. According to figures released by the U.S. Center for Disease Control in 1992, even the youngest of American teens are giving away their bodies—not to mention their hearts—in record numbers:

Among ninth-graders, 40 percent have had sex already.

By tenth grade the figure jumps to 48 percent.

By their junior year, 57 percent have.

And by the time they're seniors, 72 percent will have already lost their virginity.[2]

A number of years ago I attended one of the premier performances of Stephen Sondheim's musical *Merrily We Roll Along*. The opening scene is a cocktail party to which various friends and old acquaintances keep arriving. At first they exchange niceties and flash their costume jewelry, but as the party progresses it becomes apparent that each of these aging people carries a deep hollowness inside. The story moves away from the present back into the past lives of these people one by one, revealing, in essence, how they had become who they had become. Each of the characters had faced crossroads, and they had taken the wrong road. At the time, no one ever thought beyond the day. No one dreamed that someday they would look back and wonder why. They moved along, often glibly, as if there were no tomorrow.

But as is always the case, decisions become destinies. By the final act, every one of them had given into something. The result was a string of messed up marriages, angry children, alcoholism, broken dreams and a host of other dysfunctions. Boundaries had been breached. People had drowned.

---

[1]David Zurawik, "More Teenagers Losing Virginity on Prime Time," *The Virginian Pilot*, August 14, 1991, p. B1.
[2]*Los Angeles Times* article, January 4, 1992.

King David could have been one of those gathered there. He too understood regret.

It was all so romantic, in the beginning. It was spring. Those to whom he was accountable were off at war. It was a sleepless night, so David stepped out onto the roof of his palace for a look at the stars. And it was there on the roof that someone in another home below caught his attention.

Bathsheba, wife of a warrior. Home alone, taking her evening bath. David looked around. No one. No one but her. He watched. Then he sent for her—and the night closed in on them both. Just a stir before the storm.

Not long after, a note arrived. It contained but three words. "I am pregnant." It was then and there that David could have stopped the cyclone. He could have come clean. There was a right way, even then, that he could have followed. Yet he plotted when he should have repented. He sent for Bathsheba's husband, Uriah, to come home from battle. *Surely if Uriah comes home,* David thought, *he'll sleep with his wife, and it will appear that the baby is his. But it didn't work that way.* Uriah was an honorable man. He refused to lounge with his wife while his compatriots languished on the battlefield. So the plot had to be adjusted.

David sent Uriah back to the war, but this time onto the front lines where he was sure to be killed—and he was. David had taken Uriah's wife, now he had taken his life.

The water was rising. Not long after Uriah's death, David took Bathsheba as his wife. Scripture doesn't tell us anything here about David's feelings, maybe because there weren't any. Maybe something had died on the inside. Maybe there was only an icy river washing through his heart. Compromise has a way of starting leaks.

Then one day there was a knock at the door. It was David's longtime friend, a prophet of God. But on this day, Nathan seemed withdrawn. Nathan began, *"There were two men in a certain town, one rich and the other poor. The rich man had a very large number of sheep and cattle, but the poor man had nothing except one little ewe lamb he had bought. He raised it, and it grew up with him and his children. It shared his food, drank from his cup and even slept in his arms. It was like a daughter to him.*

"Now the traveler came to the rich man, but the rich man refrained from taking one of his own sheep or cattle to prepare a meal for the traveler who had come to him. Instead, he took the ewe lamb that belonged to the poor man and prepared it for the one who had come to him.

"The man who did this deserves to die!" David interjected. *"He must pay for that lamb four times over."* David, steeped in the story, was overcome by the thought of the rich man's selfishness—his lack of pity for the poor man. Water was seeping in under the door.

"David." Nathan's voice came like a stab through steel air.

What's the point of the story? David wondered.

"David," Nathan said again softly.

Were there tears in Nathan's eyes? What was happening here? Water was pooling at the throne.

"David," Nathan spoke with nothing more than a parched whisper.

What's he getting at? Why is he looking at me that way? What—

"David. . . . YOU ARE THE MAN!" The dam broke (2 Samuel 12:1–7).

Moral choices carry moral consequences. Every stinging word of Nathan's prophecy came true in David's life—and even more came true in the lives of his children.

- Because he killed Uriah—the sword would never depart from his house.

- Because he took Uriah's wife—David's own wives would be taken away right in front of him.

- Because he did it all in secret—his wives would be defiled in public.

- Because his actions had made a mockery of God—his baby son by Bathsheba wouldn't live (2 Samuel 12:9–14).

They sow the wind and reap the whirlwind (Hosea 8:7) was coming to pass.

While the brutal side of sin is illustrated for what it really is in David's affair, the New Testament mirrors the exact same truth:

176

But each one is tempted when, by his own evil desire, he is dragged away and enticed. Then, after desire has conceived, it gives birth to sin; and sin, when it is full-grown, gives birth to death. Don't be deceived, my dear brothers . . . (James 1:14–16).

The other morning I caught my daughter jumping on our family room couch—again. I had warned her before. I had explained what jumping does to the couch. I had spelled out the consequences if she did it again. Yet there she was. Even as I stood in the doorway, she stopped only momentarily and then, with that look of willful defiance, she jumped once more just to spite me. So we had a talk. She knew she was guilty but she argued anyway. I explained. She didn't want to hear it. I tried reasoning with her again. Then she did the only thing there was left to do in her state of defiance. She covered her ears and closed her eyes.

Kids aren't the only ones who hate being confronted with consequences. So do thirty-year-olds and sixty-year-olds. It is part of our makeup. We simply don't want to hear it. That's why prophets are unpopular. Even when it's in our best interests, we don't want anyone "raining on our parade." Yet that is exactly what love will do. It will speak the truth even when it isn't popular. And the truth is that there's death attached to depravity.

Immorality *dehumanizes* in countless ways:

America is now the world's leading producer of child porn. In the last 30 years *Playboy, Penthouse*, and *Hustler* alone have published more than 90 *billion* copies of photos, illustrations or cartoons depicting children in sexually explicit poses.[3]

Immorality is the primary cause of many of our *diseases*:

In 1993 Harvard University reported that in the next seven years, 38 to 110 million adults plus ten million children will be infected with AIDS worldwide. There are about 60 different STDs infecting people currently at the rate of millions per year. The World Health Organization estimates there are some 250 million new cases worldwide of sexually transmitted diseases each and every year. That is one billion cases every four years.[4]

---

[3]John Ankerberg and John Weldon, *The Facts on Sex Education* (Eugene, Ore.: Harvest House, 1993), p. 5.
[4]Ibid.

Immorality leads to *death* in many forms:

Every twenty-one seconds another American baby is aborted—170 every hour; 4,100 every day; 29,000 a week; 125,000 a month. Since Roe vs. Wade in 1973 the lives of more than twenty-six million babies have been taken, the equivalent of the entire population of Canada.[5] And all that doesn't take into account the millions of dying hearts and dying hopes. Despite the reality of ramifications—nobody wants to hear it or admit it or believe that it could happen to *their* family.

That certainly was the thinking in the city of Sodom. The city was proud of its moral "freedom." Alternative lifestyles were the only lifestyles in vogue. Complete freedom of choice. No judgmental religious opinions permitted. No constraints. Then two angels appeared and warned Lot and his family to vacate immediately. The judgment of God was about to unfold.

Even his family didn't want to hear it. *So Lot went out and spoke to his sons-in-law, who were pledged to marry his daughters. He said, "Hurry and get out of this place, because the Lord is about to destroy the city!" But his sons-in-law thought he was joking* (Genesis 19:14).

Sometimes the stark reality of disease or death gets our attention. But there's another form of death that happens so quietly, so subtly that we barely notice that it's happening. I think of it as heart disease. A gradual leaking away of life. A deadening of the spirit and a depleting of the will. It's a callous that grows over our soul. And soon sin no longer is called sin—it's considered an "alternative."

With the scandal and controversy surrounding the arrest of L.A. call girl Heidi Fleiss in the fall of 1993, the *Los Angeles Times* ran an article on prostitution in this one city. For the story, a number of women stepped forward and spoke candidly about life on the circuit. These were the high-priced tickets, the women who had made it to the top of their profession, who were able to rake in hundreds—even thousands of dollars for a single fling.

There's a veneer of glamour, the article explained. "Her price was $400 an hour, three-hour minimum for local calls. With a little notice, she could charge it to your corporate credit card and

---

[5]Jerry Johnston, *Who's Listening?* (Grand Rapids: Zondervan, 1992), p. 81.

make it look like you had bought roses for the secretarial pool. . . . Her nights were booked up with club-hopping and 'dates.' She lived in a cocaine-fueled world where the day began at noon and didn't end until 4:00 A.M., where you could blow $1000 on a dress and earn it all back the next day. In this world, she was 'Sheena' or 'Tiffany' or sometimes just a body with no name at all."

But behind the sequins there was another story. The real side. The side everyone wants to avoid, the consequences of compromise. "Here is what it is like to be in the service of loneliness. Here is how you become dazzled by power and glitz. Here are the fruits of oppression, the wages of sin. . . ." the real story unfolded. "They say they love you, but when it comes time to end the relationship, they're the first ones to turn around and call you a "F— -ing whore. . . . It makes you wonder what it's like not to put on an act . . . it catches up with you emotionally." All of the women interviewed had died on the inside.[6]

One of the ways Satan masquerades his agenda is to twist and pervert the clear ring of truth. He makes both the messengers and the message of a better way, look foolish. "Christians are a bunch of fighting fundamentalists." "They say that it's wrong to make love." "They impose their puritan views on everyone else." "They can't accept differences." "They act like everyone who isn't like them is going to hell."

Isn't it sadly ironic? In their mockery they completely ignore the fact that it was God who invented sex in the first place, that his boundaries were given for the protection of what is good, that it is God's love for every sinner that makes him so despise what sin does to people.

Through the haze of popular opinion, maybe a few reminders about the reality of God and his attitude toward sex are in order:

- God created it (Genesis 2:18–25).

- God commanded it (Genesis 1:26–28).

- God loves it (Proverbs 5:18–19).

- God talks about it freely (Song of Solomon 7:6–9).

---

[6]Shawn Hubler, "Fleiss Case Exposes World of L.A. Call Girls," *Los Angeles Times*, December 13, 1993, A1.

- God encourages it (1 Corinthians 7:1–5).

- God protects it (Exodus 20:14).

- God condemns its abuse (1 Corinthians 6:9–10; Ephesians 5:3–7).

Despite what the uninformed will tell you, God isn't embarrassed by sex. The point God makes throughout Scripture is simply this: Sex is so beautiful and so powerful and so meaningful that to strip it of its honored place is an abuse. Give it the honor it deserves as Hebrews 13:4 states so emphatically!

There are four foundational truths that we must be aware of and pass on to our children. Let me share them with you here.

1. There's a Right Way to Enjoy God's Powerful Gifts— It Is Called "Honoring Boundaries"

Whether it is marriage, medicine or music—all of God's gifts have a great impact on our lives. Nothing is as satisfying as being in a secure and loving relationship. Nothing means as much, when your life is on the line, than the right medication properly prescribed. Nothing moves our emotions and lifts our spirits quite the way music can. These are but three examples. The things that benefit our lives the most are beneficial because they're powerful. Taken out of bounds they are powerfully destructive. Even the best that God has given can be twisted, perverted, misused and reissued as nothing more than sex, drugs, and rock & roll. God simply asks us to "use as directed."

When it comes to the issue of sexual boundaries, God asks us not to take advantage of anyone.

It is God's will that you should be sanctified: that you should avoid sexual immorality; that each of you should learn to control his own body in a way that is holy and honorable, not in passionate lust like the heathen, who do not know God; and that in this matter no one should wrong his brother or take advantage of him. The Lord will punish men for all such sins, as we have already told you and warned you. For God did not call us to be impure, but to live a holy life. Therefore, he who rejects this instruction does not reject man but God, who gives you his Holy Spirit (1 Thessalonians 4:3–8).

Sex out of bounds is as much a spiritual issue as a physical one simply because sex is a sacred part of our whole human experience. It involves our whole being. It cuts deep into the seat of our emotions. It is the mix from which life itself is procreated in the image of God. It is the one thing that separates marriage from all other relationships—and marriage being the very illustration of God's intimate relationship with his own people.

Do you not know that your bodies are members of Christ himself? Shall I then take the members of Christ and unite them with a prostitute? Never! Do you not know that he who unites himself with a prostitute is one with her in body? For it is said, "The two will become one flesh." But he who unites himself with the Lord is one with him in spirit. Flee from sexual immorality. All other sins a man commits are outside his body, but he who sins sexually sins against his own body. Do you not know that your body is a temple of the Holy Spirit, who is in you, whom you have received from God? You are not your own; you were bought at a price. Therefore honor God with your body (1 Corinthians 6:15–20).

Take note of the key issues involved here:

- God respects every individual and doesn't want anyone to be taken advantage of. Sex outside of the commitment of marriage ends up doing just that. Without the bond of marriage, it is all too easy to use someone for our own ends—and *that* is what God is prohibiting.

- God's parameters aren't merely nice suggestions that can be adjusted when convenient. A lifestyle of taking sexual advantage of anyone in any form is a mark of those who don't even know God.

- God makes it clear, that there *will* be a point of reckoning for our willful disregard for his good boundaries. Don't be fooled into thinking he doesn't notice.

- God calls us to a better kind of life—one which is pure and clean rather than selfish and abusive. His plans for us are bigger and better. He wants us to experience the richness of pure sexual fulfillment as it was designed.

181

- God's Spirit lives within us who know him, so that to defy his boundaries is to defy God himself. Sexual sin is not simply a physical act. It is altogether spiritual in nature and impact.

So God says, *You shall not commit adultery* (Exodus 20:14). Rather, *Marriage should be honored by all, and the marriage bed kept pure, for God will judge the adulterer and all the sexually immoral* (Hebrews 13:4).

Every now and then a teenager will walk up to me and question slyly, "Where does God actually *say* I can't have sex before marriage?" I start with Hebrews 13:4, explaining that adultery constitutes sex outside of your own marriage and "sexual immorality" or "fornication" is a reference to sex between unmarried couples. Until you're married, there's a monstrously high probability that the person you're dating will end up being someone else's husband or wife. Until you've said "I do," you can never be sure if you will be the spouse of that person. Hebrews 13:4 is obviously one verse among many that reinforce the same truth: Sex is for marriage.

2. There Are Long-Term Consequences to Be Paid for Compromise—They're Called "the Wages of Sin"

Wages. Results. Consequences. Every seed grows into something. Sexual compromise has a way of springing up on us down the road. It's a bumpy road when we disregard the protective boundaries God has established. As one poet put it:

The thorns which I have reap'd
are of the tree I planted;
they have torn me, and I bleed.
I should have known what fruit
would spring from such a seed.[7]

There's that period of quiet where it seems the reaper isn't paying any attention. It appears for a time that we can plant some-

---

[7]Lord George Noel Gordon Byron, "Childe Harold's Pilgrimage," canto 4, stanza 10, in *Familiar Quotations*, ed. John Bartlett (Boston: Little, Brown and Co., 1955), pp. 453–454.

thing rotten and reap roses. But sin has a way of working its destruction back into our lives. There's a moment when it seems as though we've gotten away with our tryst. It's out the door. It's over. "That was yesterday. Today's a new day. No worries." Then something leaks out. There's a thumping on the screen door. Or a visitor at the palace door. There's a knock or a note or a Nathan.

Truth hits a home run again:

- *The mouth of an adulteress is a deep pit* (Proverbs 22:14).

- *The unfaithful are trapped by evil desires* (Proverbs 11:6).

- *A prostitute is a deep pit . . . like a bandit she lies in wait* (Proverbs 23:27–28).

- *A man who commits adultery lacks judgment; whoever does so destroys himself* (Proverbs 6:32).

Like Moses said to the Israelites, *You may be sure that your sin will find you out* (Numbers 32:23).

Or as Paul put it to the Colossians, *Put to death, therefore, whatever belongs to your earthly nature: sexual immorality, impurity, lust, evil desires and greed, which is idolatry. Because of these, the wrath of God is coming* (Colossians 3:5–6).

In light of what God has said about "wages," a great verse that every father should pass on to every son is this: *Why be captivated, my son, by an adulteress? Why embrace the bosom of another man's wife? For a man's ways are in full view of the LORD, and he examines all his paths. The evil deeds of a wicked man ensnare him; the cords of his sin hold him fast. He will die for lack of discipline, led astray by his own great folly* (Proverbs 5:20–23).

Compromises come complete with consequences.

3. There Is a Short-Term Price to Be Paid for Purity— It Is Called "Self-Control"

The Andersons have a dog, or rather, a Cocker Spaniel. This mutt knows better than to ever admit to being a dog. She jumps on company, piddles on the carpet and chews on the furniture. The same song-and-dance plays nearly every time I visit their home. Someone finally gets fed up with the dog and throws her out the front door. This doesn't fluster the dog a bit because she simply goes around the house to the back door and thumps on the screen until someone in the back of the house—who doesn't know she's just been thrown out of the front of the house—lets her back in. The people in the living room think she's out of their life and then, not more than five minutes later, she's once again prancing through the living room wagging her entire rear end. I hate to put it in print but the truth must be known. The dog is smarter than the Andersons.

The Anderson family is a silly picture of how we often conduct our lives. We court sin for a time and then realize to some degree how it is affecting us. We think it's an irritant. So we get rid of it for a time and ignore it—but leave the back door of our lives unlocked. We leave open that loophole, that possibility, that opportunity for it to come back around and dominate us all over again. The back door of our lives is where we allow things into our minds. That is where sin weasels its way back in. Unless we keep a close watch at what goes into our minds, we can be sure that sin will come bounding full force into where we live.

Control what your mind is fed on: Garbage in, garbage out.

How can a young man keep his way pure? By living according to your word (Psalm 119:9).

Control what your mind is focused on: As a man thinketh, so is he.

Finally, brothers, whatever is true, whatever is noble, whatever is right, whatever is pure, whatever is lovely, whatever is admirable—if anything is excellent or praiseworthy—think about such things (Philippians 4:8).

Control what your mind is firm on: Make some tough decisions.

Therefore do not let sin reign in your mortal body so that you obey its evil desires. Do not offer the parts of your body to sin, as instruments of wickedness, but rather offer yourselves to God, as those who have been brought from death to life; and offer the parts of your body to him as instruments of righteousness (Romans 6:12–13).

Short-term control breeds long-term joy. When will we learn

that "having it all right now" means getting so much less? We'll be doing our kids a big favor by showing them the difference.

4. There Are Many Good Reasons to Honor God's Boundaries—They're Called "the Benefits of Obedience"

Sadly, many discussions about sexual fidelity focus on the negatives. "Don't do this and don't do that and if you do you'll hit the wall and—" While warnings on the negative side are important, the benefits of righteous living deserve equal time! I've devoted the entire final chapter of this book to the issue of positive outcomes and rewards, but in the interim, please note how important it is to comprehend and to stress the benefits to our children of obedience when it comes to sexual choices. *May your fountain be blessed, and may you rejoice in the wife of your youth. A loving doe, a graceful deer—may her breasts satisfy you always, may you ever be captivated by her love* (Proverbs 5:18–19). Wow!

We need to take time to help young people think through the incredible rewards inherent in choosing to wait for sexual gratification. We need to show them how God's boundaries are inseparably linked with huge wins like:

No diseases now.

No "surprise" diseases later in life.

No shredded hearts due to shredded sexual bonds.

No loss of honor.

No lies and cover-ups.

No shame.

No explanations to a spouse (or our kids) later on.

No comparisons.

No lack of trust with our families later on.

No regret.

No unwanted pregnancy.

No abortion.

Beyond that, we can show them Scripture, which describes the internal climate of a life lived in the freedom of the Spirit rather than in the bondage to sexual sin. *The acts of the sinful nature are obvious: sexual immorality, impurity and debauchery; idolatry and witchcraft; hatred, discord, jealousy, fits of rage, selfish am-*

bition, dissensions, factions and envy; drunkenness, orgies, and the like. I warn you, as I did before, that those who live like this will not inherit the kingdom of God. Here's the contrast—life in the Spirit: *But the fruit of the Spirit is love, joy, peace, patience, kindness, goodness, faithfulness, gentleness and self-control. Against such things there is no law.* Here's the point: *Those who belong to Christ Jesus have crucified the sinful nature with its passions and desires.* Here's the mandate: *Since we live by the Spirit, let us keep in step with the Spirit* (Galatians 5:19–25).

It never hurts to do a little positive "imagineering" with your teenager. Talk about the benefits package! Talk about what it is like to be free. Talk about how great it feels to not even have to worry about all the disastrous whiplash effects of compromise. Talk about getting to go to college (without a baby) and about the thrill of security in marriage and about the peace that accompanies obedience. Talk about all that God has "saved" us *from*. Revel in it a little. God does!

Never have young people needed straightforward answers from Christian adults more than they do right now. All the boundaries for great, lasting sexual relationships have been eroded by popular culture and the flood is moving in. Please, for the sake of your kids, break the silence.

Truth or Consequences

- Have you explained the concept of boundaries to your children? Do they see how positive and freeing proper boundaries are? Do they understand how a lack of boundaries actually results in bondage?

- Are you taking back the reins of leadership in this area? Moms and dads need to be talking about sexual feelings with their kids and acknowledging how normal and positive those feelings are. Kids need straightforward answers at age-appropriate stages.

- What kinds of sexual standards are your children observing in a routine way? As they interface with popular media, what values are they absorbing? How are you stepping into that world with them in order to help control what they're taking in? How are you using what they observe as a platform for discussion and learning discernment?

- How have you exposed your kids to the harsh realities of abandoning God's protective commands regarding sexual relationships? Knowing about the consequences is helpful. Try also going beyond statistics to some real-life scenarios. Taking flowers and baked goods to people suffering in an AIDS hospice is just one way that kids could become aware of "the other side" of sexual freedom.

- Know what your children are being taught at school and church about sex! Some programs are ghastly; others go a long way toward developing good values.

- Together with your children, come up with your own list of rewards for honoring God's standards. Then, if it is appropriate, make a poster with them listing those benefits and hang it on the back of the door in their room. What other ways could you help to reinforce the freedoms gained by honoring God?

• Our church recently hosted an evening for parents and teens where the speaker was a twenty-three-year-old woman who had been raised in a Christian home but who had become pregnant as a teenager. She shared with our group some of the consequences that were attached to being unmarried and having a newborn at this stage of life. It was impactful! Do you know of someone who has endured real-life consequences as a result of their choices? Maybe they would be open to joining your family for dinner and to share about their experience. This kind of interaction can leave a lasting impression.

• Your adolescent comes home and tells you about a friend at school who is sleeping with her boyfriend and believes it's no big deal. How could you use this as an opportunity to discuss respect for God's directions? Consider questions like, "Do you think this girl feels 'free' now that she's decided to go ahead and have sex before marriage? Has she gained something or lost something? What does God (the one who invented sex) say about it? Why would he protect it within the confines of marriage? What are some of the possible consequences—physically, emotionally, spiritually, relationally—that could result from her choice to have sex at this point? What would she have to look forward to if she had waited instead?"

• As Christian parents we are more bashful talking about sex than God is. Look in Christian bookstores for good books that help you explain God's plan for sexuality to your child. Several publishers print books age-appropriate for preschoolers through college-age young adults.

13

THE TRUTH ABOUT GOODNESS

THE CONSEQUENCES OF LAZINESS

*Let us not become weary in doing good, for at the proper time
we will reap a harvest if we do not give up. Therefore, as we
have opportunity, let us do good to all people, especially to
those who belong to the family of believers.*

—Galatians 6:9–10

His name was Nick and he was mentally handicapped. And
he drove me nuts. I attended the high school where my father was
a special ed teacher. There are pros and cons to attending high
school with your father. I didn't have to take the bus because he
drove. I didn't panic when I ran short on lunch money—dad was
just down the hall. Even being sent to the principal's office (which
happened regularly) wasn't so bad. He and my dad were friends,
so he always cut me some slack. But then there was Nick.

My father's class was a curiosity for the mainstream at school.
His room contained students who were physically disfigured, a
few who couldn't speak well, one or two who couldn't hear and
a host of students who just weren't able to learn as quickly as the
rest of us. Or so I thought. I came to find out some of them
learned the essentials faster than most.

Nick was one of my father's favorites. Or else my father was

189

his favorite. I never quite figured it out. In any case, Nick always had time on his hands and hung around my dad's classroom in the afternoons. So did I. I was waiting for Dad to finish his work so we could go home. Nick was just waiting out life, hanging around a safe place in a world that doesn't have too many safe places for the mentally disadvantaged. That's where our lives intersected.

In the hours that passed after school, Nick and I would talk. I would be doing my homework in the room and Nick would plop his huge lumbering frame next to me and recount the insignificant events of his day. He usually sat too close so I would routinely move away. He would move closer. I would back up. We had this dance, you see, and we moved around the room, he and I.

Hanging out with Nick after hours wasn't all that bad. He was unimaginably friendly and although our conversations were limited by his first-grade level of comprehension, we got along.

But I told you he drove me nuts. Now I'll tell you why.

Over time Nick became ultra comfortable with me. During the day, in the halls or in the locker room, he sought me out. In my mind, this wasn't good. I was usually with my friends, my circle, my clique—and Nick would come bounding up. He was loud. He smelled bad and looked bad and he observed no social protocol. Most of all, he wasn't "cool" like my friends and I.

Worst of all was the lunch room. On occasion I would be eating with my buddies and Nick would show up at the far end of the room and yell my name over the buzz of a couple hundred students. "DANIEL! There you are!" I would be hiding. He would move in. "I've been looking for you, Daniel. Hey, Daniel, what's in your lunch? Can I sit here, Daniel?" Eyes were on me. I wanted to die. No. I wanted Nick to die. So I shunned him. After school, alone in a classroom was one thing, but in front of my friends he was an embarrassment. More than once I asked him not to approach me in public. He never really seemed to understand. By my senior year I had become an expert in avoidance. I rarely saw Nick that year and when we did meet, I acted as aloof as possible, not wanting to encourage anything that would haunt me later.

Graduation day came and I was in my glory, with robe, hat and a diploma in my hand. There was a benediction (it was legal then) and we, the graduates erupted in cheers. Hats flew heavenward. We moved en masse to greet relatives and classmates amid handshakes and hugs. Pictures popped. Buttons popped. I was for a moment immortalized in my own mind, and then—it happened. Nick walked up. He wasn't overly boisterous. In fact, he seemed strangely calm. He smiled and handed me a small envelope which I hoisted under my robe and into my pants pocket. I mumbled a perfunctory "thanks" and quickly turned back to the revelry.

I forgot all about the card until late that night. I was sorting through my pockets for keys and change. There was the card. I pulled it out. "Nick," I thought. "I won't miss him." I opened the card. It was one of those flowery, motherly looking cards with butterflies and cute snails drawn in pastels. "Probably got it from his mom," I mused. On the inside, in terrible penmanship—block letters, actually—Nick had written just twelve words.

DEAR DANIEL,
    THANK YOU FOR BEING MY BEST FRIEND.
LOVE ALWAYS,
NICK

Something changed that night. Some*one* changed that night. Twelve words tore a hole in an ice-cold heart.

A lot of years have passed since then and the card has long since been lost, but the memory of Nick and the words carefully inscribed by a shaking hand have forever been carved in my conscience. I used to wonder why God created handicapped people. I no longer wonder. He created them to teach the rest of us how to love.

Who knows what words or actions or prayers will carve out a puzzle piece of history. Who knows how God will use one small seed of kindness, of goodness—or the quiet acquiescence of forgiveness or a single act of courage.

Earlier I mentioned the fires in Los Angeles. After a night of fiery hell that snatched up 366 homes in Laguna Beach alone, homeowners returned. Along one lonely street of charred remains stood a few homes, all in a row, that were left intact. Upon closer inspection, a makeshift sign, written in charcoal, had been

propped up against one of the homes. It proclaimed:
"We did it! —George and Harry."

For hours the night before, two men who didn't even live in the area had taken up garden hoses and fought off the flames. Using garbage can lids as shields, they stood in the gap for these homeowners they had never met. They had nothing to gain. They had their very lives to lose. Yet they decided to risk it all for the hope of saving what someone else cherished so much. Through tears, one homeowner reflected, "I owe thirty-two years of memories to George and Harry."[1]

Goodness. Webster defines it as "conducting one's self according to the moral order of the universe." The Bible defines it as obedience to God, since God is the Ultimate Good. It's the outworking of righteousness. It's the idea of moving as far from evil as possible. "I just want them to be good." How many thousands of times does that phrase scroll through the minds of parents around the world each day. We want our kids to be good, to be kind, to be pure to the core in their motives, to be helpful and conscientious and righteous and godly.

At the turn of this second millennium, Christians are becoming more aware of God's power. He's doing great things in this world of ours. There are simply no boundaries on the Holy Spirit's work—except one. He most often works through people. His people. He uses us to bless the world. *For Christ's love compels us, because we are convinced that one died for all, and therefore all died. And he died for all, that those who live should no longer live for themselves but for him who died for them and was raised again* (2 Corinthians 5:14–15).

While God desires "that all men come to salvation," he uses people as his witnesses. While God desires to rescue the poor, he works through the generosity of believers to do it. While he wants to see the church built up and strengthened, he uses the members of Christ's body, you and I, to do it: *And he has committed to us the message of reconciliation. We are therefore Christ's ambassadors, as though God were making his appeal through us* (2 Corinthians

---

[1] *Los Angeles Times*, "Who Saved the Day? George and Harry Did It!" by Frank Messina, November 5, 1993, B1.

5:19b–20a). Goodness is a divine imperative. When we reach with our hands, it is God who touches others. And, as we model goodness, we teach goodness.

The decisions we make shape peoples' lives. God has loaned each of us two things: power and time. The way we sow those resources will have everything to do with what grows. *So we make it our goal* [our ambition!] *to please him . . ."* (2 Corinthians 5:9).

What difference are your efforts really going to make? Mull this one example: In the 1800s a simple Sunday school teacher took the time to lead a Boston shoe salesman to Christ. The salesman's name was Dwight Moody. Over time, Moody became an evangelist who had great influence in the life of another man, Frederick Meyer. Meyer was speaking on a college campus one day, and through that ministry Wilbur Chapman came to know Jesus Christ. Chapman served in the YMCA and through that agency, arranged to have a former baseball player named Billy Sunday come to North Carolina for an outreach. Billy Sunday was so effective that the community leaders in Charlotte decided to hold another revival meeting with evangelist Mordecai Hamm. One night while Mr. Hamm was speaking, a young man came forward and gave his life to Christ. That young man's name was Billy Graham.[2]

Small seeds. Small acts of faithfulness. We can never know who is being impacted or what will happen down the line or what will come of the good we do. One thing is sure. God is watching and the seeds we plant don't ever die.

The consequences of laziness are harder to calculate, because they consist of things unseen—all the good acts we leave undone, all that we *could* do but don't. And so Scripture calls us simply to lives of unbridled, unbounded goodness. *Let us not become weary in doing good, for at the proper time we will reap a harvest if we do not give up. Therefore, as we have opportunity, let us do good to all people . . ."* (Galatians 6:9–10).

---

[2]Max Lucado, *And the Angels Were Silent*, (Portland, Ore.: Multnomah Press, 1992), p. 56.

Goodness Is Grounded in the Heart

Goodness stems from a certain view of life. It is a paradigm shift from selfishness to other-centeredness. That's something that doesn't come to us naturally.

Jesus longs for us to learn goodness. He taught that goodness isn't an exterior quality fabricated to impress others, but rather a deep, internal character decision that impacts every relationship of our lives. Position doesn't foster it. Profession doesn't elicit it. Power doesn't guarantee it. In fact, discovering who is good and who isn't may surprise you.

Back in the Bible there was a group of men who thought they were good. They had all the trappings of religiosity but their whispers, their condescending scowls, their sharp words betrayed them. Jesus told them; *Make a tree good and its fruit will be good, or make a tree bad and its fruit will be bad, for a tree is recognized by its fruit. You brood of vipers, how can you who are evil say anything good? For out of the overflow of the heart the mouth speaks. The good man brings good things out of the good stored up in him, and the evil man brings evil things out of the evil stored up in him. But I tell you that men will have to give account on the day of judgment for every careless word they have spoken* (Matthew 12:33–36). Good stored up? Sounds like Jesus was saying that goodness is something we plant on the inside, not something we paste on the outside.

Goodness Is Learned

If you have kids, then you already know that humankind is not inherently good. Goodness isn't something innate. It's something taught and something learned. *And let us consider how we may spur one another on toward love and good deeds* (Hebrews 10:24).

A family I know embodies "protocol-plus." The father is involved in a number of local philanthropic agencies, the mom is a Bible study leader in a parachurch organization. Now and then Mrs. "Jones" stops by our office to make copies or chat with a secretary, her three young children in tow. This woman is nice. She's proper. She's beautiful. And she's deadly.

I care a great deal for this woman and her kids, so I share this not out of criticism, but out of pain. Criticism is precisely the problem. Mrs. Jones privately belittles everyone in her path. If you were a fly on the wall in our office you would hear a string of comments about someone in her study, or someone her husband deals with, or a teacher at her son's school. "This woman never. . . . Oh, you should have seen what a lousy job. . . . I've got to tell you, that teacher is an idiot, I mean to tell you, he. . . . Honestly, I've had it with. . . ." she trails on. My heart shrinks. I watch her kids. Recorders are whirring. Their young, impressionable minds log it all. The good is a veneer. The heart is filled with something else.

On the flip-side, kids are just as quickly impressed and impacted by goodness. Scripture tells us that righteousness is like a gene that gets passed onto our kids. Clearly, there are no guarantees that all children will follow in the footsteps of godly parents. But the children of the righteous live in the blessing of their parents' goodness: *But from everlasting to everlasting the Lord's love is with those who fear him, and his righteousness with their children's children* (Psalm 103:17). Often I have watched in amazement at how thoroughly good certain teenagers are. Invariably I get to meet their parents. Guess what? They have a parent or a set of parents busily loving, building, nurturing and reaching them— doing good, all the while hardly noticing the paths they're clearing for their children to walk in.

Paul refers to this process of a parent passing on goodness when he describes how he dealt with believers God had entrusted to his care. *You are witnesses, and so is God, of how holy, righteous and blameless we were among you who believed. For you know that we dealt with each of you as a father deals with his own children, encouraging, comforting and urging you to live lives worthy of God, who calls you into his kingdom and glory* (1 Thessalonians 2:10–12). Paul lived goodness and encouraged goodness. While some joke that "Insanity is hereditary. You get it from your kids," the truth is that it's goodness that's hereditary. Kids get it from their parents.

Goodness Is Sacrificial

A man once traveled the dry rocky path from Jerusalem to Jericho, a day's journey away. Like all of us, he was busy. He had business to conduct, contacts to see. But when the traveler stumbled upon another man lying hurt to the side of the path, he ran quickly to help. The injured man groaned as the other rolled him over and propped up his head. "Robbers . . . they took everything," he whispered.

The traveler reached into his satchel, pulled out his goat-skin container of precious water and gave him a drink. Ripping shreds of cloth from his own clothes, he bandaged the man's wounds and loaded him onto his donkey. They journeyed together until they reached the next village, where the man found an inn and secured a room and spent the night watching over the other.

As the hours passed, the hurt man began to come around. By the next morning he was sitting up. "You saved my life, you know." His eyes focused on his rescuer. "Are you from Jerusalem or from Jericho?"

"Neither," replied the traveler. "My home is up north," he stalled. Then he blurted out the truth. "I'm a Samaritan."

"Ah, a half-breed!" the man smiled. Then he looked down and became quietly thoughtful.

"What is it?" the good man questioned.

"Oh, I was just thinking. It's so funny . . . yesterday a number of people came along the path before you did. I saw them. They saw me. I could tell who they were by the clothes they wore. One was a priest. Another was a Levite—supposed to be a very good Jew, you know."

"Yes, I know."

"I reached out, even called out, for them to help me, but neither seemed to care. They rushed on by. I guess they didn't want to be bothered. Had religious things to do, I suppose."

"I suppose."

"But then you came. It's only funny because everyone looks down on you Samaritans. You put up with a lot. People not giving you the time of day and all, just because of your race and where you live. It doesn't make any sense." His eyes narrowed. "You're the one who should be wearing those robes. You're a truly good man."

Before long, the Samaritan put his few things back in his satchel and prepared to leave once again for Jericho. But before he did, he found the innkeeper and paid him what he had. "Take care of that man for me, would you? And on my return trip I will repay anything you spend on him" (Luke 10:30–37).

Goodness is seldom cheap. Goodness doesn't consist of religious intentions, but righteous action. When Paul reached out in love to the Macedonians he was *harassed at every turn* and endured *conflicts on the outside, fears within* (2 Corinthians 7:5). But one thing kept Paul going—his belief in the worth of every human life. He knew people were eternal souls worth any sacrifice, however costly.

The good you invest in your children is costly too. Responsible parenting means countless sacrifices. But hold onto this perspective: No moment of virtue on behalf of another human being is ever wasted. Every hospital tab picked up for another is written down in heaven.

Goodness Is Indiscriminate

Hotel guests had begun to dot the beach as Sachett opened the heavy wooden door that covered the front of his kiosk. "It's going to be a hot one," he hollered over to me. I rummaged through a barrel of life-preservers looking for an Adult Large. Sachett locked the swinging door in place and brushed sand off the counter. He stepped inside and unhooked a clipboard from the wall. I walked over with my fluorescent orange body buoy. I'd known Sachett only about 48 hours. He was the beach front manager—Polynesian by descent, and Buddhist, I had discovered in our previous conversation. He was skilled in water sports and willing to help American tourists try them all.

"Well, Daniel, what do you want? A paddle boat? Kayak? Or are you ready for a wind-surfing lesson? I can give you one at 11:00." I was engrossed in figuring out how to buckle the life preserver when an overweight middle-aged man approached the booth. "You checkin' this stuff out?" he demanded. Before Sachett could reply the man pointed, "I'll take a Catamaran."

"I'm so sorry, but our two Catamarans are reserved this morning. They're—"

"There sitting here now, so let me use one," the man cut in. I

197

stood watching with intrigue as the veins in the visitor's neck became enlarged.

"I can reserve one for you for this afternoon if you'd like but—"

"Why the h— can't I just take one now? G—, you tick me off." He stomped off in his thongs, sand whipping up the back side of his legs.

Sachett called after the man. "Come back later, and I'll set you up with one, no problem." The man was gone.

Sachett said nothing. Didn't even look at me. He went back to reviewing his clipboard. I couldn't believe the childish outburst I had just witnessed.

"That guy's a jerk." I consoled. "Makes you want to deck him."

Without looking up, Sachett replied. "I understand, but it doesn't."

"What?"

"It doesn't." He put down the clipboard and looked at me. He smiled that warm Polynesian smile. "It doesn't bother me. That poor man is hollow inside. I wouldn't say anything to harm him. It would break his spirit. It is very important not to break the spirit of people. Everyone deserves kindness."

Truly indiscriminate goodness marked the character of Christ. He wasn't a retaliator. When his own townspeople rushed at him to push him off a cliff, he simply slipped out of sight. When he stood in front of his false accusers during his mockery of a trial, he was silent "like a lamb." When he hung between two thieves being laughed at, jeered at, sneered at, spit on, his only reply was, "Forgive them for they don't even know what they're doing." If ever there was goodness, there it was. Arms outstretched. Naked. Bleeding. Forgiving the angry, selfish, mean, nasty, corrupt lot of humanity.

Love doesn't wait for other people to be good in order to show them goodness. It's proactive. Christ's goodness was sweeping, reaching to all human beings even in the darkest of conditions.

I have a small note tucked in my desk with a few simple words written on it, given to me by a friend. The words were penned by Oswald Chambers: "It is inbred in us that we have to do exceptional things for God, but we have not. We have to be exceptional in the ordinary things, to be holy in mean streets and among mean people." Amen.

Goodness Is Reciprocal

I know. In the short-run you can point to exceptions to the maxim that "goodness is reciprocal." But in the eternal scope, what goes around comes around. It may be imperceptible for a time—seeds are like that. But when Scripture repeats a principle over and over, we should take notice. When you are good, God says, good has a way of swinging back on you. When you are cruel, it catches you. *If a man digs a pit, he will fall into it; if a man rolls a stone, it will roll back on him* (Proverbs 26:27).

Plant now. Somewhere. Down the line, maybe even after your last breath, there will be life. *He who pursues righteousness and love finds life, prosperity and honor* (Proverbs 21:21).

Cultivate. Water. Let goodness root in every corner of your garden, even the rocky corner. *He who tends a fig tree will eat its fruit, and he who looks after his master will be honored* (Proverbs 27:18).

Keep the long run in view. *Commit to the Lord whatever you do, and your plans will succeed. The Lord works out everything for his own ends* (Proverbs 16:3–4a).

Sure as the sun sets, summer will pass and the harvest will come to full bloom. *For the perishable must clothe itself with the imperishable, and the mortal with immortality.* Every person continues—on the other side of the divide we call death. In light of that, Paul writes, *Therefore, my dear brothers, stand firm. Let nothing move you. Always give yourselves fully to the work of the Lord, because you know that your labor in the Lord is not in vain* (1 Corinthians 15:53, 58). Your labor isn't in vain. Your soft answers and the bills you pick up for those that can't repay you and the scoffers you've shared the Gospel with—it's not wasted. Life isn't over up there, even when it's over down here.

He who goes out weeping, carrying seed to sow, will return with songs of joy, carrying sheaves with him (Psalm 126:6, KJV).

Truth or Consequences

- Do you ask your kids about the good things they're doing? Is the "good" in their lives getting as much time and attention as the "bad?" How are you rewarding and reinforcing the good you see in them?

- Help your children internalize their importance to God's work in the world by finding ways around your church, community and beyond to minister together as a family. Help out with a church service conducted in a rest home. Volunteer to help rehab a house. Baby-sit for a single parent. Take part in a short-term mission trip as a family. Look for needy people who could use a touch of God's goodness.

- Often we envision God calling us to great acts of sacrifice. What daily needs around you provide immediate, ongoing opportunities to do good? How could you and your children help each other? Or help your extended family? Your neighbors? Your community?

- In our area, some families take a Saturday now and then to glean potato fields after harvest. The potatoes are bagged and given to poorer families. Our youth ministry sponsors a few trips across the border into Mexico each year in order to serve in an orphanage there. Our junior-highers serve the homeless in a downtown mission. Pick your own "man lying on the side of the road" and then start ripping bandages! It'll encourage them. It'll change your kids!

- When your child has a hard time getting along with another kid at school, look for ways to show indiscriminate, proactive love. Is there an enemy to whom your child can demonstrate love? Or is there an outcast to whom your family can reach out?

- One mom, a friend of my wife, was with her children driving in the rain one day. They spotted a lady walking down the road in the pouring rain getting soaked. This mom pulled a U-turn and had her son get out and give the woman their umbrella. The lady was overjoyed. But the real, lasting impact was on the kids. What are your kids observing?

- Discuss the difference between someone who does good for show, and someone who does good unto God. Look at Matthew 6:1–4. Does that mean that anything done publicly is bad? What's the difference between *doing* good and *being* good? Talk with your child about how God gets our hearts involved—that when we grasp his goodness to us, we find it easier to be good to others.

- How about adopting an older person in a rest home who doesn't have a family nearby? What would you be communicating to your children if you gave this adopted grandma or grandpa an hour every couple of weeks?

14

THE TRUTH ABOUT PASSION

THE CONSEQUENCES OF APATHY

I know your deeds, that you are neither cold nor hot. I wish you were either one or the other! So, because you are luke-warm—neither hot nor cold—I am about to spit you out of my mouth.

—Revelation 3:15–16

To get through seminary I worked for a year in a mortuary. It was an older, family-run establishment with an olive-and-gold interior reminiscent of the 60s and an exterior of cracking beige paint. With the window shades drawn, the home was bland and, I have to admit, daunting. I worked evenings with Sid, another seminary student. Our job was to manage the premises in the evenings when the funeral director/owner had gone home. We escorted relatives and friends into the viewing rooms, took the "stretch" out to pick up the deceased and, at 11:00 P.M., locked the place up tight.

One evening we had taken in an additional "deceased one," bringing the house count to four. One gentleman was lying in the viewing room, all suited up. There were three others on gurneys in the back embalming room, sheets pulled full length over their lifeless bodies. Around 10:50 or so, Sid informed me that he had to leave a little early and asked if I would lock up. No problem. I heard him go out through the side door. I heard his car start. I heard him drive away.

A few minutes later I left the front office to commence the lock-up routine. Moving down the hall I checked in on Mr. All Dressed Up and No Place to Go. I clicked off the floor lamp next to his casket. Back into the hall again and across the front of the chapel, through the crying room and into the back hall. In a small closet, I turned a knob, shutting off the synthetic organ Muzak which trailed pleasantly throughout the home all day long. It was supposed to make the place cheerier. Nothing worse than deathly silence, we were told. In an instant the music stopped and very silent it was. I could hear my own breathing. Then came the final step.

Move through the embalming room to the back door. Lock it and turn on the porch light. Sounded simple enough, but I hated it. I didn't like walking past the ghostly white sheets with human forms lying ever so still and cold—and dead, beneath. My intellect always told me how ridiculous it was to feel afraid. My heart never listened. It always beat faster as I moved next to the forms. I locked the back door. Flip. The amber porch light went on and I turned to walk back through the room.

What hit me next was like a bolt of lightning striking the core of my being. BAM! One massive sheet-covered body lunged off the gurney and tackled me to the floor. I screamed like a hysterical woman, a shriek I've never since been able to reproduce. My body hit the floor and cabinets with a thud. My arms and legs thrashed in terror while my mind went stone blank in shock. White sheet flailing, I tore for my life against this monster from the grave. And then I heard it. As if coming from another world, the real world that I had momentarily left. Laughter. It was Sid's laughter. In the same instant I saw his face. He got up, whooping hilariously, and reached out a hand to help me up. I closed my eyes and remained on the floor, breathing heavily and repenting in advance for all the things I was about to say and do to Sidney.

The dead come back to life? Can it happen? It can. For many Christians, it's time to jump off the gurney.

None of us should be satisfied if our children adopt our values

203

because of coercion from the outside. Unless values are internal-ized, they're not values—they're just somebody else's rules. Apart from God, each of us is dead, a hater of what is good and right. We care about the wrong things. When God brings us back to life, we begin to *think* and *act* rightly about what God cares about—truth, purity, goodness and all that he values. But even more than that, our aim should be to become *passionate* about all the right things. And most of all, to become passionate about God himself. Without an ongoing relationship with God, a deep love for him, we lose our moorings. Unanchored, our values become meaningless.

When I was young I played at everything. Everything was, you might say, somewhat trivial. War to me was no more than building a fort out of driftwood on the beach in front of our northwest Washington home, and guarding the outpost against pirates that might sail in off the bay.

School was another fascinating world of activity. It never oc-curred to me that I was supposed to be learning anything. We kids lived for lunch and recess. We tangled and tromped on the mon-key bars. That was as close as we got to climbing the corporate ladder, and we stepped gleefully on the groping fingers of those climbing below us.

We viewed industry in the same vein. Summer was open sea-son for us drink hawkers. I had a pitcher full of warm, sugary lemonade and a rickety wooden stand out by the road. Since rarely did anyone ever drive down our road, business was slow. Mainly my nickels came from neighbors who felt sorry for me. I remember proclaiming to one patron that I was keeping costs at a minimum by reusing the Styrofoam cups. He was so thoughtful that he didn't even finish his drink and I was able to reuse part of his lemonade as well!

Church was as equally inconsequential. Every Sunday Mrs. Hamilton walked into our tiny Sunday school room. I was usually hiding under the table before she arrived. For some reason, I loved to hide under the table. When Mrs. Hamilton walked in with those amazing high heels and bunching nylons I would reach out and grab her ankles. (At least once I even bit one of them!) She would always scream and rustle me out from under the table and give me a hug. That meant the world to me.

I usually sat next to my mom in the morning worship service. It was a time to count ceiling tiles, draw on the bulletin and analyze the hymnal. I never understood why in one song the "roll was called a piander." Finally after questioning my mother she explained that the song wasn't referring to a dinner roll as I had thought, and it wasn't a "piander." The words were actually "when the roll is called *up yonder*." One Sunday I asked her which airline Pontius Pilot flew for. She just shook her head and told me not to whisper in church.

As a kid I played at everything. I would dabble in one thing until I lost interest and then go on to the next. Whatever caught my fancy was the duty of the day and nothing of great impact really ever happened. That's how it was supposed to be. I was a kid.

But another plan was in process. My parents' plan. They were busy building an adult—especially when it came to my faith. They viewed God as truly holy, not someone to be taken lightly. They viewed church as a sacred moment in the week, not a trivial pit stop to be wedged in when convenient. I remember wanting so much to be a Boy Scout. My parents had nothing against scouting, but Scouts had meetings and outings that would have kept me from attending church with the family. So scouting was out. At the time I thought their judgment on that issue cruel and unusual. But now as I look back, my parents wanted one thing communicated without any question: Nothing replaces the Lord in our lives. It wasn't legalism. It was a way of life called "passion." They simply loved God too much to let anything steal away those precious few hours of worship.

Passion. Webster fleshes it out eloquently: "fervor and ardor, burning intensity, zeal, affection, enthusiasm, a strong emotion that has an overpowering or compelling effect." When it comes to our life with God, it means being so filled with love that our lives burst with motivation. God longs for people like that—passionate people.

More than anything else, parents who love God desire their kids to be fueled from within. We want our children to desire God, to obey God, to pursue God. Not because we stand behind them with a stick, but because of an inner drive, because burning within is an inner passion for his presence.

The whole drama of the Jewish nation is a story of a God, intense in his love for his people, and a people who wander away. Losing their inner drive, the Israelites turned ritualistic.

It's always the case: when passion wanes, it's replaced with ritual. Going through paces. Once compelled from within, now complacent. Once profound, now trivial. Call it "ritualism," or "meaningless repetition" or "religiosity devoid of realness." It's when the fire of faith dies down. We all fight the tendency, don't we?

Why is passion so elusive? Why is it a struggle to lift our eyes and behold—and be held? I've identified at least six reasons and I'll list them for you as I see it:

1. *Unbelief*: "I just can't believe that God's love for me is that intense—so why should it matter how I feel about him?"

2. *Self-preoccupation*: "I'm so busy with this and with that. . . . I simply don't have the time to stop and get deeply involved in my faith."

3. *Pride*: "I'm doing fine. God is there. I am here. We sort of just do our own thing."

4. *Fear*: "I'm comfortable with my routines. I don't want to upset anything or get into anything I can't handle."

5. *Laziness*: "I feel like if I get too involved with God it's going to cost me. The sacrifice may be more than I want to make. He might force me to be a missionary or something."

6. *Habit*: "I've been out of touch for so long, why change now?"

Someone has written this about spiritual apathy:

> I would like $3 worth of God, please. Not enough to ex-plode my soul or disturb my sleep, but just enough to equal a cup of warm milk or a snooze in the sunshine. I want ec-stasy, not transformation. I want the warmth of the womb, not new birth. I want a pound of the eternal in a paper sack. I would like to buy $3 worth of God, please.

Like helium balloons drifting off on a lazy summer afternoon, we float from our Father with hardly a notice. And the consequences? They are profound. To be sure, the darkest periods in church history have been times when the hearts of God's people grew cold while the ceremonies of faith continued.

It was to just such a gathering of believers that the words of Revelation 2 were written. The church at Ephesus had been established by Paul and nurtured by Apollos, Timothy and John. Over time they had made great advances on the pagan community that surrounded them and even resisted the false doctrines of an insidious immoral group called the Nicolaitans. The Ephesian church was a zealous, righteous, hard-working bunch of people. But God rebuked them. Why? *Yet I hold this against you: You have forsaken your first love. Remember the height from which you have fallen! Repent and do the things you did at first. If you do not repent, I will come to you and remove your lampstand from its place* (Revelation 2:4–5).

A congregation of people. From the outside, a model. On the inside, moldy. They had fallen from where they had begun. The joy in their hearts as they served their Lord had died. That gleam of love in their eyes was gone. They were going through the paces and had forgotten their passion.

Have you been there? A slow leak. Nothing at first. Ignore it. Then it becomes a hissing away of life. Or maybe a spiritual blowout. Faith goes flat. We question everything and feel nothing. The Presence is gone, replaced by the eerie whistle of a breeze through a dry soul and the banging of shutters on internal windows that used to let in God's light.

It's happened before. Long ago God spoke through his prophet Isaiah:

The Lord says: "These people come near to me with their mouth and honor me with their lips, but their hearts are far from me" (Isaiah 29:13a).

God crashes in, invading neat systems and upsetting rituals. His are the words of a deserted lover. The one who has sacrificed all and received nothing in return—lifeless co-habitation, not relationship. This is no distant demigod, but God *the Father* who lingers over humanity like a parent hovering over his children.

Do you hear the agony in God's voice? "These people." Not only agony, but distance. Not *"my* people" but *"these* people." They

207

were his people, but now they weren't. The distance was killing them. God offers three examples—three symptom of this disease of distance. The first symptom? Dead worship!

Their worship of me is made up only of rules taught by men (Isaiah 29:13b). They skipped to the temple. They carried their Bibles. They recited the creeds. They repeated the hymns. They slept through the sermon. The lights were on, but no one was home. They had substituted form for function—a complete replacement.

Outward religiosity can look an awful lot like genuine passion. The difference is the motivation of the people involved. Invisible stuff. Hard to pinpoint. But there was a second symptom. They claimed to be wise, but it was only from the neck up.

The wisdom of the wise will perish, the intelligence of the intelligent will vanish (Isaiah 29:14).

Theological scholarship gone sour. All the right answers. Machine-like information banks, without a soul to speak of. They astound you; they amuse themselves; they shame me, says God. They're a sham! They know facts about me, but they don't know ME. They've got their degrees and their classes but it stops there. It's hollow wisdom!

But he's not finished. There's a third symptom of their spiritual apathy: shallow work. *Woe to those who go to great depths to hide their plans from the Lord, who do their work in darkness and think, "Who sees us? Who will know?"* (Isaiah 29:15).

They assume they can live and make plans and carry out their religious work without God knowing or caring. It's as if he weren't there. "Woe" from the throne of God. "They're in a delusion. Their work is shallow and senseless and I am about to bring them to their senses."

You turn things upside down, as if the potter were thought to be like the clay! Shall what is formed say to him who formed it, "He did not make me"? Can the pot say of the potter, "He knows nothing"? (Isaiah 29:16).

"You've got the whole thing backwards," God says to them. "You're acting as if the potter is as stupid as the clay. I made you. I know you inside and out. I know your little thoughts before you think them. I know what is behind your credentials and creeds and cryptic repetitions. Nothing!"

When Jesus quoted Isaiah in Matthew 15, the religious elite were still in the same fog. When Christ came on the scene he did an X-ray of them. When held up to the light, they proved to be hollow on the inside. Their status, their image, their knowledge, their traditions, their respectability meant nothing to Jesus. In fact, it angered him. *Woe to you, teachers of the law and Pharisees, you hypocrites! You are like whitewashed tombs, which look beautiful on the outside but on the inside are full of dead men's bones* (Matthew 23:27).

The Czechoslovakian philosopher Gardavsky Vitezslav, who was martyred for his faith in 1978, campaigned against a society that carefully planned every detail of material existence but eliminated mystery and miracle, and squeezed all freedom from life. He wrote a book entitled "God Is Not Yet Dead" in which he states our dilemma with great accuracy:

> The terrible threat against life, is not death, nor pain, nor any variation on the disasters that we so obsessively try to protect ourselves against. The terrible threat is that we might die earlier than we really do die, before death has become a natural necessity. The real horror lies in just such a premature death after which we go on living for many years.[1]

The problem is a heart problem, not a program problem. A passion problem, not a procedure problem. God reaches out for our hand and we hand him an operations manual. His response is singular. "I don't want your lists or your lesson plans, I want your love."

God chipped away the veneer, and what was the true nature of his people? Dead worship. Hollow wisdom. Shallow work.

Yet in the midst of this graveyard comes a resounding, thunderous cry, *Therefore once more I will astound these people with wonder upon wonder* (Isaiah 29:14a). Lethargy will be electrified! Indeed, God's power was seen again by all of Israel. God's power will be seen by every one of us as well. We will experience it now by choice, or we will see it one day when he reigns.

---

[1]Eugene Peterson, *Run With the Horses* (Downers Grove, Ill.: InterVarsity Press, 1983), p. 17.

Some do decide to live in light of his presence. They experience an infusion of God himself. But what does that look like? In the words of the Psalmist, *The sacrifices of God are a broken spirit; a broken and contrite heart* (Psalm 51:17).

What Passion Looks Like

Who are those who have a true heart? When they come before God

- they don't strut their stuff.

- they don't dress to impress. They come spiritually naked and willing to be clothed.

- they don't talk about all their great deeds. They come listening in a mind-set of humility.

- they don't stand at his throne. They come kneeling.

- they don't approach with arms folded. They come with empty hands raised.

- they don't pretend to worship while they're preoccupied. They come prepared to encounter the eternal.

There was a woman who came before God like that. *While [Jesus] was in Bethany, reclining at the table in the home of a man known as Simon the Leper, a woman came with an alabaster jar of very expensive perfume, made of pure nard. She broke the jar and poured the perfume on his head* (Mark 14:3).

A pouring of perfume—an outpouring of love! The name of the perfume? "Passion." A little extravagant? A little gushy? A little outrageous? You bet.

Some of those present were saying indignantly to one another, "Why this waste of perfume? It could have been sold for more than a year's wages and the money given to the poor." And they rebuked her harshly (Mark 14:4–5).

A year's wages down the drain. At least that's how they viewed it. Calculating. Reserved. Distanced. Judgmental. "Hey, she isn't keeping form! She's outta line! If she were spiritual she'd give that money to the poor." There's not a hint that this woman cared what they thought. She was alone—in worship. Something on the inside had completely taken over the outside. Jesus always sees the inside. He saw hers—and theirs.

"Leave her alone," said Jesus. "Why are you bothering her? She has done a beautiful thing to me. The poor you will always have with you, and you can help them any time you want. But you will not always have me. She did what she could. She poured perfume on my body beforehand to prepare for my burial. I tell you the truth, wherever the gospel is preached throughout the world, what she has done will also be told, in memory of her" (Mark 14:6–9).

And so it is. One woman who loved deeply, who gave everything she had—every last drop, to her Lord.

The story begs one question. Would we have joined her or would we have jeered?

If we are a passionate people who love God more than anything in the world, that passion will revolutionize our walk of faith in at least five vital ways:

Passion Prompts Confession

Joe Aldrich, President of Multnomah Bible College, used to say that "maturity is simply a return to the reality about ourselves. About who we really are and who God really is." We who are God's have the Spirit of God. But often we shut off and shut out his overpowering, flesh-defeating, inner-working and outer-working. Being passionate as a people starts with a humble submission on the inside, followed by a quiet confession on the outside.

When we're intense in our love for God, we become uncomfortable with masks. They itch and we take them off. We long for truth. Truth that sets the heart free. That is what confession does.

Those who love God, love to obey him purely. *Whoever has my commands and obeys them, he it is who loves me* (John 14:21).

Eugene Peterson writes:

God's love is passionate and seeks faithful, committed love in return. God does not want tame pets to fondle and feed; he wants mature, free people who will respond to him in authentic individuality. For that to happen there must be honesty and truth. The self must be toppled from its pedestal. There must be pure hearts and clear intelligence, confession of sin and commitment in faith. Adoration of God is full-blooded and soaring.[2]

Love makes us thirsty for righteousness. We long to come back to our senses when we sin and get things right. We're willing to be honest, thoroughly honest, before our holy, all-knowing God.

Passion Fosters Contentment

True lasting contentment is unattainable without an intimate inner connection with our Lord. When our hearts and minds are set on things above rather than on earth, says Paul to the Colossians, then the peace of Christ can rule in us. The book of Psalms says the same. *He who dwells in the shelter of the most high will rest in the shadow of the Almighty. He will cover you with his feathers* (Psalm 91:1, 4). And Ephesians 2:14 affirms that it is God himself who brings about peace in our lives.

People ask me all week long "How's it going?" Do you ever have trouble responding to that question? I do. I have a hard time knowing what to say. I feel like a hypocrite saying "fine," when the fact is, the world is not all fine. Usually there's a family in crisis on my doorstep . . .

and I'm struggling to program effectively in this culture . . .

and there's a mountain of phone calls I haven't gotten to . . .

and there are kids who need more attention . . .

and I've barely had any study time for my next lesson . . .

and I have staff people who are struggling to disciple well . . .

and I have a trip that is requiring legions of preparation time and . . .

and what I really want to say is, "Well, to be honest, all is not fine, but I feel God's peace. That's all. I just feel his peace. Without

[2]Eugene Peterson, *Run With the Horses* (Downers Grove, Ill.: InterVarsity Press, 1983), p. 89.

him I'd fare about as well as a Ritz cracker that has just been stepped on. But, in God, I feel at peace in the midst of it all."

Passion Creates Compassion

When love runs deep we begin to see with God's eyes. And when we do, feelings of grace and empathy emerge. The fruit of the Holy Spirit—love, joy, peace, patience, kindness, goodness, gentleness, faithfulness and self-control—well up from within and overtake the way we relate. Nitpicking at others loses its appeal.

Passionless people devoid of the Spirit's control always turn petty. They argue and bite and wheeze about the brand of creamer the church picks for the coffee. But when a body of people are ruled by the Spirit and thirsting after the Almighty God, they have far less time or attention to bark at each other. They are busy serving and giving and proclaiming and winning and releasing others from their plight of sin. They're busy doing eternal work. Instead of breaking people's hearts, their hearts break over people.

When our focus is on God himself we lose our preoccupation with what others do or don't do. We can stop playing God in other people's lives, because before their Master they will stand or fall (Romans 14:4). Instead, we can love them intensely.

Passion Inspires Confidence

To stem the chewing and sputtering and spitting grief we feel when faced with insurmountable challenges, God gives us Jeremiah, the weeping prophet. He loved God with a passion in the midst of persecution, rejection and bewilderment. Again, Peterson writes:

> Jeremiah didn't like his suffering. He yelled at God in his pain. He didn't like it, but he wasn't afraid of it because the most important thing in his life was God—not comfort, not applause, not security, but the living God. What he did fear was worship without astonishment, religion without commitment. He feared getting what he wanted and missing what

God wanted. He feared the waste of taking these few eternity-charged years that we are given and squandering them in cocktail chatter when we can be vehemently human and passionate with God.[3]

The Bible confronts us with a startling truth. The power that raised Christ from the dead is resident in us (Philippians 3:10). Believe it! Being filled with an awareness of God's presence in us gives us the *guts* to face the heat of ungodly opposition, the *willingness* to fight the good fight, the *motivation* to speak boldly about the good news of Christ.

The following was given to me a while ago. The story goes that it was found by a missionary, tacked on the wall of a young African pastor's home. Whether or not that's true, it prompts me to rethink my own commitment:

I'm a part of the fellowship of the unashamed. I have Holy Spirit Power. The die has been cast. I have stepped over the line. The decision has been made. I'm a disciple of his. I won't look back, let up, slow down, back away, or be still. My past is redeemed, my present makes sense, my future is secure. I'm finished and done with low living, sight walking, small planning, smooth knees, colorless dreams, tamed visions, mundane talking, cheap living, and dwarfed goals.

I no longer need pre-eminence, prosperity, position, promotions, plaudits, or popularity. I don't have to be right, first, tops, recognized, praised, regarded, or rewarded. I now live by faith, lean on his presence, walk by patience, am lifted by prayer, and labor by power.

My face is set, my gait is fast, my goal is heaven, my road is narrow, my way rough, my companions few, my Guide reliable, my mission clear. I cannot be bought, compromised, detoured, lured away, turned back, deluded or delayed. I will not flinch in the face of sacrifice, hesitate in the presence of the adversary, negotiate at the table of the enemy, ponder at the pool of popularity, or meander in the maze of mediocrity. I won't give up, shut up, let up, until I have stayed up, stored

---

[3]Eugene Peterson, *Run With the Horses* (Downers Grove, Ill.: InterVarsity Press, 1983), p. 93.

up, prayed up, paid up, preached up for the cause of Christ. I am a disciple of Jesus. I must go till he comes, give till I drop, preach till all know, and work till he stops me. And when he comes for his own, he will have no problems recognizing me—my banner will be clear!

Passion Results in Celebration

Our prayers and our songs and our reading of God's Word and communion with God will be consuming! Sacred moments. Supernatural realities. To think that our words are uttered to the God of the Universe—who should have nothing to do with rebellious people like us, and yet in his mercy has chosen to hang on to us! And to realize that God has spoken. He's extended himself to humanity.

When Ezra stood before the people of Israel to read from God's Word, look what they did! *Ezra opened the book. All the people could see him because he was standing above them; and as he opened it, the people all stood up. Ezra praised the Lord, the great God; and all the people lifted their hands and responded, "Amen! Amen!" Then they bowed down and worshiped the Lord with their faces to the ground* (Nehemiah 8:5–6). Wow! The Israelites stood, lifted their hands, responded with their voices, and bowed low to the ground! They were moved. What a scene!

These were people who had felt the resultant dullness due to their drain of passion. Because of their insolence they had lived lives of bondage in Babylon. And now they had been freed! They had returned to their land and to their Lord and they felt the fervor of being free once again to hear the Scriptures read aloud. Their worship service was full and soaring, and every last one of them was involved to the core.

When we approach God in the same frame of mind, we too will be "caught up" in him rather than in ourselves. Our prayers won't be nicely cut out like a string of paper dolls. They will reflect real thought, some real pauses, and some real tears from time to time. Words will get garbled in the rapture of it all, but the meanings will come through louder than ever.

Let us be thankful, and so worship God acceptably with reverence and awe, for our "God is a consuming fire" (Hebrews 12:28).

Our worship will be passionate. Not trite or thoughtless. True worship bursts on the inside. Sometimes it bursts on the outside as well. But either way, it fills the mind with a longing for holiness. It prods and moves and fills and floods. It is concentrated and contagious.

The Jews wanted to know what God thought was the most important thing about their life with him. Which was his favorite law? How could they live to their fullest potential as God's people? How could they please a perfect and holy God? Moses wrote down God's thoughts in Deuteronomy 6:5: *Love the Lord your God with all of your heart and with all your soul and will all your strength.* Not a little but with the entirety of your being.

Later the New Testament believers wanted to know the same thing. Okay, God, *now* what is the most important thing in all of life? Could you whittle it down for us—give us the bottom line of being a Christian? Jesus repeated the same admonition. Love the Lord with everything you've got! (Matthew 22:37; Mark 12:30; Luke 10:27).

In my own journey of faith I have come face-to-face with this issue. When I truly face God, I realize his face is bigger than my face and I have been humbled into asking myself some lean questions:

- Am I real or have I become ritualistic?

- Am I passionate or predictable?

- Am I thinking or tinkering?

- Am I discipling others or just dabbling in their lives?

- Am I awestruck in the presence of God or a little bored?

The Swedish diplomat Dag Hammerskjold, who became the highly respected Secretary General of the United Nations, kept a journal. He died in a plane crash en route to Africa, and in the wreckage his journal was found. In it Hammerskjold wrote, "God does not die on the day when we cease to believe in a personal deity, but we die on the day when our lives cease to be illumined by the steady radiance, renewed daily, of a wonder, the source of which is beyond all human reason."[4]

Spiritual apathy. As opposite of passion as death is to life. Here is it's outcome: *A sluggard does not plough in season; so at harvest time he looks but finds nothing* (Proverbs 20:4). Apathy claims the lives of believers slowly, like a cancer that steals away life one day at a time. Like leprosy, it deadens cell by cell, eating away, eroding what once was Spirit-filled. It saps motivation. It causes near-sightedness, then blindness. It drains all the joy and leaves only a shell, a crust—a cadaver.

Where do we go from here? How do we inspire passion within our families?

1. *Recommit* yourself to a life filled with passion. Commitment, dedication, inner drive—it all stems from a decision, actually, from a series of decisions made daily. Have you decided that God is worth your very best? Are you deciding daily that the sacrifices are worth it? Is how you answer reflected in what you're doing? Do you talk to your children about what they love the most? Is it a daily part of your conversational diet?

2. *Remember* all the good that God has done in your life and in the lives of believers throughout history. Like Moses did with the Israelites, as recorded in the book of Deuteronomy, *Remember well what the Lord your God did. . . . Remember how the Lord your God led you. . . . Remember that you were slaves. . . .* Over and over, Moses laid claim to the faithfulness of God in the lives of his people. Are we taking time to reminisce in our homes as well? Remember back and reaffirm what God has done.

3. *Recapture* the drama of God's Word. Let it rehydrate your soul on a daily basis. Drink it in. Feel it go down. Don't stop. If it seems dry, maybe you're only skimming the surface. Go deep and see what is really there and then go deeper and see what it is saying to you personally. As James exhorts, don't walk away too quickly. Take the time to ask, "So what?" in response to the Word. "What difference does this make? How will I think differently, act differently? How am I being conformed to the image of Christ

---

[4]Linda Lawrence, *Rare Beasts, Unique Adventures*, (Grand Rapids: Zondervan, 1991), p. 51.

because of this?" Those are the questions our children need to hear us asking.

4. *Reorient* your schedule so that eternal pursuits get primary focus once more. Look at your planner, your calendar. What priorities does it mirror? Make the hard choices about what you and your family will do and won't do with your time and resources while you have them.

5. *Rekindle* the flame of love in your worship and prayer. Sing louder than you've sung in the past. Taste every word of praise as it rolls across your tongue and thank God that he's given you one more moment, one more breath, with which to sing. Show your children the magnificence of God. Watch how you refer to the Lord, and to gathering with his people. Has it become a form, a function, a habit—or is it a drive? Is it compelling? Do you spend time after church talking about it all, wondering how you might bring about change in your lives because of it all? What are you modeling here?

There's no time like the present for change. You may have heard the following tongue-in-cheek story. There's truth behind it.

Satan was planning a strategy for carrying out his purposes on the earth, and he called three demons to assist him in devising a plan. The first suggested that they tell humanity that there is no heaven. "The heart of man knows that it is true," Satan objected, "the Bible describes it over and over and the earth is full of believers spreading the message of eternal hope. Won't work."

The second demon suggested they tell people there is no hell. Satan objected again. "The Bible is even more explicit about the reality of hell. The earth, after all, shows evidence of the fact that rebellion against God and his laws brings about utter destruction and despair."

The third demon moved forward and offered his advice, "Let's tell them there's no hurry."

"That's it!" cried Satan.

And so it is. Life ebbs away when believers choose to do nothing for yet another day.

The dead come to life. Can it happen? Yes it can! But will it? That is where our volition comes in to play. We can saunter ap-

athetically through life, avoiding anything that smacks of the un-
manageable. We can retain our forms and pretend that the function is there as well. Or, we can get completely real about God's
presence in the day-to-day. Where the Spirit of the Lord is, there
is life! Jump off the gurney.

Truth or Consequences

- How do you demonstrate for your children God's first place in your home? What lines do you draw in the sand regarding behaviors such as church attendance? What real sacrifices is that priority costing you and your family members on a daily basis? Are they learning that whatever is first place in your lives will cost you?

- Are you taking the time to explain the connection between your church involvement and your love for God? Do your kids see your lifestyle as an outgrowth of passion or as a series of religious habits to be maintained? Give your kids ten honest reasons why you go to church. (And make sure God truly is at the top of the list!)

- Give your kids some examples of how true faith could easily degenerate into dead worship, hollow wisdom and shallow work. When older kids or teens complain about how boring your church is, go visit some others. Don't be critical, but compare and contrast them. What's good? What's bad? Why? Which evidence real passion for God?

- Whether it is going to church or serving the Lord in some way, have you discussed the "whys" behind what you do?

- Why not take the five characteristics of passion listed in this chapter and use each as a topic for discussion during the week. Have your kids come up with examples of how true passion will be seen in the way we live our lives. Some families keep a journal of answered prayer and God's power made evident.

- At church, are your kids aware that what happens in them is far more important than what happens in the service? Help them by discussing what they felt, prayed, confessed or learned during their time of worship rather than what happened "up front."

- If you attend a sporting event with your child, help them notice how excited everyone is over their team. They stand in line for tickets, battle crowds for a seat, eat overpriced bad food, sit for hours on hard chairs and endure every imaginable inconvenience simply because of the their passion for the game. Draw a parallel to our relationship with God. Consider the following kinds of questions: Do we complain when church causes an inconvenience? Are we excited about giving God our attention or do we drag ourselves "to the altar"? Is our love for God obvious by the way we praise, worship and pray? Like we would with our favorite sports team, are we anxious to talk with others about our love for God?

15

THE TRUTH ABOUT REWARDS

THE CONSEQUENCES OF SHORTSIGHTEDNESS

The faithless will be fully repaid for their ways, and the good man rewarded for his.

—Proverbs 14:14

Beverly Hills. We rarely go there, but one night we did. It was a posh little Italian trattoria, designed and priced for the upper crust, or for those who aren't but who decide to go someplace special with someone special anyway. The latter was why we were there. From the way we were greeted by the valet, to the tuxedoed waiters who served flawlessly, to the exquisite cuisine—this wasn't just "food"—everything was "magnifico!" It was a memorable treat from my wife's parents in honor of her mother's birthday. We patted our lips, placed our napkins on the linen covered table, stretched a little and praised the meal as we got up to go.

The women in our group excused themselves to visit the rest room before the long ride back home. We, the men, went outside into the cool night air to flag the valet for Bob's car. Bob, my father-in-law, handed the young man our parking stub and we waited and chatted. We were the only ones leaving the restaurant at that time.

Now to realize the impact of what happened next, you need

to picture my father-in-law's car. It's a Buick. It's not a bad Buick, really. You might call it "fine" or "functional" or maybe even go as far as "comfortable" but you would never use words like "lavish" or "luxurious," or even "leased." It's just a car.

Within moments we heard a car pull up next to us, so we turned, expecting to see our car. But it wasn't ours. It was a big, brand new, jet black Mercedes, polished to a gleam, its engine purring invitingly. The kind of car you would describe with words that begin with the letter "L." My trance was broken when the valet jumped out of the front seat, held the door open wide, motioned to my father-in-law and waited for us to get in and drive off. In "our" car. There was a moment of silence. A truly strange moment where we were caught in a juxtaposition between the world as it is and some wild flight of fantasy.

Now if it were you, what would you do? I think I would figure, "Oh, how the Lord does provide for his own." Then I'd grab my wife, get in, and drive like a man outta prison! But my father-in-law isn't as opportunistic. He explained to the valet that we owned a maroon Buick. He did, however, add that if something had happened to it, we would consider taking this one and call it even. We got the Buick.

Think about something with me for a moment. What if it actually were restaurant policy to replace old cars with new cars during dinner? Imagine it. You drive in with a beater and you get something better. You give him the keys to your decade-old Fiat (short for "Fix it again, Tony") and he hands you back the keys to a brand new Ferrari. In with a Volkswagen—out with a Volvo. Does that kind of thing only happen in our dreams? Not according to God.

Scripture says that after death, those who are children of God will wake up to a whole new world beyond the biggest and best of our imaginations. Before he left this earth to rejoin the Father, Jesus assured us, his followers, that he was going to build another world. No matter how dark or broken or dismal this world seems to be, our sights should be set on what's ahead, because it is all being laid out for us even now.

The King who came once is coming back. And when he comes, there's going to be a party, complete with gifts (sometimes called "rewards") and party hats (sometimes called "crowns") and feasting and singing and celebrating without bounds! This is exciting stuff!

And the King has already sketched out the future. *Everlasting joy will crown their heads. Gladness and joy will overtake them, and sorrow and sighing will flee away* (Isaiah 35:10).

Have you ever read an intensely enthralling adventure novel that continues to spin and spiral your emotions as you move closer and closer toward a climactic ending? It's great! But imagine how you'd feel if the final chapter were missing. On the cover, a sticker: "Caution: Final Chapter Not Included." Would you immerse yourself for weeks in a novel that had no ending? No! You would hate it and so would I. God understands that. He didn't leave us to go through life ignorant of what the future will hold for the faithful. No! He gave us the final chapter. He gives us a glimpse of what's beyond the finish line. He explains in advance who wins. And it's not "the one with the most toys." Your kids need to know that ahead of time!

One of the components missing in the faith of too many young people today is a thorough understanding of what awaits those who love God. The fact that they don't, seriously undermines their motivation. The fact is this: People respond to rewards. It's no mystery to God. Maybe that's why he told us about the rewards he's set aside for us. Maybe that's why Satan doesn't want us thinking about this. We might, just might, be enticed into doing something meaningful in this world—something that would seriously impact the next.

Rewards Are a Powerful Motivator

What in the world do you and I do that isn't prompted by some reward? Let's be honest. We go to school—to be trained, to get a degree, to get a job. We help someone who is hurting—to see them relieved, to feel good inside. We work—to get paid, to use our skills, to feel the significance of contributing to something. We invest heavily in our children—so they'll grow up to be a blessing to us, not a curse! On and on it goes.

If there were no perceived benefits down the line, much of

what we do would cease immediately. Sadly, that's what has happened to many children today. How can we expect motivation in the here and now from kids who have no comprehension of the then and there? Let's wake up to the new world right around the corner. What we see isn't all there is!

Paul pictured this life as a race. He explained that a clear focus on the prize at the finish line is what keeps us going. In fact, it keeps us going even when the going gets really rough! *Do you not know that in a race all the runners run, but only one gets the prize? Run in such a way as to get the prize. Everyone who competes in the games goes into strict training. They do it to get a crown that will not last; but we do it to get a crown that will last forever. Therefore I do not run like a man running aimlessly; I do not fight like a man beating the air. No, I beat my body and make it my slave so that after I have preached to others, I myself will not be disqualified for the prize* (1 Corinthians 9:24–27).

The race itself is usually exhausting. What do you do when the journey becomes unbearable, when the jeers of the opposition are exceptionally shrill? Jesus looked out toward his own horizon and saw the cross—but he also saw beyond it. He comforted his followers with what he saw: *Blessed are you when people insult you, persecute you and falsely say all kinds of evil against you because of me. Rejoice and be glad, because great is your reward in heaven* (Matthew 5:11–12).

In the eternal scheme of things, every single wrong will be made right. Every insult, every sneer, every lost opportunity, every sleepless night, every hurt inflicted upon any of God's children because of their faith will be repaid! Can you imagine what the first-century believers martyred by Emperor Diocletion have in store? Or those chained to cinder block walls in a Siberian prison because of their love for Jesus? Or how about that woman in Vermont who is tucked away on a farm, loving and forgiving a husband who daily mocks her simple faith in a good God? Nothing good will go unrewarded. That gives us focus even when our eyes are blurred in suffering.

If you're an athlete, says Paul, you have a prize in mind. Recall it and it keeps you in training. Lose your vision of victory and you lose your steam. Start staring at your feet and you trip. Take your eyes off the prize and your passion turns to passivity. It's the reward that keeps us running. Don't lose sight of it!

Rewards Are a Reality, Not Just a Vague and Distant Maybe

He who sows righteousness reaps a sure reward (Proverbs 11:18).

Whenever I travel I try to find some small thing I can take back to my kids. I realize a lot of dads do this, but when I go on the hunt for those little gifts, it feels like mine are the only kids in the world. I call home often to check up on them and to reassure their mom I'm returning soon. Then I go out on my mission. What little thing would they love? I want them to know I'm thinking of them. I want them to know that they're special and that I appreciate them behaving while I'm gone.

When I do arrive home all eyes fix on my suitcase. There's expectancy. There's anticipation. "What's in there?" There's no masked bashfulness in asking, "Daddy, did you bring me something?" Children know a gift when they see one coming. And me? I'm ecstatic. Nothing is more fun than to see the wonder on their faces when I pull out that crumpled bag that contains their surprise. "I've been thinking of you. I love you. Here's something for you. It's good to be home."

I'm not so sure that our heavenly Father doesn't have some of the same kinds of feelings for us. He's thinking about us, you know. And he says that we're his children. And that he loves us. And that he's preparing things for us right now. It's a sure thing. It's in the bag.

In his book *Everything You Ever Wanted to Know About Heaven*, Peter Kreeft writes about the general view of heaven held by those living in the medieval era—during the "dark ages."

> Earth was Heaven's womb, Heaven's nursery, Heaven's dress rehearsal. Heaven was the meaning of earth. . . . Medieval man was still his Father's child, however prodigal, and his world was meaningful because it was "my Father's world" and he believed his Father's promise to take him home after death. This confidence toward death gave him confidence toward life, for life led somewhere.[1]

---

[1]Peter Kreeft, *Everything You Ever Wanted to Know About Heaven* (San Francisco: Harper & Row, 1982), p. 3. Quoted in Stacy and Paula Rinehart, *Living for What Really Matters* (Colorado Springs: NavPress, 1986), p. 16.

Imagine what was going through Christ's mind when he said to his followers, *In my Father's house are many rooms; if it were not so, I would have told you. I am going there to prepare a place for you. And if I go and prepare a place for you, I will come back and take you to be with me that you also may be where I am. You know the way to the place where I am going* (John 14:2–4).

A mansion in the making now. A place for you in God's celestial blueprint. You're his and he's coming for you. Another image God gives us is a bridegroom coming for his bride. Believers are called the bride of Christ. *Let us rejoice and give him glory! For the wedding of the Lamb has come, and his bride has made herself ready* (Revelation 19:7). Get your dress on!

Rewards Are Exciting to God—It's Really Okay for Us to Get Excited Too!

For the Son of Man is going to come in his Father's glory with his angels, and then he will reward each person according to what he has done (Matthew 16:27).

Jesus was describing the end of the world to his disciples. He explained that he would be returning to the earth. In the same breath, he mentions what he'll be bringing with him. When God speaks of rewards it isn't in hushed tones, the way people talk at a funeral. It is we who get tongue-tied and embarrassed, as though contemplating a reward at the end of the line somehow diminishes the purity of our motive.

Kids love rewards. Kids live for rewards. So do adults, but we don't readily admit it. Whatever that reluctance stems from, we need to put it away. God isn't embarrassed to tell us the wonders he's planning for us.

The writer of Hebrews speaks lavishly of our heavenly kingdom to come. In fact, in parts of chapter 12 he speaks of it as if it's here already—as if the perfect future is already superimposed on the imperfect present. Scripture takes us beyond the here and now and exhorts us to live in the now in light of the then, for what is ahead! We keep our destiny clearly in view, and *since we are receiving a kingdom that cannot be shaken, let us be thankful . . .* (Hebrews 12:28). Don't be bashful, be thankful! No need to cower in false humility. Run up to your Father. Climb onto his lap. Look into his eyes—and smile.

Rewards Are Given Exclusively to Those Who Belong to God Through Christ

For we must all appear before the judgment seat of Christ, that each one may receive what is due him for the things done while in the body, whether good or bad (2 Corinthians 5:10).

"I'll see you on Judgment Day" goes the phrase. But most people don't understand the various types of "judgments" by God. As you speak to your kids about God's final day of accountability, be sure to explain that a completely different kind of judgment will be faced by those who belong to Christ and those who don't. Those who have accepted Christ have already "judged themselves" by admitting their need for a Savior. That's what it means to "be saved." We are "redeemed" or *bought back* from the dead. We who were headed for destruction were intercepted by the sacrifice of Christ, the perfect Lamb of God. We are "children of God" and will spend eternity with him because we're his. When we stand before Christ, our eternal life with him won't be the issue. His concern will be our lives on earth. He'll be rewarding us for what we've done with our time.

On the other hand, there is a judgment clearly for those who have refused God's offer of a Savior. Everyone who has ever died will be raised up for this final moment before their Maker. *Then I saw a great white throne and him who was seated on it. Earth and sky fled from his presence, and there was no place for them. And I saw the dead, great and small, standing before the throne, and books were opened. Another book was opened, which is the book of life* (Revelation 20:11–12). Everything that has ever been hidden will be brought to light—the good, the bad and the ugly. It is significant that earth and sky will be gone—there's no place to run to, no place to hide. It is simply individual men and women before God.

Ultimately, *If anyone's name was not found written in the book of life, he was thrown into the lake of fire* (Revelation 20:15). I realize that there are times when the truth isn't popular. When it comes to this issue of accountability, the Bible states reality, regardless.

Those who have chosen separation from God in this life will be resigned to separateness for eternity. Hell was never intended for people. It was intended for Satan and his angels. Still, the fact remains: People who reject God will be themselves rejected. They will be forever lost and the loss will be torment (Luke 21:22–24). Hell is a reality despite popular opinion.

Rewards Are Given in Direct Relation to the Works of Believers on Earth

Behold, I am coming soon! My reward is with me, and I will give to everyone according to what he has done (Revelation 22:12).

My brother was the athlete. I was the klutz in our clan. When I was in high school I heard about a freshman who wore his athletic supporter backwards in P.E. Some of the guys got together and decided they had better point it out to him. When they did he said he thought the tag was supposed to go in the back. I can identify with that guy.

So my brother was sort of a hero to me. He played all the sports I was never picked for. He was always bigger, stronger, and far more disciplined than I. Consequently, he had a shelf full of trophies in the room we shared. Dave never knew it then, but when he wasn't around I used to sneak over to his side of the room, pull down one of his trophies and set it carefully on *my* shelf. Then I would stand back and gaze at it with pride.

"Well, thanks, I really couldn't have done it without those of you who sacrificed so much. Really. I never believed I'd make it to the finals, but you, my fans, just kept believing for me and, well, here I am, accepting this beautiful trophy. Thanks, Mom. Thanks, Dad. And, thank you, Coach. None of us would have—" Slam! The screen door would bang shut. My brother was home. I grabbed "my" trophy and returned it to its shelf—and its rightful owner.

I have since learned you can do all the imagining you want, but it doesn't alter reality. Trophies go to those who win and winning is determined by how you play the game.

Scripture tells us there is a way to live in which you win, ultimately and completely. Regardless of how the score looks at half-time, you *will* win if you follow the game plan. In a culture rife with shifting values and vague concepts of character, kids need to understand that some things indeed work in the long-run, and some things don't. Fortunately, God has already defined how to play to win.

Picture a gold-processing plant. Workers heat gold until it becomes molten liquid, then pour it into a furnace that rages at hundreds of degrees. The impurities burn away, only the purest gold remaining.

Keep that image in mind as you consider our life on earth. First of all, the basis for a life of goodness is simply Jesus himself. *For no one can lay any foundation other than the one already laid, which is Jesus Christ* (1 Corinthians 3:11). We find our acceptance in Christ. But we also find the possibility for growth in goodness in Christ. *For we are God's workmanship, created in Christ Jesus to do good works, which God prepared in advance for us to do* (Ephesians 2:10). God opens to each of us opportunities to live in a way that matters for eternity. It's as though the days of our lives will be poured into a "refining furnace" and . . . what will be left? What have we done that matters to God?

Paul continues, *If any man builds on this foundation using gold, silver, costly stones, wood, hay or straw, his work will be shown for what it is, because the Day will bring it to light. It will be revealed with fire, and the fire will test the quality of each man's work* (1 Corinthians 3:12–13). God's complete insight will reveal the truth about our lives. It will serve as a sieve. Our days will be poured through the grid of his perfect knowledge. He knows every small act of kindness. He has recorded every motive and movement. And he has been waiting to reward you. *If what he has built survives, he will receive his reward. If it is burned up, he will suffer loss; he himself will be saved, but only as one escaping through the flames* (1 Corinthians 3:14–15).

Many times the Bible speaks of rewards using the imagery of a crown. Just exactly what these rewards will look like is yet to be seen. What is clear, however, are the reasons that they're given. Scripture speaks of a "crown of life" (Revelation 2:10) and a "crown of glory" (1 Peter 5:4). We're told that believers will be rewarded for sharing the truth about Christ (1 Thessalonians

2:19) and for living righteously (2 Timothy 4:8). And unlike earthly rewards, heavenly crowns last forever (1 Corinthians 9:25).

Rewards Will Be Missed Due to Our Shortsightedness

There was an incredibly rich king who packed his bags for a trip. Before leaving his estate he decided to do something amazing, even a little risky. He rounded up his staff, sat them down, and proceeded to dole out responsibility for his property. Some of his servants got huge fields to maintain, some got gardens. To some he entrusted a great deal of leadership, others had oversight for only a few things. As far as his finances were concerned, he gave different amounts to various servants so that they could invest his fortune wisely for a good return on his money.

Finally everything had been given away. His final instructions were simple: "I've given all of you something," he said. "Now, do your very best with what you've got. I'll return one of these days, and when I do I'll reward you for your faithfulness." And with that, the rich man left.

As the story goes, the days passed. Some of the servants got to work and began planting their fields. Others decided that their master could handle things just fine once he returned and so they decided to take life easy and hope for the best. Some invested what they had and some didn't do a thing. Some sowed while others sat. Then one day the master returned. Some were excited because they had done their best with what they had. Some were a little nervous. And just as the master had promised, those who had invested their time and resources wisely were amply rewarded. In fact, they were invited to share all the wealth that had been accumulated due to their perseverance.

Then the master called in those who hadn't done a thing. "Why have you been so lazy?" he questioned. One spoke up and explained, "Well, er, uh, well, you see, sir, we knew you had a lot of power and could handle things fine on your own so we, well, you see, we kind of just figured it really didn't matter what we did. And besides, we only had a little to work with, I mean, we were real limited in what we could accomplish." The master then replied, "I gave each of you the opportunity to be faithful with what you had. The issue was not how much you had but what you did with what you had." And with that those servants were banished from the kingdom. The faithful servants, on the other hand, were invited in to the king's private quarters, and everything the king had was theirs.

Sound familiar? Jesus shared a similar story with his followers (Matthew 25:14–30). His point? Everyone has a limited number of days. Yet every life has its opportunities. Everything done will be rewarded—handsomely. Tending too closely to the immediate and the material blurs our vision for the eternal. Heavenly honors are forever.

Right now the patience of God remains—for a time. It won't always be so. A day is coming when what we see will be gone, and what is now unseen will become present reality. Conduct your life accordingly, writes Peter, *Since everything will be destroyed in this way, what kind of people ought you to be? You ought to live holy and godly lives as you look forward to the day of God and speed its coming. . . . In keeping with his promise we are looking forward to a new heaven and a new earth, the home of righteousness. So then, dear friends, since you are looking forward to this, make every effort to be found spotless, blameless and at peace with him* (2 Peter 3:11–14).

In the now famous words of missionary Jim Elliot, "He is no fool who gives what he cannot keep to gain what he cannot lose." Elliot, martyred for his faith by the bushmen he loved, lived his words. He lost his life—and won the prize.

The stuff of this world is going to burn. At the instant of death, that wounded refugee in Bosnia and the "Trump"ed-up tycoon in Manhattan are equally as wealthy. The great Pharaohs of Egypt were buried with their wealth tucked in around them so they would have it in the afterlife. Now archaeologists exhume their tombs. Guess what they find. A party? No. A worm-eaten Pharaoh, with all of his trinkets sitting unused and his gold unspent.

No one carries a cent from this planet. It's time we started talking with our children more about the value of life on the other side of "the great divide." And it's time we began living as if *our citizenship is in heaven* (Philippians 3:20). The Landowner is coming back sooner than we think.

Rewards Are Better Than Any Earthly Thing We've Ever Encountered or Imagined

No eye has seen, no ear has heard, no mind has conceived what God has prepared for those who love him (1 Corinthians 2:9).

The rewards believers will receive are beyond anything we've ever even imagined—yet it never hurts to try, because God has given us some astounding glimpses into our future. God has ripped a corner off the wrapping paper. He's pulled back the curtain just a tad:

We'll become perfected people: *Dear friends, now we are children of God, and what we will be has not yet been made known. But we know that when he appears, we shall be like him, for we shall see him as he is* (1 John 3:2).

We'll live in a perfect place: . . . *the Holy City, Jerusalem, coming down out of heaven from God. It shone with the glory of God, and its brilliance was like that of a very precious jewel, like a jasper, clear as crystal. . . . The wall was made of jasper, and the city of pure gold, as pure as glass. The foundations of the city walls were decorated with every kind of precious stone. . . . The great street of the city was of pure gold, like transparent glass. . . . On no day will its gates ever be shut, for there will be no night there. . . . Nothing impure will ever enter it, nor will anyone who does what is shameful or deceitful . . .* (Revelation 21:10–27).

We'll serve a perfect King. *Now the dwelling of God is with men, and he will live with them. They will be his people, and God himself will be with them and be their God* (Revelation 21:3). And *to him who sits on the throne and to the Lamb be praise and honor and glory and power, for ever and ever!* (Revelation 5:13).

We'll experience perfect peace. *He will wipe every tear from their eyes. There will be no more death or mourning or crying or pain, for the old order of things has passed away. He who was seated on the throne said, "I am making everything new!"* (Revelation 21:4–5).

Don't read these verses too quickly. Let them sink into your heart and life. No pain. No tears. No injustice. No lies. No racism.

No hunger. No sadness. No end. This is what's beyond the finish line. This is what's behind the door we call death. This is our destiny. Let it grip you. Let it shape you. Let it become your desire.

We'll enjoy perfect fulfillment. Some worry heaven will be boring. Hardly! Heaven isn't a back corner of the universe where angelic beings float like metaphysical globs in a sea of emptiness (playing harps, of course). Scrap that image. It isn't biblical. It isn't true. Your kids need to know that!

The book of Revelation describes heaven as a huge new world complete with nations of people. Those who have been faithful on earth will rule and reign with Christ forever. In fact, of the thousand-year millennium, when Christ's kingdom is established here on earth, Revelation 5:10 tells us this: *You have made them to be a kingdom and priests to serve our God, and they will reign on the earth.* Being in the service of the King of the Universe will outstrip any excitement we've experienced here on earth. Including splatball, parachuting and riding jet skis. Better than closing a big deal or finishing your first novel or winning the Super Bowl. Even the love we experience in marriage and family is only a foretaste of what is to come. Life beyond this world will be entirely purposeful, fulfilling and satisfying. Count on it.

I'm no botanist, but I have read that in China there's a bamboo tree with a highly peculiar existence. The inhabitants of the remote Chinese villages where it grows understand the tree, so they deal with it accordingly. They plant a tiny sapling and for the first year it apparently does nothing. They patiently water it and fertilize it and wait. The second year, same thing. It doesn't grow. It just sits there. They come out the third year and give it more water and continue to feed it and, well, nothing. It's about the same size as it was in year one. Amazing. Year four, same song-and-dance. Nothing happens. Then, around the fifth year of the tree's small life, it EXPLODES in growth! In one year the tree can shoot as high as 40 feet into the air, towering above those who faithfully tended it.

Hopefully someday my kids will get to visit China, to see the ancient cities and the rickshaws and the Great Wall. But really to see a tree. Then they'll remember what their daddy told them about seeds and saplings that don't appear to pay off in the short-run. They'll remember that the winning is in the waiting. That faithfulness today brings a flourish tomorrow. They'll recall that the rewards for effort aren't always immediate, but they come. And when rewards do come, they reach far beyond this earth.

Truth or Consequences

- How do you talk about death with your children? Even those who don't deliberately shelter their children from the reality of death often leave many questions unanswered. What is death—besides funeral homes and flowers? Who do you know who "died well," confident of eternal life in Christ? Share his or her story and the fact that believers don't need to fear death.

- Talk about "destiny" with your children. Actually, our eternal hope can and should be woven quite naturally into many different life discussions. What happens, for example, when you throw something away? We don't just die, as some say, and we aren't recycled—reincarnated into another life-form. God snatches us back from the trash heap of death and brings us into a new life.

- Can your kids describe heaven and hell as the Bible does? Has what we don't know about the future prevented you from talking about it at all or in very vague terms? How about doing a word search with a commentary and your Bible and taking your kids on a "futuristic adventure" of the truth about what's ahead.

- Are your children aware of the heavenly rewards that await God's people? Do they make the connection between earthly choices and eternal rewards? With younger children, try cutting out crowns from construction paper. Then on each one write about one type of crown, or reward, that Scripture says will be given to believers in heaven. Discuss the kinds of actions that would warrant such a crown.

- If your son or daughter has trophies from past sporting events (or if you have a few dusty ones in the garage yourself) try this. Take one positive character quality you see emerging in your child and write it on a slip of paper the same size as the placard on the trophy. Tape the piece of paper over the placard making the trophy a reward for a character quality in your child's life. Talk about how who we are and what we do will be rewarded in heaven. Nothing goes unnoticed by God.

- Take a prominent, positive role model like Mother Teresa and talk about what she has done with her life. Ask, "What's different about her life than, say, the life of someone who has lived selfishly for material gain? Do you think she's happier about her life choices or the one who has accumulated a lot of wealth or clout? How about after they die—who will be the winner then? What choices could you be facing right now that may have a big impact eternally?"

16

THE TRUTH ABOUT PERSEVERANCE

THE CONSEQUENCES OF QUITTING

The one who sows to please the Spirit, from the Spirit will reap eternal life. Let us not become weary in doing good, for at the proper time we will reap a harvest if we do not give up.

—Galatians 6:8–9

In England, a short distance from a place called Aviemore, is a grassy field. A walk in this field reveals a strange and amazing monument of the ancient past—the remains of a Druid temple of pagan worship erected before the time of Christ. It consists of two circles of standing stones, an inner and an outer circle, respectively twenty-four and sixty feet in diameter, the stones projecting about three to four feet above the ground. As the wind sweeps across the moor and whispers among these stones, there's an empty sense of lostness—of ancient blindness.

However, just a short distance away in the same field, stands a small Presbyterian church. Each week those who live in the area come to worship the Lord—the Creator of the universe. There's an intriguing contrast between these two shrines. One built centuries ago as an altar to the sun god, the other to the God who made the sun. They stand together, side-by-side, in a field of grain.

Matthew 13 takes us to another field. A farmer has planted wheat all day and is now sleeping—confident that the seeds he has planted will grow strong and productive. But a villain approaches the scene. An intruder sweeps across the field, scattering weeds in the blackness of the night.

Months later. The scene opens on the same field. The wheat has sprung up, but just as you might imagine, it is pockmarked with the weeds. So the good farmer's servants come to him and ask him if he wants them to yank up the entire field in order to get rid of the weed infestation. "No" he replies, "because in pulling up the weeds you'll also uproot the wheat. Let it go until harvest. At that time, the harvesters will separate the wheat from the weeds. The weeds will be burned and the wheat will be gathered into my barn."

Two problems constantly confronted the farmer, no doubt—impatience and discouragement. It would have been easy to give up, to plow up the field and shout, "That's it! There's too many weeds in this world. I quit! I'm not even going to try to farm anymore." But the point Jesus was making was just this: hang on.

God is at work even when his hand is difficult to see. His activity is ample even in the darkest of days. Wait on the Lord. Don't lose heart. Keep farming. Keep going through those dark nights this side of eternity, because God takes care of the harvest as Augustine wrote centuries ago:

> Whoever learns to do God's work well in this world—this valley of tears and troubles—becomes hearty, like the sturdy farmer who sows seed even in the dead of winter. Do cold winds, or harsh weather prevent him from working? Not at all!
>
> Thus we should see the troubles of this world as they are: diversions thrown in our path by the evil one, meant to turn us away from the good works we are created to do. See what the psalmist says: "He who goes out weeping. . . ." We will indeed find cause for weeping, every one of us. And yet we must go, doing the good works of God.
>
> But we know that some operation of the Spirit is at work, when we continue sowing even in our tears. For the Spirit promises, through the psalmist, that we will return—aston-

ished with joy!—and carrying the fruit of our labor as an offering to him.[1]

In the summer of 1989 the eyes of the world were fixed on the Tour de France. They should have been. The unbelievable took place. Champion cyclist Greg LeMond had become the first American ever to win the grueling twenty-three-day, 2000-mile race.

But what many didn't know was that in 1987 Greg was nearly killed in a hunting accident. After four months in recovery, he was readmitted to the hospital for an emergency appendectomy. Once again Greg began training, sorely behind all the competition, only to be brought down by an acute inflammation of his shin. Greg attempted some initial races but didn't perform. His Dutch sponsors were ready to cut off his support. He just didn't have it anymore.

But he kept on. Day after day, Greg recalls, he squeezed out every ounce of endurance he had and then went beyond it. Finally the Tour de Italy came—and went. He didn't do that well, disappointing those who were counting on him, and after that race a medical exam revealed that Greg was anemic. He had pushed so hard the exertion was eating into his muscles.

Then in May 1989, before the Tour de France, Greg rode in the Tour de Trump but couldn't keep his speed up on the hills. He came in twenty-seventh. Anyone else would have quit. Except Greg. Win or not, he was determined to compete to his greatest ability in the final round.

LeMond wasn't even mentioned in the press pre-race favorites to win the Tour de France in 1989. In the first twenty-one days of the race, though, people began to take notice. His strength was surprising, but for Greg every minute was a fight. The world watched as he descended the alpine slopes of the Pyrenees at a dangerous 60 mph. This was the moment Greg had worked for all his life. He raced against the clock, the other riders—and the odds.

The final day. The final hours. Greg was in the top three. An-

---

[1]Homilies on the Psalms: 2, by Augustine, as quoted in *Early Will I Seek You*, by David Hazard (Minneapolis, Minn.: Bethany House Publishers, 1991), pp. 106–107.

other rider led by 50 seconds going into the short with Paris fifteen miles away. No one imagined Greg could break past what seemed to be an insurmountable barrier.

Total concentration. Every muscle, every tendon, every nerve operating at maximum output. Finally, unbelievably, LeMond inched past his opponent, crossing the finish line first. He had beat the second man by a mere eight seconds in an 87-hour race.

Once on the platform, receiving the winner's prize, Greg LeMond spoke these words: "I kept thinking about how I almost quit two months ago and what a good thing it was that I never gave up early. That's what it taught me. Never give up early." LeMond, by the way, won again in 1990.

When the going gets tough, the tough keep going. But what about the rest of us? Few of us feel like "hard men" for Christ. Few of us feel strong under pressure. I really can't imagine that Joseph felt much different than you and I do. After all, from what we read it appears he was probably a little spoiled. Remember the coat?

Now Israel loved Joseph more than any of his other sons, because he had been born to him in his old age; and he made a richly ornamented robe for him. When his brothers saw that their father loved him more than any of them, they hated him and could not speak a kind word to him (Genesis 37:3–4).

We're talking a bad case of favoritism and an equally daunting stack of sibling rivalry. Not a good setup for building character. Yet one thing becomes apparent as the story unfolds. Joseph had a deep-seated trust in God.

Things went from bad to worse. Joseph had a dream that one day his brothers would bow down to him. He even told his brothers. That was the last straw as far as they were concerned and they plotted to kill him. They captured him, threw him in a pit, and later sold him to a band of slave traders en route to Egypt. That's when things went from worse to *much* worse.

Joseph was put in the ranks of the Pharaoh's slaves, yet because God's blessing fell on everything that Joseph touched, Potiphar, Pharaoh's captain of the guard, put him in charge of the household. Great—aside from one big obstacle: Potiphar's wife. She attempted to seduce Joseph on more than one occasion.

And though she spoke to Joseph day after day, he refused to go to bed with her or even be with her. One day he went into the house to attend to his duties, and none of the household servants was inside. She caught him by his cloak and said, "Come to bed with me!" But he left his cloak in her hand and ran out of the house (Genesis 39:10–12). Enraged at his rejection, Potiphar's wife lied about Joseph, claiming that the coat she held was evidence that he had attacked her. Joseph was imprisoned.

A perfect setup for anger and bitterness. But the narrative indicates that Joseph continued to honor God. In fact, due to his exemplary behavior in prison he was once again appointed to a position of oversight—this time of the prison itself. It was while there in prison that by the power of God Joseph interpreted the dreams of two inmates (the Pharaoh's baker and his cup bearer). Just as Joseph had foretold, both men were soon released and placed before the King. This could have been Joseph's lucky break. Surely one of the men would put in a good word for him. But Scripture records that *The chief cup bearer, however, did not remember Joseph; he forgot him* (Genesis 40:23). The baker? Well, he didn't say anything either. Potiphar had the guy hanged.

Quite a saga! I've taken the time to relay these key events in Joseph's life to make a singular point. Everything, humanly speaking, was against him. Think about it:

- He was spoiled as a child.

- He was hated by his brothers.

- He was abandoned in a pit to die.

- He was sold as a slave to be beaten and used.

- He was thrust into a completely different culture.

- He was lied about even though he behaved admirably.

- He was misunderstood by his boss and thrown into a dungeon.

- He was forgotten by the very men that he had helped while in prison.

Often when I speak to a group of parents I ask how many of

them grew up in a family that was dysfunctional to some degree. Most hands go up. It's true. Most of us come from imperfect homes with imperfect parents and have wandered through a myriad of life's land mines prior to getting where we're at right now. Don't get me wrong. I in no way discount the genuine tragedies many of us have encountered. But *many* of us have encountered them. We're all in the same boat. Most of us could point to a past of pain and claim that we have good reason to give up.

A man I am close to in my ministry has come out of a lifestyle of extreme alcoholism. As a child he was abandoned by his father, nagged by his mother, held responsible for the actions of his siblings (he was the oldest), and ultimately not allowed to go away to college because he was needed at home. When he did leave home to get married his mother accused him of not loving her anymore. His marriage eventually failed and he lost more than one job due to his drinking. His life was a whirling disaster. I must add, too, that my friend was a Christian even during these years.

In time my friend, who I'll call "Bob," was admitted to a rehab program. It was there that he met an administrator in the program who was also a Christian and began seriously investing himself in Bob. Day after day he worked with Bob, counseled Bob, loved Bob, believed in Bob and eventually was able to place Bob back into society with the strength to survive.

One day Bob and I were talking and he said to me, "Daniel, my biggest problem was that I always had my family to blame. I looked at my past and said, 'See, you've got an excuse to be a drunk.' It wasn't until I was in that program and started hearing the stories of everyone around me that a change began to take root in my heart. We all had a similar past. I finally started to realize that I could go on through life being controlled by my past or I could press on in the strength of God despite the past. It was there that I decided that God's power really was able to heal me. Once I believed that, the healing began."

There are always so many good reasons to give up.

In *The Complete Book of Running*, Jim Fixx wrote:

> When we race strange things happen to our minds. The stress of fatigue sometimes makes us forget why we wanted

to race in the first place. In one of my early marathons I found myself unable to think of a single reason for continuing. Physically and mentally exhausted, I dropped out of the race. Now I won't enter a marathon unless I truly want to finish it. If during the race I can't remember why I wanted to run in it, I tell myself, "Maybe I can't remember now, but I know I had a good reason when I started." I've finally learned how to fight back when my brain starts using tricky arguments.[2]

God asks us to hang tough despite what's happened to us in the past. And despite what is happening to us now. He says, "Keep going!"

The Mandate to Keep Going Despite the Masses

How many times have you heard your kids say, "That's not what so-and-so's mom makes him do" or "Everybody else is doing it." So you say, "If all your friends jumped off a cliff, would you jump off too?" Most younger kids say no, they wouldn't. By the time they're teenagers, though, they think hard about taking a dive with the rest of their friends.

Peer pressure is nothing new. The early Christians were intimidated into a first-century form of religious peer fear. To them Paul wrote this: *So then, just as you received Christ Jesus as Lord, continue to live in him, rooted and built up in him, strengthened in the faith as you were taught, and overflowing with thankfulness* (Colossians 2:6–7).

Their issue was their faith. Paul encouraged them on: Don't water down what you believe! Sink your roots in deep, keep growing, remember what you've learned, thank the Lord for what you've been given! It's a "stay strong" message. And then Paul identified two enemies of faithfulness, two leviathans that lurk in the dark, intent on taking his readers captive.

See to it that no one takes you captive through hollow and deceptive philosophy, which depends on human tradition and the basic principles of this world rather than on Christ (Colossians 2:8).

---

[2]Quoted in Charles Durham's *Temptation* (Downers Grove, Ill.: InterVarsity Press, 1982), p. 99.

There are two traps waiting to snap shut on you: One is called "What everyone does" (human tradition), the other is called "What everyone thinks" (principles of this world). Both, Paul argues, are hollow and deceptive. They promise an easier route than what God has mapped out as the right way to live. Don't be fooled. Abundant life is found in Christ, not in human designs.

There's another crowd, though, a celestial cheering squad rooting for you and waving a banner up ahead. They have run the course and they know what awaits you—so they're pulling for you now. *Therefore, since we are surrounded by such a great cloud of witnesses, let us throw off everything that hinders and the sin that so easily entangles, and let us run with perseverance the race marked out for us. Let us fix our eyes on Jesus . . .* (Hebrews 12:1–2a).

In an article written a few years back, Larry Libby recalls a little-known Bible character named Demas. When Paul wrote to the believers in Colosse from a Roman prison, he sent his greetings to Dr. Luke and Demas, his friend. Paul referred to Demas as a close associate, a faithful fellow worker. "What these friends must have endured together!" Libby writes. "The frown of Rome. The anxiety of imprisonment. The sting of rejection. The smell of blood and the bite of the whip. Yet through it all they clung together and clung to their Lord."

But a careful reading of 2 Timothy 4:9–10 will stop you cold. Paul concludes his letter to Timothy and adds this remark. *Do your best to come to me quickly, for Demas, because he loved this world, has deserted me and gone to Thessalonica.* What?

> Demas threw it all overboard. Everything they had fought for, everything they had endured together. And for what? For a few perfumed, sultry nights in Thessalonica? Or was it that job offer with the multinational corporation? Or his buddy's offer of a condo on the Aegean? How could it be? Demas had labored and suffered and triumphed at the side of the Great Apostle—the man who brought the gospel to the Western world, the champion of the faith who wrote a third of our New Testament. Yet he trashed it all for some pallid preoccupation.[3]

---

[3]Larry Libby, "When Spiritual Apathy Sets in . . . and You Couldn't Care Less," *Discipleship Journal*, No. 48, 1988. p. 6.

The "world." It's swept along in a spiritually unconscious state. It's easy to become a part of the flow, to heed its entrancing voice. But it never delivers on the contentment it promises.

Clearly, the only way our kids will know how to race is by watching us. If we don't race, neither will they. And if we do, we can be sure they will be watching how well we run, and in which direction, and for how long, and how we feel about it all and what we do when we fall down.

The Call to Keep Going Despite the Costs

The Christian life isn't a leisurely stroll through a garden of flowers. One of the greatest struggles of our times is that our culture is saturated with go-the-path-of-least-resistance thinking. We encounter that mind-set full force when confronted with the hard realities of following Christ. "Christianity has not been tried and found wanting," G. K. Chesterton wrote. "It's been found difficult and not tried."

Many are willing to run the race as long as the race isn't too difficult or too long or too costly or too uncomfortable:

> Religion in our time has been captured by the tourist mind-set. Religion is understood as a visit to an attractive site to be made when we have adequate leisure. For some it is a weekly jaunt to church. For others, occasional visits to special services. Some, with a bent for religious entertainment and sacred diversion, plan their lives around special events like retreats, rallies and conferences. There is a great market for religious experience in our world; there is little enthusiasm for the patient acquisition of virtue, little inclination to sign up for a long apprenticeship in what earlier generations of Christians called holiness.[4]

The only way that long obedience is attained is by a willingness to make short-term sacrifices.

In chess the queen is the most important offensive player.

---

[4]Eugene Peterson, *A Long Obedience in the Same Direction*, (Downers Grove, Ill.: Inter-Varsity Press, 1980), p.12.

During an international competition a number of years ago a man named Frank Marshall made what has been called the most beautiful move ever made on a chessboard. He was matched with a Russian player. The Russian attacked Marshall's queen relentlessly. Spectators assumed Marshall would observe convention and move his queen to safety. He considered all the options, then picked up his queen and placed it on the most illogical square of all—a square from which the queen could be captured by any one of three hostile pieces. Dismayed, everyone began to realize he had made a brilliant move. No matter how the queen was taken his opponent would be put in a losing position. Seeing the inevitable, the Russian conceded the game. Marshall won by sacrificing what the masses would have treasured. He sacrificed his queen.[5]

When I share that story with my teenaged audiences I ask, "What queens are you holding on to? What person or thing in this life is keeping you from living in light of the next?" To live for God will mean making some tough decisions about what's ultimately important. Scripture invites us to sacrifice some queens in honor of the King.

As Jesus said, *Whoever finds his life will lose it, and whoever loses his life for my sake will find it* (Matthew 10:39). There are always reasons to give up in the face of opposition. But once we come face-to-face with ultimate realities, none are good enough. While some bad people appear to prosper for a season, the harvest is coming and then their true character will be brought to light.

Blessed is the man who does not walk in the counsel of the wicked. . . . He is like a tree planted by streams of water, which yields its fruit in season and whose leaf does not wither. Whatever he does prospers. Not so the wicked! . . . For the Lord watches over the way of the righteous, but the way of the wicked will perish (Psalm 1).

Few things worth having are easily had. Following a concert by the immortal pianist Paderewski, a woman came up to him and said, "I'd give my life to be able to play like you do." Paderewski

[5]Robert Fulghum, *Maybe, Maybe Not* (New York: Random House, 1993), pp. 193–195.

simply looked at her and replied, "I did." Perseverance, sown at great cost, reaped a bounty.

A Firm Resolve to Keep Going Despite Feelings of Frailty

Why couldn't any of Saul's men defeat Goliath? Because they looked at their puny spears, their garbage-can-lid shields and their war-strategy maps. Then they looked up at the opposition and said, "Nope—no can do!"

Anyone attempting to defeat Goliath with human resources would have been ground into hamburger by the lug—but God never intended for us to attack giants with human weaponry. David never dreamed of going it alone. But with the power of God behind him he couldn't imagine not going! He understood the power of God. It was God's power that delivered that fire-breathing Philistine into David's hands.

There's a certain mind-set we must have if we're going to persevere against the odds. It's encapsulated in 2 Corinthians 4. I think of it as "wall talk"—the kind of words we need to hear when we "hit the wall."

But we have this treasure in jars of clay to show that this all-surpassing power is from God and not from us. We are hard pressed on every side, but not crushed; perplexed, but not in despair; persecuted, but not abandoned; struck down, but not destroyed. We always carry around in our body the death of Jesus, so that the life of Jesus may also be revealed in our body. For we who are alive are always being given over to death for Jesus' sake so that his life may be revealed in our mortal body (2 Corinthians 4:7–11).

We're desperately inadequate for the road ahead, Paul affirms, but God is in us. The treasure of our lives isn't our power or prestige or anything personal. The spark of life that exists in us is due to his presence in us. He is the energy and the Energizer. If not for him we would be smashed like old clay pots. But because of him we're spiritually alive. Our bodies may be wasting away but our inner man, the part of us that lasts, is becoming stronger every day!

Paul was likely from a wealthy Jewish family. He had been trained by Gamaliel (a costly private tutor). He had accumulated degrees and honor and had the potential of living in fat city. But Paul made a revolutionary discovery—he had *learned* something:

I can do everything through him who gives me strength (Philippians. 4:13).

God assured Paul, *My grace is sufficient for you, for my power is made perfect in weakness.* God was saying, "Paul in an environment of realized weakness, my power flourishes!" So how does Paul respond? *Therefore, I will boast all the more gladly about my weaknesses, so that Christ's power may rest on me. That is why, for Christ's sake, I delight in weaknesses, in insults, in hardships, in persecutions, in difficulties. For when I am weak, then I am strong* (2 Corinthians 12:9–10).

It was Paul, too, who experienced insurmountable temptation, yet found that God indeed offered the power to overcome what seemed overpowering. He wrote, *No temptation has seized you except what is common to man. And God is faithful; he will not let you be tempted beyond what you can bear. But when you are tempted, he will also provide a way out so that you can stand up under it* (1 Corinthians. 10:13).

2 Peter 1:3 says, *His divine power has given us everything we need for life and godliness through our knowledge of him who called us by his own glory and goodness.*

These are great refrigerator verses, or for wherever your greatest battles are fought. Put them on a sticky note. Attach them to your attaché case. How about one on your car visor? These are the reminders of a power that is beyond us and always available to us if we're willing to *remain in him* and persevere under pressure.

The Determination to Keep Going Despite Difficulties

God made no promises that our following him would be easy. *In fact, everyone who wants to live a godly life in Christ Jesus will be persecuted* (2 Timothy 3:12). Did you happen to catch the certainty in that verse? There's no other possibility. If you live with an intense righteousness in an unrighteous world—it *will* cost you. When you're wading upstream, there's *always* a drag.

According to Romans 8, suffering is one of God's most effective tools for deepening our intimacy and our identification with Christ. In our suffering we identify in a whole new way with the Christ who suffered for us, and when we are suffering he is aware! Stephen understood this too as rocks were being hurled mercilessly against his body. Scripture usually speaks of Christ as being seated at the right hand of God, yet when Stephen was being attacked, Christ was *standing*. Stephen died with these words on his lips: *I see heaven open and the Son of Man standing at the right hand of God* (Acts 7:56).

Remember Joseph? His past was one grief after another, and his future was entirely uncertain. Yet he was driven ahead by desire—a determination that kept him at the helm even when the gale was flapping at his sails. Peter also understood suffering. You might say he wrote the book on it. Take a look at the following for example:

In this you greatly rejoice, though now for a little while you may have had to suffer grief in all kinds of trials. These have come so that your faith—of greater worth than gold, which perishes even though refined by fire—may be proved genuine and may result in praise, glory and honor when Jesus Christ is revealed. Though you haven't seen him, you love him; and even though you do not see him now, you believe in him and are filled with an inexpressible and glorious joy, for you are receiving the goal of your faith, the salvation of your souls (1 Peter 1:6–9). What's beyond the finish line? Praise, glory, honor, joy and eternal life!

We heard Nancy Kerrigan's name over and over in connection with the 1994 Winter Olympics. We imagined her pain—heading for the Olympics as an accomplished skater, only to be attacked by an assailant slamming her legs with a pipe before she ever hit the ice.

But imagine being Nancy Kerrigan's mother, living out dreams through her daughter, applauding her victories, holding her through defeats. Nancy's mother, Brenda, rose for years at 4:30 A.M. with her daughter in order to get her ready for skating lessons. She was waiting in the wings, day after day, year after year, standing at Nancy's side. Brenda watched her daughter work her way through state competitions, and regional competitions, and national competitions—right toward the Olympics. There were preliminaries, semi-finals, and finally the Olympics.

She stood by, worn from years of faithfulness but unflinching, as her daughter skated with almost a magical grace. A perfected art. An amazing feat of endurance and strength. And there was Brenda watching her heroine ascend the platform where she was awarded an Olympic medal. Yet, amazingly, Brenda had become legally blind. Many of those dreams and years of sacrificial love and commitment were shrouded in physical darkness. Every move, every moment was as real and as clear as the day. She saw it all, but only with the eyes of her heart.

There are times in "the race" when we feel as though our heavenly Father can't see us either. But he does. He's there when we get up in the morning and he's there when we hit the ice. While there's a temporary physical separateness for now, he's watching with eyes of the heart, closer than any human ever could. *He holds victory in store for the upright, he is a shield to those whose walk is blameless, for he guards the course of the just and protects the way of his faithful ones* (Proverbs 2:7–8). Our Father is aware of our triumphs. He's holding us when we pace dark hallways in the night. And now and then we get a glimmer, a glimpse of what's in store for us, his children, and we realize that it is *we* who don't yet really see. But we will. *The path of the righteous is like the first gleam of dawn, shining ever brighter till the full light of day* (Proverbs 4:18).

So we walk—every day, planting seeds. We walk by his side. We hold on to his hand in the field. This season is turning a corner. Harvest is almost here.

Truth or Consequences

- Have you spoken to your children about eternity? Do they realize that the race isn't simply a physical one—limited to this earthly journey? Do they view physical death as simply a passage, as an entrance into another very real and important future?

- What are some times and places you or your kids have been tempted to give up but have stayed at the task and succeeded? What are the benefits of "pushing past the pain" and of taking hold of even those challenges that seem beyond our strength?

- Many storms threaten to set us back—the sway of the masses, the incredible costs en route, our feelings of frailty and the constant difficulties involved in taking the right path over the easy path. How are you preparing your kids for each of these stressors? Help them accept the fact that what is best won't usually be the easiest by letting them try difficult things, standing with them as they do. Are you showing them by your example as well as illustration, that long-range benefits result from perseverance in the short run?

- Get out and get some physical exercise with your teenager—or take them to work out at a gym if you're able to. Talk about the parallel between perseverance in a workout routine to get results and the similar truth about our spiritual journey.

- Like Joseph, we all can think of reasons to quit. What are yours? What would your children list as theirs? Study the life of Joseph together as a family. Call it a study of "triumph over tragedy" and help them come up with specific ways that they can overcome pressures and difficulties in God's power.

ACKNOWLEDGMENTS

I feel so much gratitude to so many people that selecting a few to mention here seems impossible—but I'll try. Mike Hyatt, Martin Culpepper, and the InterAct team have believed in and backed my dreams from the moments we talked. Their insight has been invaluable. I want to thank Kevin Johnson and Nancy Renich of Bethany House Publishers for performing editorial magic, and Peter Glöege of The Lookout Design Group for applying his creative talents to the cover.

For over ten years the staff, elders and congregation of Mission Hills Church have envisioned, encouraged and enabled the kind of family ministry that changes lives for eternity. People like Doug Haag, Chuck Swindoll, Jay Marshall, Jack Monroe, Mark Strecker, Dave Holmes, Milan and Kay Yerkovich, and Jon and Mary Alyce Johnson have invested generously in shaping who I am as a pastor and the thoughts that fill these pages. Each of you knows how special you are to me. I am indebted to Ken Garland, along with the other faculty members and students at Biola University, who never cease to inspire me. And finally—thank you, Lori, for freeing me to write past dark and for loving me so purely.

Dr. Daniel Hahn
September, 1995